A WORLD WITHOUT WAR

Praise for *A World without War*

'Sundeep Waslekar's *A World without War* is a book that every adult on the planet must read. It not only warns us of the threat to the survival of human civilization posed by our morally repugnant use of science and technology to escalate the arms race, but it also provides a new global social contract, a new vision and a new hope for the future of humanity.'

—Jody Williams, Nobel Peace Prize laureate

'This is a seminal and timely book focusing on the existential danger humanity faces because of nuclear and other weapons of mass destruction. Sundeep Waslekar refuses to give in to the grim status quo. His in-depth analysis and rigorous research provide a visionary "escape hatch" grounded in reality and informed by human ingenuity. A must-read for all those who care about a better and sustainable future.'

—Mohamed ElBaradei, Nobel Peace Prize laureate

'While the dangers of climate catastrophe are urgent, the existential threat of nuclear destruction is becoming immediate. More than describing the danger in frightening detail, the author serves us well by pointing to possible ways to rescue humanity before it is too late. This kind of challenge to status quo thinking is just what we need today.'

—The Rt. Hon. Lord Alderdice, John, senior research fellow at Harris Manchester College, University of Oxford

'A sweeping historical exegesis that describes contemporary dynamics of war, peace and the challenges of social cohesion and political accountability time and again. Waslekar excels in leaving no stone unturned in every corner of our globe, using his unique perspectives to inform and narrate.'

—Azza Karam, secretary general of Religions for Peace

'In times like these, when everything is uncertain and shaky, when regional conflicts multiply, international law norms are challenged, principles of multilateralism appear obsolete and prospects of global governance look dim, *A World without War* is particularly important. Not only does it make us more optimistic about our common future, but it also gives specific guidance on what each of us could and should do to contribute to building this future. The book is a must-read for anyone who is not ready to listlessly observe the current suicidal trends in world politics.'

—Andrey Kortunov, director general of the Russian International Affairs Council

A WORLD WITHOUT WAR

THE HISTORY, POLITICS
AND RESOLUTION
OF CONFLICT

SUNDEEP WASLEKAR

HarperCollins *Publishers* India

First published in India by HarperCollins *Publishers* 2022
4th Floor, Tower A, Building No. 10, Phase II, DLF Cyber City,
Gurugram, Haryana – 122002

www.harpercollins.co.in

2 4 6 8 10 9 7 5 3 1

Typeset in 11.5/15.5 Bembo Std
Manipal Technologies Limited, Manipal

Printed and bound at
Thomson Press (India) Ltd

For Ilmas

Contents

Preface

Caen is a picturesque town in the Normandy region of France. It has witnessed wars for thousands of years. In Roman times, it was known as 'Catumagos', meaning battlefield. It was the scene of the hundred-year war between the English and the French kings in the fourteenth and fifteenth centuries. It was one of the main theatres of the Battle of Normandy in the Second World War.

Caen is now transforming into a town where people from all over the world are invited to reflect on the horrors of war and the need for constructing a world without war. It has a peace museum, which welcomes you with a sculpture of non-violence. The local university has established a chair in peace studies. The 1,000-year-old abbey in the centre of town hosts an annual peace forum on its grounds. On one of its walls rests the Normandy Manifesto for World Peace.

I am one of the six signatories of the manifesto. The other five are Mohamed ElBaradei, Leymah Gbowee, Anthony Grayling, Denis Mukwege and Jody Williams. ElBaradei is the emeritus director general

of the International Atomic Energy Agency and was awarded the
Nobel Peace Prize in 2005. Gbowee is a pioneer of an African women's
movement for non-violence and was awarded the Nobel Peace Prize in
2011. Grayling is a philosopher and the author of several books on war,
peace and ethics. Mukwege, a gynaecologist, was awarded the Nobel
Peace Prize in 2018 for giving life and honour to thousands of women
raped in the Congolese war. Williams is the architect of the international
landmines ban treaty and was awarded the Nobel Peace Prize in 1997.
She now chairs the Nobel Women's Initiative for spreading peace
around the world along with other female Nobel laureates.

The six of us came together in Caen in June 2019, on the seventy-
fifth anniversary of the Battle of Normandy, to issue the Normandy
Manifesto for World Peace because we wanted to warn the world
that the arms race was escalating to a degree beyond human control
and our species was at the risk of extinction in a future global war by
accident, incident or intent. It is still possible to withdraw from the
precipice if we are willing to consider a new global contract and a new
architecture for global security with the phased elimination of weapons
of mass destruction from all over the world as its cornerstone. If we
are imprisoned by our competing national ego, greed and the pursuit
of power, we will sleepwalk into a war of human extinction. If we
transform our mental frameworks, new technology and philosophy can
help us enter an era of summum bonum.

My friend Ilmas Futehally, co-founder of the Strategic Foresight
Group (SFG), was present in Caen when we issued the manifesto. We
went for a walk around the abbey and she suggested that I elaborate
the thoughts underpinning the manifesto into a long essay or a book.
We had together led several studies of the SFG in measuring the cost of
conflict in different parts of the world. We had realized that the cost of
a war is not only to be understood in terms of death, destruction and
military expenditure. There are many other costs—of a psychological,
environmental, diplomatic, cultural and educational nature. Wars lead

to the destruction of the civilization where they take place. A world war in the future will ravage human civilization. If the human race has to survive, there is no other option but to begin thinking about a world without war, and the pathways to build one.

John, Lord Alderdice, director of the Centre for the Resolution of Intractable Conflicts at Oxford University, invited me to give a public lecture on Mahatma Gandhi's 150th birth anniversary, 2 October 2019, on the prospects of peace in the twenty-first century. Mahatma Gandhi is known for his non-violent struggle for India's independence. It is not much known that he was also the pioneer of the concept of a world federation of free nations renouncing their weapons and enjoying peaceful coexistence. His proposal was a progressive revision of Immanuel Kant's framework for a federation of states presented in the eighteenth century. It is necessary for scholars to study Gandhi's concept of a world federation. I argued in my oration at Oxford that it was possible to build the vision of a world without war, by taking ahead some of Gandhi's ideas and adapting them to the twenty-first century.

Ilmas was also present at Oxford on this occasion. As we walked with Lord Alderdice for dinner at Arlosh Hall of Harris Manchester College, she suggested that the manifesto and the speech now make way for a book. In the months that followed, we spent hours deliberating the idea of a book on the vision of a world where wars could only be found in films, books and museums.

Thoughts about the book were rolling in my mind while I was preoccupied with my routine work in the last few weeks of 2019. The period around Christmas 2019 shocked me. Russia announced that it had inducted Avangard hypersonic missiles in its combat forces. These are not ordinary ballistic missiles—they travel at twenty-seven times the speed of sound, disguise their trajectory and carry a nuclear payload. They are the weapons of a global nuclear war. Why did Russia include them in its arsenal with such fanfare? It was an omen clearly indicating that Russia was thinking about a world war. I thought this would prompt a global debate on the risk of a war involving Russia, but nothing of that sort happened. In the West, the immediate obsession was with China. In the rest of the world, countries were bothered about their regional strategic competitors. In fact, nobody was willing to talk about war. Whenever I gave talks and interviews about the risk of a major war, I was criticized for being alarmist. Moreover, a virus suspended our civilization. The media was justifiably obsessed with it. We were also worried about climate change with heat waves, forest fires and floods in the most unexpected places. When Russia invaded Ukraine in February 2022, the risk of a war appeared on the world's policy agenda. As the war showed no sign of abating even after weeks, people seemed to forget about the pandemic and climate change. Germany decided to arm itself to the teeth for the first time since its unification. Even the pacifist Scandinavian countries contemplated joining a military alliance.

Meanwhile, I was watching Russia, the United States (US) and China as they were involved in an intensive hypersonic missile race from 2020 to 2022. Since these missiles can alter their trajectory on their own, artificial intelligence (AI) takes over from military commanders. In the past few years, algorithms have gradually started either guiding or taking control from human commanders in many aspects of military affairs. We as a species are surrendering the ability to annihilate our civilization to machines. We are blindly walking towards a precipice.

The world's scientists have been watching these developments. Unlike media persons and politicians, they can see the threats posed by nuclear weapons, climate change and pandemics in an integrated way. Every year since 1947, the Bulletin of the Atomic Scientists—founded by Albert Einstein and other nuclear scientists—has set the Doomsday Clock. The clock uses the imagery of apocalypse (midnight) and the contemporary idiom of nuclear explosion (countdown to zero) to indicate humanity's vulnerability to human-made disasters. In January 2022, the Bulletin's Science and Security Board set the clock for the third consecutive year at 100 seconds to midnight, marking the closest humanity has come to extinction in the past seventy-five years. In the spring of 2022, Prince El Hassan bin Talal of Jordan and I argued, in a joint article published by *Project Syndicate*, that the clock should be set at one minute to midnight. Rachel Bronson, president of the Bulletin of the Atomic Scientists, circulated our proposal among the members of the Bulletin's Science and Security Board. We will see if the clock is set closer to midnight later in the 2020s.

Despite the warnings issued by the Doomsday Clock, the evidence of nine states possessing more than 13,000 nuclear weapons, the dismantling of arms control treaties, the risk of killer pathogens, the risk of weaponization of AI and the evidence of the use of lethal autonomous weapons, we still live in denial. We do not worry about the threat of human extinction because we do not see anyone using nuclear weapons. Just as we lived in denial about terrorism until Al-Qaeda hit the Twin Towers in 2001, about pandemics until the coronavirus affected 500 million people since 2019, and about wars until Russia invaded Ukraine in 2022. On the other hand, there is evidence of how leaders, movements and individuals have prevented a nuclear Armageddon over the years, especially at times of heightened tensions. There is equally impressive proof available of how civil society groups have forced the world to abolish many categories of weapons, including landmines and cluster munitions. Just as we live in denial about the risk of universal death, we live in the rejection of hope for a paradigm change. We somehow believe in the power of status quo. In the discourse dominated by deniers and fatalists, the world needs a way out.

I decided to write this book as a wake-up call for deniers on both sides of the argument. Those who close their eyes to the risk of our collective extermination, as well as those who want to remain blind to the potential of universal transformation. The coronavirus pandemic in 2020–21 was for me, ironically, a great opportunity. I was unable to travel. My office was closed. I could not even leave my apartment building for several months. There was no better moment to process

my thoughts and convert them into words. I used the metaphor of the
Doomsday Clock to navigate my thesis of a movement from midnight
to morning, from a world at the doorstep of the apocalypse to a world
without war.

In Chapter 1, I discuss the existential threat posed by a cataclysmic
arms race, the constant increase in military expenditure and the
development of new weapons using nuclear, biological, chemical and
lethal autonomous technologies. If we look at the next few decades,
is there any guarantee that a group of leaders such as Hitler will not
emerge, in possession of a ready stockpile of weapons of mass destruction
in their hands? What do common people want as evidence available
from public opinion surveys on the use of weapons of mass destruction?

In Chapter 2, I examine the risk of future wars from national ego,
national interest and leaders spreading hypernationalism to consolidate
their hold on power. I will particularly discuss nationalism in the
countries that possess nuclear weapons.

In Chapter 3, I examine deep philosophical questions concerning
the nature of war and of man. It is possible to renounce wars, since war
is a matter of choice, as proved by historical records of several centuries.
If wars can be waged as a choice, they can also be rejected as a choice.

In Chapter 4, I examine how transformation for peace takes
place. Enlightened leaders, courageous military officials and people's
movements worked tirelessly in the Cold War to bring down the
stockpiles of nuclear weapons, though still above dangerous levels, and
prevent catastrophic wars. It was not by fluke that the Cold War avoided
nuclear Armageddon—it was the dedication of many men and women.
What lessons can we learn from their exceptional contribution to the
history of the past century?

In Chapter 5, I outline the historical discourse of the past several
hundred years. Scholars have proposed, for over 500 years, federations of
states in different forms to resolve conflicts peacefully and prevent wars.
The United Nations (UN) is the most successful expression of these
efforts in its universal acceptance. It has made significant contribution

to socio-economic progress, ranging from eradicating polio to raising awareness of climate change. But the UN does not have the capacity to resolve conflicts between big powers, abolish weapons of mass destruction and end the scourge of war. We need to reform the UN or develop an alternative to address its limitations.

In Chapter 6, I propose a new global social contract, whereby a mechanism is developed to address issues that threaten the survival of humankind. People need to commit to their humanity while being loyal to their states. Such a transformation can be brought about by leaders and citizens alike, with a new philosophy, new politics and new activism, which I discuss in detail. It will result in the emergence of a new era of hope. If we do not change ourselves, we face the prospect of universal death.

While the words in this book are mine, the thoughts have evolved in conversations with innumerable friends. It is impossible to mention them all here. Mohamed ElBaradei convinced me of the existential risk from a global nuclear war. Since he has dedicated his life to averting the misuse of nuclear energy for weaponization, his views have high credibility. Martin Rees and many others reiterated this argument. Jody Williams introduced me to the risks posed by AI and autonomous technologies. Leymah Gbowee explained the power of ordinary people, especially women, in transforming the world. Anthony Grayling helped me raise a bar for global ethics. Thomas Greminger explained the value of cooperative security in several discussions. Lou Marinoff engaged in debates on the nature of war and the nature of man. His masterpiece, *On Human Conflict*, had a profound impact on me. Prince El Hassan bin Talal always emphasized the centrality of human dignity in structuring our visions of the world in our myriad conversations in Amman, Mumbai, London and Geneva. John, Lord Alderdice, exposed me to the psychological aspects of war in personal conversations, as well as the annual conclaves of the Centre for the Resolution of Intractable Conflicts. Jean-Yves Ollivier and other colleagues on the board of the Brazzaville Foundation helped me understand African perspectives on military conflicts. Kabine Komara's conversations and work on the ground demonstrated that conflicts between nations can be resolved without violence. Maropene Ramokgopa introduced me to the southern African concept of 'Ubuntu'. Paula Miksic introduced the philosophy of Soka Gakkai and shared extremely valuable stories of the survivors of the nuclear war in Hiroshima and Nagasaki. Francois-Xavier Priollaud has been walking with me every step since we began working together on the Normandy Manifesto for World Peace, encouraging me to develop a blueprint of a world where wars such as the ones they experienced in Normandy do not recur again.

The sojourn of my words into a book was only possible because of the cooperation of several colleagues. Jayantika Kutty and Maitreyee Avachat, research analysts at the SFG, produced volumes of data and analysis that have gone into this book. I would like to thank my editors Stephanie Hale and Binita Roy. Stephanie made it possible for me to carve a sculpture out of the block of marble that was my first draft. Jeppe Olsen read an earlier draft and offered very useful suggestions. My friend Shrikant Menjoge provided constant encouragement to complete the manuscript. Once I wrote the manuscript, I could only take it to the publisher because of Kanishka Gupta, my dynamic literary agent. He has an outstanding knowledge of the publishing industry and an exceptionally helpful nature. Millions of thanks are reserved for him. I am most grateful to HarperCollins India, particularly Executive Editor Swati Chopra, who deserves all credit for bringing this work to readers. I must particularly thank my copy editor Shreya Chakravertty.

I cannot express my debt of gratitude to my closest friend Ilmas Futehally for making this book possible. She has been my compass for a quarter of a century, shaping my ideas and values. She urged me to write this book at Caen and again at Oxford, and again and again in Mumbai. She read every draft, meticulously helping me improvise. She gave me confidence in my moments of doubt. Ilmas, this book is for you.

This book is also for generations who were born much after me and who will endure the twenty-first century if a global war does not terminate their lives. When I look at my sons, Saahil and Rahul, I feel very deeply my responsibility to the future. I know that my generation has failed the younger generations, whether it is with regard to pandemics, climate change, inequality or the arms race.

This book is a way to say to my sons, their friends and successive generations that it is possible to save our civilization from the scourge of war, a hollow promise that was made to us in the charter of the UN. The naysayers will tell you when Donetsk is being bombed and Damascus is living in the shadow of death, to imagine a world without war is utopia. They will ask you to walk the trodden path and acquire more weapons to protect yourself from demons. They will instigate you to hold your flag and think of nothing more.

They will not tell you that Jean-Jacque Rousseau gave birth to the idea of social contract when monarchy and theocracy reigned supreme, and citizens did not really matter. They will not tell you that Rabindranath Tagore appealed to us to rise above nationalism when competitive nationalism was dominant enough to spark the First World War. They will not tell you that John F. Kennedy and Nikita Khrushchev had agreed on a world without weapons at the height of the Cold War.

We need a world without war not merely because of the fear of our survival. We need it because hope is feasible. We need it because dreaming is good and aspirations are essential. We need it because tomorrow is ours. We need it because the impossible is often possible.

I was once on an aircraft that almost crashed. I was once at a hospital when the world's best doctors told me that my son would immediately die. I was once surrounded by terrorists with loaded guns in their hands. On the aircraft, I joined a spontaneous small team that helped the wounded and the shocked. At the hospital, I mobilized knowledge resources from around the world. The result is that my son is now a healthy young man. And some of the terrorists who pointed their AK-47s at me have actually given up guns.

These little experiences have taught me a few big lessons. It is possible to turn death into life. It is possible to convert violence into peace. It is possible to transform darkness into light. It is possible to change despair into hope. It is possible to end wars and unite the world. It is possible to make '*Vasudhaiv Kutumbakam*' a living truth.

Sundeep Waslekar
Mumbai, September 2022

1

Approaching Midnight: The Threat of Human Extinction

We are now in the most dangerous epoch of our species' history. After living in the shadow of nuclear weapons for over seventy-five years, the insatiable thirst for power has found some of us in a perilous race to create an even more cataclysmic arsenal that can exterminate our entire civilization within a few hours. We are preparing to abdicate human control on our species' existence, handing over this ultimate power to machines and algorithms. And thus we find ourselves at the edge of a black hole, staring at extinction. When we have the ingenuity to transform our planet into a paradise, why are we on a relentless march to commit collective suicide?

In March 2022, UN Secretary General Antonio Guterres warned that nuclear war is 'within the realm of possibility'.[1] In January 2022, and in the earlier two years, the *Bulletin of the Atomic Scientists* set the Doomsday Clock at 100 seconds to midnight—the closest the

1

symbolic clock has been to Doomsday ever since it was created in 1947. The Bulletin was founded by Albert Einstein and scientists who had worked on the Manhattan Project. It has a dozen Nobel laureates on its board. It declared in January 2020, 'Civilization-ending nuclear war— whether started by design, blunder, or simple miscommunication— is a genuine possibility.'[2] The statement echoed the sentiment in the Normandy Manifesto for World Peace, which I had co-signed with four Nobel Peace Prize laureates in June 2019: 'The risk of a war by accident, incident or intent remains a distinct possibility . . . We face the risk of human extinction.'[3]

This book is necessary to shake people from their slumber, because most of us are not willing to see that we are at a treacherous precipice. We are blinded by hyper-nationalism: the glory of our nation is what matters the most. We are willing to sacrifice life and annihilate humankind so that the nation's flag can fly high in the middle of the graveyard that our planet is becoming.

We can certainly pull back from this knife edge and chart a new trajectory to eventually create a world without war. But if we wish to solve the problem, first we must recognize that there is one.

It seems as if the world's 7.8 billion inhabitants are afflicted by tunnel vision. To give an analogy, it is as if our perspective is confined to what we see on the computer screen, ignoring the information that rests in the computer's central processing unit (CPU). What we do not see, we do not believe. If at present our highest attention is not engaged in containing the risk from the deadly race for building and acquiring nuclear and post-nuclear weapons, it is because we are blindfolded— just as we were about terrorism until Al-Qaeda hit the World Trade Center in the US; pandemics until COVID-19 virus crippled the world economy; and about climate change until Texas and Florida began to be flooded by cyclones and hurricanes. With terrorism, pandemics and climate catastrophes, there will be grave damage, but humankind will survive their impact. But, if nuclear arms and post-nuclear weapons are to be used in the defence of a nation's honour, we await universal death.

Before we understand the impact of post-nuclear weapons, let us look at the familiar dangers posed by nuclear warheads and missiles. Because there has not been any nuclear war since the bombing of Hiroshima and Nagasaki in 1945, we believe that we need not worry about one in the future. Also, those bombs only destroyed two cities. Humankind as a whole was spared. But this is an illusion. Little Boy and Fat Man were minor experimental bombs. Their destruction capacity was 15 kilotons each, and they killed around 2,00,000 people—though we will never know the real number because counting the dead bodies was difficult in the aftermath of the explosions. The survivors of the world's first nuclear weapon attack we may meet today were young children at that time.

Setsuko Morita was one such twelve-year-old student at Second Hiroshima Prefectural High School. She was at the Eastern Drill Ground with other girls, 1.7 km from the hypocentre of the Hiroshima blast. She recalls how, after the detonation, 'her friends staggered to their feet, looking like ghosts, with eyeballs popped up and skin peeling off'. Ryoko Iwanga was 1.1 km from the Nagasaki hypocentre. She still lives with the pain of countless shards of glass piercing her body that morning and seeing all her loved ones killed.[4]

Most nuclear weapons today have a destructive capacity of over 100 kilotons, several times that of the bombs dropped on Hiroshima and Nagasaki. According to the International Campaign to Abolish Nuclear Weapons, a 100-kiloton bomb will kill almost everyone within a 5 km radius of ground zero within minutes. The detonation will spread the radioactive fallout to territory within an 80 km radius, causing death from radiation sickness and cancer over several years.[5] What do these indicators mean in terms of real life in London, New York, Moscow, Beijing, or any other place in the world?

If a single 100-kiloton nuclear bomb hits Westminster in London, initially, a fireball of 100 million degrees Celsius will erupt. All buildings, people, vehicles, statues and streets as far as Kensington in the west, the financial centre in the east, London Zoo in the north, and Clapham Town in the south will be vaporized within minutes. There will be nothing but rubble, smoke and radiation an hour after the explosion. People present in the area from Kew Gardens to the Royal Observatory, Greenwich—outside the 5 km radius of the totally ravaged zone—will suffer from third-degree burns, shock waves and radiation, and at least half of them will die over the days that follow. Radiation fallout will spread as far as Oxford and Cambridge. Many people will suffer from radiation and cancer over months and years. If a warhead with a 50,000-kiloton blast yield, such as the Tsar Bomba, is detonated over central London, everything in the entire area extending as far as Reading and Chelmsford will evaporate in a matter of hours. Windowpanes will break in York and Glasgow. Radiation fallout will spread all over the United Kingdom (UK), Ireland, France, Belgium, and some parts of Europe. In a real war, the bombs are likely to be larger than 100 kilotons and smaller than the Tsar Bomba. They are likely to have a blast yield of 1,000, 5,000 or even 10,000 kilotons. Moreover, the enemy is unlikely to use only one warhead. There will most probably be a shower of bombs at different locations, which would destroy Great Britain, killing the entire population and ravaging most structures within a couple of hours, and radiation will contaminate Europe in a few days. I have only used London as an example here since Prime Minister Boris Johnson's decision in March 2021 to accelerate the nuclear arms race has made it vulnerable.[6]

A similar fate awaits other cities in the world in the eventuality of a nuclear war. If a 100 kiloton bomb is detonated over Manhattan, all its inhabitants will be incinerated, and most buildings from Central Park to Washington Avenue will collapse within a few minutes. A comparable bomb would destroy Beijing from Baiyunguan in the west to Chaoyang in the east, and in the case of Moscow, from the Bolshoi Theatre in the north to the Kremlin in the south. Bigger bombs will devastate larger territories. Radioactive fallout will spread across large parts of a country, depending on the blast yield and winds. Since, in a war, several bombs will be detonated at various locations, entire countries will be ruined. The health and environmental impact of any nuclear attack will spread far beyond the conflict zones, encompassing almost the entire Earth (as we shall see later in this book).

Nuclear bombs will not merely result in physical destruction, economic collapse, health crises and environmental devastation. They will ravage our minds, rupture our hearts and tear apart human civilization. A single nuclear attack can demolish every one of us, wherever we may be living, even if our abode is far away from ground zero.

Let us now consider post-nuclear weapons. Since the end of the Cold War, new kinds of weapons and their delivery systems have been developed. Hypersonic missiles, which look like wedge-shaped rockets, are operated using AI, where algorithms enable the machines to determine their own targets, change trajectories and evade radars. In the race to develop more such weapons, Russia and China have taken the lead, followed by the US. In December 2019, for example, Russia inducted Avangard into its defence services. It is a hypersonic glide vehicle that travels at twenty-seven times the speed of sound and carries a 2,000 kiloton nuclear payload. It can withstand temperatures of 2,000 degrees Celsius and manoeuvre in its trajectory to avoid missile defence systems.[7] Meanwhile, the US tested its own hypersonic missile in March 2020, when the country, along with the world, was being ravaged by the COVID-19 pandemic. In fact, even the pandemic did not halt the deadly hypersonic missile race between the big powers, in which nobody was the winner. In August 2021, China tested a nuclear-capable hypersonic missile, which went round the Earth in orbit. Around the same time, Russia tested the deployment of a hypersonic missile from a nuclear submarine.

The US, Russia and China are engaged in a race to deploy AI to enable the operation of unmanned submarines and other unmanned underwater vehicles. In a future war, algorithms will move underwater delivery vehicles and fire missiles at other underwater or over-the-surface targets. This may sound like a science fiction story where oceans are the theatre of catastrophic warfare. Unfortunately, it is a priority for the three big powers in their military planning for the 2020s and the 2030s.

Lethal autonomous weapons, or killer robots, are not the humanoids that they are portrayed to be in movies and computer games. They are guns and delivery vehicles often shaped like flat aircraft. Outwardly, they may even resemble some conventional non-nuclear weapons. However, internally, AI enables them to act on their own without human intervention. Add to this the proliferation of cyberweapons in recent years. These are malware capable of overriding the command-and-control systems of the user's adversaries. We will only become aware of other, more advanced weapons that are currently being designed when they suddenly become visible in the defence market one day. It is quite plausible that weapons of biological warfare such as killer pathogens are under development at this very moment, as we will discuss later in this chapter.

Since information on nuclear weapons is treated with utmost secrecy, we do not have official data on the exact number of weapons held by each country. The *Bulletin of the Atomic Scientists* has been able to compile limited statistics and estimates in this regard (Table A1 in the Appendix). However, data on the numbers of hypersonic missiles and lethal autonomous weapons (killer robots) in the possession of different countries is not available as these programmes are, as of 2022, in the early stages of development and shrouded in secrecy.

Scientists, military planners and diplomats know only too well the havoc these cataclysmic weapons can wreak; they can envisage the collapse of civilization in gory detail. But ordinary citizens do not have information on how their cities and towns will be ravaged in case of an all-out nuclear war—the question of human extinction from the planet is beyond imagination.

Even when experts inform us about the development of weapons of final destruction, we do not really care because, by default, we believe in the goodness of human nature and expect that it will deter a nuclear catastrophe. Human beings are intrinsically hopeful. We naively feel certain that no situation will arise in the next few decades that will motivate the US to launch a pre-emptive attack on China or North Korea. But, if anything, the evidence is to the contrary. For example, in September 2017, Donald Trump, then President of the US, threatened North Korea on the floor of the UN General Assembly: 'We will have no choice but to totally destroy North Korea.'[8] Similarly, we optimistically believe that no terrorist attack, no violation of borders, no rhetorical escalation of the domestic agenda will lead to a nuclear war between India and Pakistan. We innocuously trust that no leader of Russia will try to expand the nation's sphere of influence to capture some of the countries earlier belonging to the Soviet Union. And we assume that the nuclear command-and-control system will work brilliantly well; the algorithms that drive hypersonic missiles and early warning systems will not fail; and autonomous weapons will never go awry.

A prime reason people in general do not anticipate a war leading to human extinction is that nobody, except North Korea's supreme leader, is threatening one. It would be naive to expect that any nation in the world will announce its plans for pressing into action terminal weapons months in advance of the event. Such a decision would be sudden, secretive and swift. The option to use nuclear or hypersonic missiles will be exercised at an advanced stage in a conventional war. The missiles will leave their silos within ten to fifteen minutes of the leader taking the decision to launch them. If biological agents are used, that will happen in stealth. It is likely that there will not be a premeditated intent but a chain of incidents in a conventional war that will unexpectedly cross the nuclear threshold. There is also a possibility of misinterpretation of data by the command-and-control system, due to a cyberattack or the failure of the AI used by the early warning system. The US, Russia and China are concentrating on using AI for the early detection of threats to enable a swift response. While AI might provide inputs that humans cannot gather, a rush in using it to detect threats and launch attacks can lead to miscalculations by men and machines. In either case, we will come to know of a nuclear war only after it starts. The impact of a biological weapon will be revealed much after its effects have started spreading. Nukes and killer robots do not make appointments. Neither do pathogens send visiting cards in advance. Believing that attacks of nuclear weapons, lethal autonomous weapons or killer pathogens are not on the anvil because nobody is openly threatening to use them is being ingenuous.

War takes place in the backdrop of simmering tensions between parties, which just needs a single spark to act as a trigger. It is impossible to anticipate the triggers of even non-nuclear wars years or months in advance. As a result, there is a tendency to treat the tensions as the routine management of relations. But the absence of a vivid signal of global confrontation involving weapons of final destruction does not mean that we have eliminated such a risk.

We are currently in a twilight zone, where we cannot make out the definitive trajectory of any future global war. However, we cannot completely rule out such a catastrophe either, as many sets of rivalries and tensions are at play globally, especially between countries that possess weapons of final destruction. At best, we can concur with astrophysicist Martin Rees, Astronomer Royal of the UK and one of the greatest scientists on the planet, who has reiterated in several of his articles and in his book *Our Final Hour* that the threat of human extinction in a world war is merely in abeyance. Russian scholar Alexey Arbatov disagrees. Writing for the Carnegie Moscow Centre in March 2019, he announced that the danger of nuclear war is much greater in the 2020s than it was in the 1980s.[9]

In the US, France, China, Russia and North Korea, a single leader can decide to launch a nuclear attack. In Britain, India, Pakistan and

Israel, a small group would decide when to order the launch of a missile or the detonation of a weapon carrying a nuclear payload. If Iran, Saudi Arabia and other states acquire nuclear weapons in the future, we may not even get to know their decision-making structures. Our species' survival is mortgaged to a handful of persons. And yet, people trust that their wise leaders are aware of the catastrophic impact of the weapons of final destruction and, therefore, will never use such an arsenal.

In reality, there is not only the risk of erroneous judgement by a leader, but also a risk of interest groups within the government manipulating the uppermost decision-makers. In many countries, intelligence agencies, a few civil servants and defence personnel believe that they are the real patrons of the state. They try to control state policies and function in a secretive way—unlike the head of state or government overtly responsible to the nation. They are known as the 'deep state'. They may convince the leader of the need for a war out of their own beliefs or to protect their institutional interests. Some of them may even sense that the role and very existence of the military and intelligence agencies will be threatened in the absence of the threat of war and so may advocate for it. The deep state may find it in its interest to manipulate leaders to create rivalries that can unexpectedly go wrong and trigger a war. It is even possible for the deep state in a nuclear-armed country to create a chain of events that leads to military confrontation. One does not have to look far for a classic example of the deep state manipulating a country's affairs: we need only consider the operations of US intelligence agencies to destabilize Fidel Castro's Cuba in the early 1960s, which led to the Cuban missile crisis that could have caused the Third World War. In 2014, the Russian deep state possibly played a critical role in fuelling the conflict in Ukraine, which could have transformed into a war between Russia and the US, but fortunately it did not.

Can mere awareness of the dangerous nature of any weapon prevent its deployment? Many certainly seem to have thought so.

Alfred Nobel, the inventor of dynamite, had expressed a wish to produce a material or a machine that would have such a devastating effect that war from then on would be impossible. In 1891, referring to his dynamite factories, he said to the Austrian Countess Bertha Von Suttner, 'Perhaps my factories will put an end to war sooner than your congresses: on the day that two army corps can mutually annihilate each other in a second, all civilised nations will surely recoil with horror and disband their troops.'[10] Earlier, Richard Gatling, the inventor of the Gatling gun—the first-ever machine gun—believed that his invention from the days of the American Civil War would put an end to wars and armies. He was convinced that the deadliness of machine guns would make their use unthinkable due to the horrible carnage they caused. He also believed that the increased lethality of machine guns would reduce the number of soldiers required on the battlefield; armies would be made redundant. Richard Gatling's idealism proved to be entirely misplaced.

Not only have dynamite and machine guns been routinely used, but nuclear bombs have also been detonated—not once but twice within a week. Since the end of the Second World War, many world leaders have seriously contemplated using nuclear weapons, as we will see later in this book. It would be, therefore, foolish to believe that global leaders will never use nuclear and post-nuclear weapons and whatever other weapons they might secretly be making.

This brings us back to our initial question of whether the nearly 8 billion people in the world can trust a few leaders in nuclear-armed states with the survival of humankind. Adolf Hitler, Joseph Stalin, Mao Zedong, Pol Pot and Slobodan Milošević are only a few among several leaders who have ordered the massacre of thousands of their own countrymen. They were all too eager to wage wars with other nations and slaughter millions of people outside the boundaries of their own countries. There were no nuclear weapons, hypersonic missiles, killer robots or deadly pathogens during their time. What if a future leader with the psychology of Hitler, Stalin or Mao finds weapons of final destruction readily available in his stockpile? How can we be sure that no such leader will come to possess ultimate power in the twenty-first century?

Another reason this book is necessary is to explain how we can turn back the clock and gradually find a way to liberate the world from the menace of wars. Many believe that the fact that the Cold War concluded with the fall of the Berlin Wall instead of a nuclear Armageddon was humanity's good fortune. But to credit fluke for our survival in the Cold War is humbug. Our way out of the disaster was carefully constructed by dedicated individuals and groups. They proved that it is possible to prevent the ultimate tragedy of nuclear annihilation. Such was the success of these groups that there was a brief moment in time when the top leaders of the US and the Soviet Union almost agreed to abolish all nuclear weapons within a definitive time frame.

Our way forward cannot be confined to signing treaties to abolish specific types of weapons. Such arms control arrangements are essential but not enough. We must go beyond structures that aim to curtail the supply of nuclear weapons to address the factors that contribute to the demand for such a deadly arsenal. We must remove the cobwebs from our mental frameworks and international relations. It is in this context that this book will examine how to establish the foundation of a peaceful new era of *summum bonum*.

This book is a moral imperative.

William Faulkner said in his Nobel Prize banquet on 10 December 1950: 'I believe that man will not merely endure; he will prevail. He is immortal, not because he alone among creatures has an inexhaustible voice, but because he has a soul, a spirit capable of compassion and sacrifice and endurance.'[11]

Faulkner was speaking in a red-brick building in Stockholm known for its shining crown and golden hall. It was surrounded by water that had frozen in the winter. The sun had set in the early afternoon. Yet, when Faulkner spoke, the crown on top of the building shone.

We need to help mankind to endure, not perish, for millions of men and women before us have built and shaped the civilization that is here today, even though some of them sometimes went astray. To help humankind rise to the challenge of our collective survival is not a choice. It is an ethical obligation to our species.

An Appetite for Arms

Many people believe that the risk of a global war has receded with the end of the Cold War, when in the second half of the last century, two powerful military blocs armed with nuclear weapons confronted each other, and then thankfully abandoned the path of escalation. Thus, we think that we are now out of danger. The evidence could not be more to the contrary.

In 1949, at the beginning of the Cold War, the global military expenditure was around $250 billion in terms of the 2016 constant value of the US dollar. It had increased more than threefold by 1952 when the first hydrogen bomb—several times more powerful than an atomic bomb—became part of the American arsenal. Global military expenditure, mainly on account of the US and the former Soviet Union, further increased significantly around the mid-1980s. It was in the range of $1,300 billion to $1,500 billion (2016 constant) from 1983 to 1988. That is when the Cold War was at its height, with cruise and Pershing missiles stationed in Europe. During the Cold War, Mrs Pershing and her friends needed to be fed because they protected the Americans from the scary Soviet Union. Additionally, the Soviets wanted to pamper their SS-N-20 Sturgeon missiles and TU-160 stealth bombers to feel secure. In the 1990s, the military outlay temporarily declined following the fall of the Berlin Wall but started rising again by the end of the decade. If there indeed exists no threat of virulent attacks since the end of the Cold War, why is the worldwide military enterprise guzzling more dollars than ever before? As compared to $1,000 billion in 1999, the global military expenditure is expected to double to $2,000 billion by 2025 (2016 constant). Tables A2 and A3 (in Appendix 1) explain the pattern of arms expenditure during and since the Cold War, respectively.

The expenditure pattern that was observed at the beginning of the twenty-first century is reminiscent of a similar one a hundred years earlier. All the major European powers gradually increased their expenditure on armaments from the 1890s to 1914 when the First World War took place. See Table A4 in the Appendix.

Sir Edward Grey, British Foreign Secretary from 1905 to 1916, used to say that excessive spending on arms would lead to a catastrophe.[12] The First World War did take place following the growth of military expenditure in the preceding few decades, though there were many reasons for it besides the arms build-up. Or was the growing outflow of armaments a symptom of what was happening beneath the surface of the geopolitical landscape? If indeed the military budget is an interpreter of the maladies poised to be unleashed on us, what does the doubling of the worldwide military outlay from 1999 to 2025 foretell?

It may be argued that military expenditure by countries follows economic growth. The emerging economic powers of our time are suddenly able to splurge on their national security needs. These countries are China, India, Saudi Arabia and South Korea, in addition to old-timers the US and Russia. Undoubtedly, a fat purse can enable a country to buy lethal toys, but whether it would buy the weapons depends on if it has enemies. In the 1990s, the US and Russia temporarily reduced their military expenditure thanks to the decline in mutual hostilities. Germany, Japan and France are three other significant economies that since the end of the 1980s have maintained their arms expenditure at a constant of around $45 billion to $50 billion per year. In recent years, the Trump administration in the US used diplomatic and political pressure on its European allies to force them to increase their military spending. As a result, Germany increased its military outlay by 10 per cent over the previous year in 2019 to cross $49 billion.[13] In 2022 in the aftermath of the Ukraine war, Germany decided to increase its military expenditure further by a whopping 50 per cent.[14]

Many rich countries such as Switzerland, Canada, Sweden, Norway and Denmark try to reduce wastage of resources on arms by mitigating enmity with others. But, on the other hand, emerging economies such as China, India, Saudi Arabia and South Korea want to be equipped with weapons as they are engaged in strategic competition with their rivals. So, it is fair to say that economic growth does not automatically lead to an increase in spending on bombs and missiles, but an increase in hostile enemies certainly does. There is an underlying relationship between the will to spend and the intent to kill.

Military expenditure alone does not reveal the entire truth. Spending $10 billion on swords and daggers is different from spending that amount on machine guns and dynamite. Or an outlay of $100 billion for tanks and guns is not the same as splurging on nuclear weapons and hypersonic missiles. Countries are not only burning more and more funds, but are also producing increasingly lethal weapons. The last 500 years have constituted an era of competitive destructive potential, where not only money but also science and talent have been deployed to develop the potency to murder greater numbers of people per hour or per million dollars. Military historian Trevor N. Dupuy's Lethality Index demonstrates how each level of technological development has led to an increase in killing capacity.[15]

Dupuy's Lethality Index gives the following illustration. It reveals that from approximately 1500 BCE to 1500 CE, there was hardly any change in the lethality of weapons. Swords, spears, and arrows—used in combat for a few thousand years—could kill twenty to twenty-five persons in an hour. An arrow was the only missile that could be used to attack a target from a distance. Arson was the only weapon of mass destruction—it was used by Persian forces under Xerxes while attacking Athens; by the Crusaders of the fourth Crusade while attacking Constantinople; and by Genghis Khan and his Mongol descendants while invading Central Asia and the Middle East, among others. The combination of cavalry, bows and arson was lethal but limited in its massacring capacity in comparison with what was to follow.

With the discovery of gunpowder, firearms were invented, and their destructive potential gradually augmented from the sixteenth to the early twentieth century. In the First World War, several deadly weapons were introduced for the first time, including aircraft, poison gas and tanks. Following the Second World War, a nuclear arms race produced so many weapons that they could destroy the earth several times over.

Eventually, arms control talks resulted in reducing the number of nuclear warheads with the US and the former Soviet Union from 66,000 in the mid-1980s to roughly 14,000 now, out of which 9,500 are in active military service. There are mutual inspections by American and Russian experts of each other's military bases to monitor and verify the disassembling. The nuclear waste generated through the deconstruction of weapons is normally buried to prevent radiation. Some of the aircraft earlier used for deploying nuclear bombs are now being modified for non-nuclear use. All this has been possible under bilateral treaties between the two countries. But now, as the treaty regime is being eroded, there may not be any legal and technical framework available for dismantling weapons in the future.

In the event of a nuclear attack, it is important to bear in mind that beyond the immediate damage caused in the first few hours, there would also be long-term health and environmental impacts due to radiation and global cooling. Some scenarios predict that the Little Ice Age can recur. Further, it is impossible to generalize the medium- and long-term impact of a nuclear war, not only on the combating countries, but also on surrounding countries. It would depend on yield, type and number of warheads used, the altitude at which they are detonated, wind speed and direction, and many other such factors. What is certain is the complete annihilation of the target zones and long-term damage to life, environment and economy in the countries involved in warfare, as well as in several others.

Another aspect that requires attention, along with nuclear bombs, is the use of delivery vehicles for nuclear warheads. Intercontinental ballistic missiles (ICBMs) were developed by the US and the former

Soviet Union in the 1950s, and China followed a few decades later. The speed of an ICBM is up to 20,000 km per hour. The speed of a commercial aircraft is 900 km per hour. Thus, an ICBM moves at more than twenty times the speed of an aeroplane on an intercontinental flight. The US can deliver a nuclear bomb to a target in China or Russia within half an hour and vice versa. The US, the UK, China, Russia and North Korea have missiles that can travel over a 10,000 km range. Multiple independently targeted re-entry vehicles (ITRVs) make it possible to send several warheads using a single missile. Even though the total arsenal of nuclear weapons has declined since the 1980s, the possibility of deploying multiple warheads with every missile has increased the lethality of each attack.

During the Cold War, we not only invested our financial, scientific and technological resources in producing weapons capable of blowing up the planet several times over, but we also invested in the power of words to spread callousness to justify a political culture of mass annihilation. In the 1950s, the new term 'megadeath' entered the nuclear lexicon. One megadeath equals 1 million deaths. It was an acknowledgement that the world was now thinking in terms of millions of deaths in future wars. Politicians and scholars showed ethical and intellectual bankruptcy in failing to reject the term and the policies that necessitated it. It was left to guitarist Dave Mustaine and bassist David Ellefson to form a heavy metal band by that name (Megadeth) to parody the concept. The band became very popular and sold 40 million records worldwide. They released albums titled *Killing Is My Business . . . and Business Is Good*, *Countdown to Extinction*, *The System Has Failed* and *Endgame*.[16] Musicians and art lovers demonstrated their deep feelings of regard for humanity, but decision-makers and their scholarly propagandists lived in a different world. They do so even today.

The end of the Cold War a quarter century ago should have heralded the end of the desire to build destructive capacities. As there is no significant conflict between Russia and the US, there is no need to maintain nuclear forces on high alert. According to the Union of Concerned Scientists, nuclear missiles that are perpetually kept in a state of readiness, so that they can be launched within minutes of a decision being taken, are commonly said to be on 'hair-trigger alert'.[17] This term indicates that the US's land-based missiles can be launched within five minutes and submarine-based missiles within fifteen minutes of a presidential decision to do so. Russian officials informally claim that their land-based missiles can be launched within tens of seconds; it is not known whether that claim is an exaggeration or if the Russian launch procedures allow faster launches than do the US's procedures.

At the beginning of 2021, the US had deployed 1,350 such strategic warheads on 652 ICBMs, SLBMs (submarine-launched ballistic missiles) and strategic bombers.[18] Russia had deployed 1,444 warheads on 527 ICBMs, SLBMs and strategic bombers.[19] In 2022, almost 2,800 American and Russian nuclear warheads are ready to destroy the human civilization at a minute's notice. Since the time required for a weapon on hair-trigger alert to be set is only five to ten minutes, and the time required by an ICBM less than an hour, it would be impossible to negotiate with the enemy and reverse the decision. Moreover, if there is a hypersonic glide at the tip of the ICBM carrying the nuclear payload, it will not be detected until mushroom clouds begin to move up in the atmosphere after detonation. It is possible that scores of nuclear bombs will hit the enemy country, killing several million people in a few hours. If the adversary notices the attack in its direction, it is bound to launch a pre-emptive attack and perhaps a huge one aimed at crippling the offensive capacity of the rival. This can, in turn, attract a massive counterattack. Within an hour of the first attack, an all-out nuclear exchange will take place, causing innumerable megadeaths on both sides. This can damage the atmosphere of the earth, with catastrophic consequences for the countries that are not even remotely involved in the conflict, and make large swathes of humankind perish. The 2,800 nuclear weapons on hair-trigger alert, backed by a stockpile of another

7,000 warheads, missiles and bombers, have thus come together to form the most dangerous moment in our species' history.

Speed and Stealth

The main difference in the arms race of the twenty-first century, as compared to the Cold War era, is that we have learnt to operate weapons by stealth. In the years following the Second World War, the US and the former Soviet Union competed in making ever bigger bombs. Eventually, they realized that the big weapons were difficult to deploy and might, in the end, prove to be unusable. So they changed the strategy to produce small weapons with big impact. Enter the nuclear earth-penetrating weapons (EPWs) and low-yield nuclear weapons. The EPWs penetrate earth and concrete structures and explode beneath the surface with twenty times the impact of its yield level. If a warhead has a 100-kiloton yield, its impact will be the equivalent of a weapon of 2-megaton yield. As EPWs are used to destroy underground structures, it is not clear what impact they would have on life on the surface; the fallout would also depend on specific characteristics of the location. Along with the EPWs, the nuclear weapon powers have also developed a fondness for low-yield weapons. In 2020, the first year of COVID-19, the US administration deployed an unknown number of low-yield warheads, known as W76-2, on submarine-launched missiles. These bombs have a destructive capacity of 5–15 kiloton of TNT and are comparable to the bombs used in Hiroshima and Nagasaki. However, the newer warheads will inflict much greater damage because of the increase in population density all over the world since 1945. The greatest danger posed by EPWs and low-yield weapons is that they will instigate a terminal war. It is relatively more tempting to use these weapons as they are capable of damaging a small town, which can be treated like a warning shot and can come in handy to force an adversary to surrender. Weapons such as these aim to bypass the stigma currently associated with the use of nuclear weapons. It is naive to believe that the country that is made a target will take the attack lying down, without opting to launch a full-scale nuclear attack of its own. In fact, a determined nuclear power may just find the justification in retaliating with 1,000-kiloton (or larger) bombs, which will destroy several cities and population centres, with the radiation causing utter mayhem. This will, in turn, invoke reprisal. Thus, within hours of any country using low-yield nuclear weapons against another nuclear power, a full-blown nuclear exchange is inevitable.

We are also learning to produce arms that can move at unprecedented speeds. Let us take the example of the hypersonic missiles mentioned earlier. They are fast cruise missiles moving at 5–20 Mach speed (1 Mach equals 1,235 km per hour). Hypersonic weapons have the advantage of speed, precision, manoeuvrability and low-altitude travel at ranges that are incomparable to existing ballistic missiles. Besides hypersonic cruise missiles, there are hypersonic glide vehicles. They are small missiles on the tip of ICBM vehicles. They can determine their own path, changing directions and avoiding radars, as they are steered by algorithms and not through human control. Thus, hypersonic weapons have an advantage over other kinds of missiles in that they can design an unpredictable trajectory, making it harder for them to be detected. Some hypersonic weapons can be used to strike small nuclear arsenals. This can escalate a conflict if countries with smaller arsenals feel threatened and compelled to use or lose their nuclear capabilities. It can also result in nuclear-capable countries investing in clandestine facilities. Deploying missiles that can move with speed and stealth will take strategic warfare to higher levels than we have seen so far. Already, there is stiff competition between three major powers—the US, Russia and China—to make and use hypersonic missiles.[20] If these missiles are deployed in hair-trigger-alert positions, the future of the world's population will become unpredictable.

Hypersonic missiles belong to the new generation of post-nuclear weapons. Other weapons in this category include 'killer robots', technically known as lethal autonomous weapons. They are still in their infancy, but they may dominate the military scene in the second quarter of the century unless something more vicious takes over. As of today, there is no international consensus on what constitutes a lethal autonomous weapon system. It is often defined as a system that can target and fire independently, without meaningful human control.[21] The essential feature of these weapons is that they operate based on algorithms, choosing their own actions and targets; there is no human intervention, though all countries producing killer robots insist that they will have a human in the loop. This is to downplay the risk involved in delegating decisions of life and death to a machine.

The story of Harpy, an Israeli-made killer robot, has recently been reported by the media. It operates autonomously as an unmanned aircraft, without precision guidance from (human) controlling authorities. It loiters in the air for several hours and looks for radar signals. Whenever it does detect such a signal, it hits and destroys the radar. A band of these weapons are to be deployed in a war to destroy the enemy air defence system. The air force can then operate and do what it likes with impunity. Azerbaijan deployed several Harpy robots in a war with Armenia in October 2020, even while the world was being ravaged by a pandemic. According to some other media reports, South Korea has a killer robot stationed on its border with its northern neighbour. This is a gun acting as a surveillance mechanism and firing at the target when necessary.[22] This is only the tip of the iceberg; there are bound to be many more such weapons in operation, though hidden from the gaze of the media.

Unlike Harpy or the South Korean killer robots, which may be described as not so sophisticated, much more advanced lethal autonomous weapon systems are being developed and produced by the US, the UK, France, Russia, China, South Korea, Australia and certainly Israel. They will soon be available for sale across the world, from Azerbaijan to India.

Just as killer robots use AI for identifying and eliminating targets, there are ways in which the armed forces use AI for data interpretation and speeding up military decisions. The main strength of AI is in collating and interpreting vast amounts of data in relatively short spans; it can help military commanders and fighter pilots filter available data and act fast. Reportedly, this is being done on F-35 fighter planes by the US air force, where AI is used to evaluate data from multiple sources before it is shared with pilots.

Military planners are aware of the risk associated with using AI in a nuclear war and are reluctant to allow it to be used in the command-and-control systems of nuclear weapons. AI can at best be treated as a decision support system; it may not be used to launch a nuclear weapon. The decision to launch nuclear weapons is still a human prerogative. But AI may be used in evaluating data to advise human decision-makers when initiating a nuclear attack. With the race for early detection of and response to threats using AI, the lines between machines and humans in nuclear decision-making structures are getting blurred at a fast pace.

There are two risks associated with the present use of AI in the nuclear theatre. First, given the speed with which AI is encroaching on the military decision-making processes, it is difficult to predict how the technology will be used in the future. We may well find that the current reticence in using AI to launch a nuclear attack may vanish soon. Second, if in anticipation of war, nuclear decisions are delegated to the field level, the use of AI cannot be ruled out. Will decisions supported by AI be better than those prompted by the whims of a psychopath leader or military commander? The answer will define the fate of the 7.8 billion inhabitants of this planet.

It is some measure of the looming problem facing us that more than 4,500 AI experts have called for a new treaty to prohibit lethal autonomous weapons systems in various open letters since 2015. Civil society activists have launched a Stop Killer Robots Campaign.[23] But the countries that have been investing resources in the ongoing research and development of weapons systems with minimal human control over important functions (including recognition, selection and engagement of targets) refuse to ban such weapons. These countries might settle for a code of conduct in their production, deployment and use, but absolutely abhor the idea of a legally binding treaty. The refusal of killer robot–producing countries to go beyond a voluntary code proves their moral erosion and avarice for death and destruction.

Good into Evil

The journey of man from stones, spears and fire to nuclear weapons during the Cold War, and nuclear-armed hypersonic missiles and killer robots in the second quarter of the twenty-first century, proves our increasing willingness to use science and technology for our own annihilation. The original intended purpose of science was to harness the forces of nature to improve human life. But warmongers have been using discoveries and inventions to conceive and build destructive arsenals.

Examples of such subversive uses abound, chlorine being one. It was used in the eighteenth century as an antiseptic for cleaning water and in the dyes and the textile industry. However, by the First World War it had been used as a weapon in the form of a poison gas even though an explicit ban on the use of toxic gases had been introduced in the Hague Declaration of 1899.[24] Similarly, TNT was originally invented as a yellow dye in the 1860s. Within decades, it was being used as an explosive to fill artillery shells in wars.[25]

Consider the example of the radio, which was invented as means of entertainment and information in the 1890s. But one of the first orders for Marconi's radio sets was placed by the British War Office for use in the Boer War.[26] Subsequently, others put it to the much more sinister use of spreading hatred and propaganda, such as the Nazis targeting the Jews.

It is the same story with the invention of the aircraft. Wilbur and Oliver Wright made the first powered flight in December 1903. Within a mere six years, by 1909, both France and Germany had a military air branch for reconnaissance as well as bombing. And by the First World War, which began in 1914, the use of planes in warfare was common.[27]

Continuing in a similar vein, we see that after barely half a decade of Otto Hahn and his research assistant Fritz Strassmann discovering the nuclear fission of heavy elements (in December 1938) and explaining it publicly,[28] the first atomic bomb was dropped on Hiroshima.

It used to take several decades to convert an invention or discovery made for the good of humanity into a devastating force. In the first half of the twentieth century, it took less than a decade, particularly with complex technologies such as aircraft and nuclear fission. In this century, the time lag between an invention and its misuse for destruction has further decreased.

Over the next few decades, new technologies that are expected to facilitate human progress are AI, 3D printing, supercomputers, synthetic biology and space exploration. It remains to be seen how these may be adapted to find more and more ways of scaling up our destructive capabilities.

One of the technological frontiers being explored extensively is outer space, mainly to use satellites for communication, education and remote sensing, and to look for new habitats for mankind. In the 1950s, the US and the former Soviet Union began to militarize space. They also quickly developed the capability to destroy satellites, attacking their own for experimental purposes. China and India have followed in their footsteps in the last two decades.

In March 2019, India destroyed its own satellite in the lower orbit and announced that it had done so to demonstrate its technological prowess.[29] Indians received the news with great applause as evidence of the country's advancing position in the geopolitical sphere. Plans for developing such anti-satellite (ASAT) missiles were in the offing since 2007, when China successfully tested an ASAT missile destroying one of its own satellites. India's logic in pursuing the ASAT weapons programme was not too different from its motive in developing nuclear weapons; it was the same reaction as in 1964 when a Chinese nuclear test at Lop Nor had motivated India to develop its own atom bomb within the next decade.[30] India will continue to watch carefully further developments in the militarization of space and try to follow or overtake China. At the same time, the Chinese will try to overtake the Russians and the Americans. Pakistan or other countries will try to catch up with or bypass India. It is unfortunate that instead of focusing on the many benefits space exploration can provide—including in the fields of communication, global positioning, weather forecasting, health and education—a vicious chain is evolving to use this treasure of resources for war preparedness.

In the next few decades, cyberspace is likely to become another frontier for conducting warfare. Already, cyberattacks to cause digital damage are commonplace. Tricking unsuspecting internet users to secure their bank account details is an everyday affair. How many of us have not received the offer of being paid millions of dollars by a strange widow of a rich former ruler or an oil company executive? But now, cyberattacks have progressed to cause physical damage in the real world. There are widespread reports on how the Industroyer malware shut down a power grid in Ukraine in 2016 and how Stuxnet damaged the physical structure of centrifuges of a uranium plant in Iran.[31] It is possible that some of this malware may be adjusted to attack other kinds of infrastructure by terrorists or rogue states, or even the so-called civilized states, albeit incognito. The ability of the attacker to remain anonymous and operate in a borderless world makes cyberattacks that are capable of causing physical damage particularly vicious.

The most hazardous scenario that we can perhaps foresee is that of the three most powerful states of the world possessing nuclear and cyberattack capacities—China, Russia and the US—engaging in brinksmanship. The difference between the use of cyberattacks for the surveillance and destruction of the rival's nuclear infrastructure is disappearing at a fast pace. If one state uses AI to launch a cyberattack to render the nuclear weapon capacity of its rival ineffective, that will open up a new and much more sinister possibility. The rival would not like its defensive potential and billions of dollars in investments over decades to be nullified so easily. It may, therefore, launch a pre-emptive attack on the AI capacity, the nuclear weapons manufacturing sites and missile silos of the other state. This can lead to an all-out war involving nuclear weapons, missiles and algorithms, with an unpredictable catastrophic outcome.

Michael Klare explains in *Arms Control Today* (November 2019) that the US, Russia and China are involved in developing malware to undermine the nuclear command, control and communication systems of their rivals, while trying to protect their own systems from potential strikes by an enemy:

> Although activity in cyberspace is much more difficult to detect and track than conventional military operations, enough information has become public to indicate that the major nuclear powers (notably China, Russia, the United States), along with the secondary powers (such as Iran and North Korea), have established extensive cyberwarfare capabilities and engage in offensive cyberoperations on a regular basis, often aimed at critical military infrastructure.

Klare describes possible pathways for cyberwarfare leading to nuclear war:

> The first and, possibly, most dangerous path to escalation would arise from the early use of cyberweapons in a great power crisis to paralyze the vital command, control and communications capabilities of an adversary, many of which serve nuclear and conventional forces. The recipient of such an attack might fear more punishing follow-up kinetic attacks, possibly including the nuclear weapons, and fearing the loss of its own arsenal, launch its weapons immediately.[32]

There is known mistrust between the US, Russia and China about the cyberwar capacities and intentions of the adversaries. There is a constant risk of one country overestimating or underestimating the cyber capabilities of the other two and inducting AI into its military decision-making apparatus. Such a risk has triggered a race between the US, Russia and China which will significantly increase the exposure of humankind to a machine-driven war in one or two decades. It has enhanced the risk of the three countries hastening to deploy AI-driven systems in a premature way.

It is possible that a cyberwar between X and Y nuclear-armed countries may not be initiated by either X or Y. A third country, say, Z, may create mistrust between X and Y by generating deepfakes and poisoning data in the nuclear surveillance and communication systems, escalating tensions between the two. The country Z can also use deepfakes to pollute the political atmosphere and public opinion in X and Y, leading to a demand for war, which could inadvertently cross the nuclear threshold. The cost of producing such menace would be hardly any for Z whereby the consequences would be catastrophic for X and Y.

The risk of a planned, accidental or inadvertent nuclear war will increase with the introduction of AI-enabled unmanned platforms. These would include underwater vehicles, aerial vehicles and space planes. Such vehicles without human control can intentionally or unintentionally collide, sparking a war.

The emergence of supercomputers complicates future possibilities. There is intense competition between the US and China to make petaflop computers. A petaflop computer is capable of making at least a 1,000 trillion calculations per second. In 2021, Japan's Fugaku was the fastest petaflop computer in the world, with a speed of 400 petaflops.[33] The US and China have computers that can make more than 100 petaflop calculations per second. China has more than 200 such computers and the US almost 150. Japan has around thirty to forty. With the ability to perform several tasks at the same time, supercomputers have applications in almost all fields—from medicine to meteorology, from astrophysics to security. They can also be used to simulate nuclear explosions and test nuclear warheads on a molecular level.[34] Lawrence

Livermore Laboratories in the US already has some petaflop computers that simulate nuclear tests,[35] and the US is openly engaged in expanding nuclear testing capacity on petaflop computers. There is no information available on similar endeavours undertaken by China and Russia, but it would be very surprising if they are far behind. This has the potential to propel a new-age nuclear arms race.

Space weapons, supercomputers and killer robots, much like nuclear weapons and ballistic missiles, require large infrastructure, financial resources and political support. It is not easy to develop these programmes in complete secrecy because of the scale of infrastructure and resources involved. They are bound to be detected in a democratic society in this information age. However, in closed societies such as China, North Korea and Russia, all sensitive research is undertaken under government auspices and closely monitored by intelligence agencies. On the other hand, synthetic biology and gene editing do not require huge resources. It is possible for big and small players alike to use these technologies to produce a sort of Frankenstein's monster in the form of a biological weapon without the information becoming public knowledge. And this brings a bioterrorist attack well within the realm of possibility.

Scientist Martin Rees once wagered that a bioterrorist attack would kill millions of people in the early part of the twenty-first century.[36] Such an attack has not come to pass in the first two decades of this century, but there is no guarantee that it will not happen in the remaining eight decades, especially with the phenomenal speed at which advancements are being made in synthetic biology and gene editing.

Synthetic biology is a new interdisciplinary area where scientists apply engineering principles to biology. This enables them to produce artificial biological elements such as chromosomes, DNA and microbes in a laboratory. The experiments in this field so far have succeeded in the creation of the first artificial biological cell in a laboratory. As is evident, this science can be extremely valuable in developing new vaccines and energy resources; some even consider it a panacea for global warming. But the other side of synthetic biology is dangerous. It is now increasingly possible to modify pathogens and increase their virulence, transmissibility and resistance to antibiotics. It is also possible to create an entirely new pathogen. The greatest risk from synthetic biology is its ability to produce, either knowingly or unknowingly, an artificial pathogen capable of self-replicating at an unprecedented speed and spreading disease. Currently, efforts are being made in a laboratory in the US to create a pathogen capable of absorbing CO_2 from the atmosphere.[37] The intention is to address the problem of global warming, and therefore energy companies are supporting research in this field. But imagine if someone else produces a pathogen capable of absorbing O_2 from the atmosphere a few decades later! Once humans learn the art of creating self-replicating DNA in a laboratory with the combined application of AI and synthetic biology, it is theoretically possible to give birth to new or extinct species. One of the greatest dangers facing humankind in the twenty-first century is that the science of modifying genes to eliminate disease can be misused to create new forms of viruses, pathogens, bacteria and even species.

Modern science has generated a capacity for gene editing using CRISPR CAS9 technology, blending genomes of two different species to create a chimaera, and producing a genome in a lab. The goal is to conquer disease, save lives and improve health and medicine. Advances in gene editing can deliver precision medicine, obliterate currently incurable diseases such as cancer and Alzheimer's, and save human life by growing limbs and organs in the bodies of animals on new kinds of farms. Some of these experiments can go terribly wrong and give birth to strange creatures—unnatural animals with the capacity to think like humans, malformed or designer babies, or dangerous viruses and germs.

As there are ethics committees assisting the work of many synthetic biology companies, they are not expected to cross a moral threshold. But is that an adequate safeguard, especially in closed societies such as China, North Korea and Russia? In November 2018, He Jiankui, a Chinese scientist, gene-edited the embryos of twins to emancipate them from the risk of contracting AIDS. There were protests among scientists around the world, and He Jiankui was punished for crossing ethical boundaries.[38] The episode demonstrated that a single researcher with a small support team could successfully edit genes. It also showed that the scientific community would not accept such an aberration if they came to know of it. There is no guarantee that a future He Jiankui will announce his experiment, especially if he is secretly backed by any state for military purposes.

In this context, we have to consider a *PLA Daily* report from October 2015, according to which China's national strategy of military–civil fusion (*junmin ronghe*) has highlighted biology as a priority.[39] Chinese military scientists and strategists have consistently emphasized that biotechnology could become the 'new strategic commanding heights of the future revolution in military affairs'. The Chinese People's Liberation Army's (PLA) Academy of Military Medical Sciences, or AMMS, which China touts as its 'cradle of training for military medical talent', has been placed directly under the purview of the Academy of Military Science, which itself has been transformed to concentrate on scientific and technological innovation. This change could indicate a closer integration of medical science with military research. In 2016, an AMMS doctoral researcher published a dissertation titled 'Research on the Evaluation of Human Performance Enhancement Technology', which characterized CRISPR CAS as one of three primary technologies that might boost troops' combat effectiveness.[40]

It is also possible that a state-of-the art laboratory established to research biological problems may ironically prove to be a source of disaster. The most advanced laboratory is known as a BSL-4 level lab, which undertakes highly sensitive research on hazardous viruses and pathogens. There is a risk of a virus accidentally or inadvertently escaping from such a laboratory. There is also a risk of some scientists— either under the sponsorship of the state, or a criminal group, or on their own—hacking the technology and producing and spreading dangerous pathogens. If there were only a handful of such laboratories, it would be possible to govern and monitor them in a safe way. However, in 2022, there are almost sixty such laboratories across twenty-three countries, and more and more countries want to set them up. There is no international regime to regulate their functioning. The world's attention is drawn when nuclear plants are built even for peaceful energy purposes, but nobody notices anything when one more BSL-4 lab is set up in some corner of the world.

Critics might deny such alarming possibilities. They might suggest that overreaction can create obstacles in the path of genuine scientific developments. They are right. We must be careful in imagining future risks. The problem is that our own current habits don't inspire confidence. The species that turned chlorine, aeroplanes, radio and nuclear fission into instruments of obliteration; that turned AI into the power behind killer robots and hypersonic weapons; that turned petaflop computers into devices for testing nuclear weapons is the same one that can misuse advances in medicine, biology and chemistry to produce pathogens that can spread pandemics or absorb elements from the atmosphere without any defences to stop the spread of such an unnatural product.

Critics might also argue that military research is not the villain it is made out to be, converting good science into demonic technologies, and that it has in fact produced many tools, goods and services useful for humanity. These include the internet, GPS, drones, weather radar, microwave ovens, digital cameras, jet engines, synthetic rubber tyres, canned food, penicillin, night-vision cameras, jerrycans and ambulances. It is true there is a two-way relationship between the research and development efforts of the military and the civilian economy. However, just because military research helps in human progress, does not mean that we can absolve it of using scientific advancement for the destruction of humankind.

Since military research and development takes place in utmost secrecy, we never know what is in the pipeline. By the time the world comes to know about new weapons, they are already being readied for deployment. The latest hypersonic missiles, killer robots and EPWs may soon be overtaken by something that is being secretly created now, which we can simply call the neXt Weapon. Such a device may be in the form of drone swarms that can be despatched to kill the decision-makers in an enemy capital, or synthetic genomes capable of absorbing oxygen from atmosphere, or something else completely beyond our imagination until we see it used once a war breaks out.

Close Calls

If you feel that fears of Armageddon are exaggerated, let's examine the evidence. A simple Google search will reveal that there have been many close calls when a nuclear weapon was on the brink of being pressed into action, which could have led to the Third World War. The catastrophes were averted by very narrow margins in each case.

Max Tegmark, a leading AI researcher, is a founder of the Future of Life Institute. The Boston-based institute specializes in assessing existential risks to humankind from AI, biotechnology and nuclear weapons. Tegmark has described many such close calls, or nearly missed nuclear war episodes, in his writings. Two such episodes have been highlighted in his book *Life 3.0*, as well as by Bryan Walsh in his book *End Times*.[41] One of these incidents occurred during the Cuban missile crisis. On 24 October 1962, a Soviet satellite exploded in outer space. The US believed it to be an ICBM attack. Why it did not retaliate is a subject shrouded in mystery. Two days later, an American U-2 pilot flew over Siberia by mistake. Immediately, the Soviet MIG interceptors took off to bring him down. In response, the US despatched F-102 A jets loaded with nuclear missiles that they could shoot at their own discretion. The pilot whose error had triggered this massive and dangerous response reached American airspace safely, and a war was averted. But a few more false alarms about missile launches were issued that day. The next day, 27 October 1962, another event took place, which has now become part of history.

A Soviet B-59 submarine had lost contact with Moscow for several days. It had a nuclear torpedo, which the submarine crew were authorized to launch without consulting authorities in Moscow, but only through a consensus decision of the three senior officers on board. USS *Randolph*, an aircraft carrier, and American navy destroyers spotted the submarine and began to drop small depth charges at it, with a view to force it to come to the surface. The Soviet crew believed that a war had started, and decided to use the nuclear torpedo without consulting Moscow. Captain Staviski and Officer Valentin Gregerovich voted in favour of launching the torpedo. However, they could not complete the decision-making process as Sub-Captain Vasili Arkhipov determined that there was some misunderstanding and ruled against propelling the perilous weapon. If Arkhipov had agreed, a nuclear torpedo from the B-59 would have been set off. It would have attracted retaliatory strikes on Soviet targets in the mainland, not merely on Soviet assets near Cuba. Arkhipov came to be celebrated as the man who averted the Third World War. The next day, two more false alarms were detected as the North American Aerospace Defence Command (NORAD) received wrong alerts from its computers about separate Soviet nuclear strikes on Florida and Georgia.

The second incident took place on 26 September 1983, in the aftermath of the Soviets downing a Korean aircraft that had entered its airspace by mistake, killing 300 passengers. It was a time of great suspicion. The Soviet early warning satellites showed that the US had launched five missiles. Stanislaw Petrov was the officer at the monitoring station who had to report the attack to the command structure and a retaliatory missile attack would then be launched on the Americans. Petrov followed his gut instinct and determined that the US would not launch only five missiles at a time. He, therefore, reported it as a false alarm. It indeed turned out to be so as the satellites had misinterpreted certain reflections of the sun. Petrov, like Arkhipov, is known as the man who saved the world. Films have been made about both men.

Within a few weeks of Petrov's courageous decision, the Soviets again misinterpreted NATO (North Atlantic Treaty Organization) war games and moved their nuclear missiles to attack-ready positions, but fortunately, the real facts were revealed before it was too late.

Tegmark believes that the world was lucky that such episodes took place during the Cold War, when AI for military decisions had not been deployed. In the 2020s, AI is poised to occupy an increasing space and importance in early warning systems. Imagine if there had been robots in place of Arkhipov and Petrov, and if they had misinterpreted the signals. The Third World War would have been inevitable, and perhaps the human race would have come to an end.

Daryl Kimball, executive director of the US Arms Control Association, has reported another episode in the editorial of *Arms Control Today* (December 2019). On 9 November 1979, the NORAD computers reported that 2,200 Soviet missiles had leapt towards the US.[42] Just one minute before the National Security Advisor was to call the President to recommend an immediate nuclear retaliatory attack, it was clarified that the NORAD message was a false alarm caused by the malfunctioning of simulation software.

The world has continued to face similar close calls since the end of the Cold War. The listing by the Future of Life Institute includes the following episodes.[43]

On 25 January 1995, the launch of a scientific rocket by Norway was perceived to be a submarine-launched Trident missile belonging to NATO, and Russian President Boris Yeltsin activated the nuclear briefcase to prepare for a retaliatory strike. The nuclear briefcase is a black box, which only a head of state can use to activate a code that launches a nuclear strike on the enemy. The Russian observers determined, just in time, that the rocket was not moving towards Russia, and it fell in Norway as planned. In fact, proper notifications had been issued for this scientific experiment but had not reached the radar technicians in Russia. It shows the extent to which the world is vulnerable to a nuclear exchange with very small margins of error in the procedure.

A few incidents have taken place in the US. On 29–30 August 2007, six American nuclear warheads went missing. It turned out that they were mistakenly loaded on a B-52 bomber and transported from North Dakota to Louisiana. Originally, they were supposed to be removed at the base in North Dakota from the missiles that were transported to Louisiana. The warheads were accounted for as being on a wrong trip, during which they were outside the scope of safeguards. On 23 October 2010, the Warren air force base in Wyoming, US, lost contact with almost 50 Minuteman III ICBMs, fully loaded with nuclear weapons, for an hour due to problems with a computer chip somewhere in the system. During this period, theoretically, they could have been launched. In 2013, several officers commanding missiles in the US were found to be involved in inappropriate behaviour, such as excessive consumption of alcohol or cheating in proficiency tests, and were deemed not capable of taking responsible decisions. American democracy, particularly freedom of the press, has brought these incidents to light. How do we know if authorities in China and Russia never lost control of their arsenal at any point in time?

We have to remember that the incidents of close calls may not necessarily have declined since the end of the Cold War. It is only that information about recent incidents is not as easily available as on ones in the distant past. The Future of Life Institute concludes, 'With all of this combined, it becomes clear that the risks of a small problem escalating into a full-scale nuclear war are much greater than most people realize.'

Such examples are mostly of accidents that were averted. Other than close calls, there have been 'broken arrow' incidents when nuclear safety was endangered. A 'broken arrow' incident means accidental detonation, theft or loss of a nuclear weapon. At least thirty-five to forty such incidents during the Cold War are mentioned in open sources on the internet. These include a Soviet nuclear submarine sinking near the Norwegian coast in 1989, and another one sinking near Spain in 1970.

There were also 'broken arrow' incidents involving the American military. In January 1966, an American aircraft collided with a tanker during routine mid-air refuelling in Spain. The B-52 was carrying four nuclear weapons. Of these, one was recovered on the ground, one was recovered from the sea and two of the weapons' high explosive materials exploded on impact, releasing some radioactive materials. In December 1965, an A-4 aircraft loaded with one nuclear weapon rolled off the elevator of an American aircraft carrier and fell into the Pacific Ocean, more than 500 miles from land.[44] The pilot, aircraft and weapon were lost.

There is no information available on incidents that might have occurred since 1995. More dangerous than close calls and 'broken arrow' incidents are instances of government leaders wanting to use nuclear weapons as a deliberate choice. Bryan Walsh has enumerated incidents of the likely use of nuclear weapons by intent.[45] There have been instances where a see-saw between the US President and his senior officers has occurred on plans to use nuclear weapons. In 1968, General William Westmoreland activated a plan to move nuclear weapons to Vietnam, but he was overruled by President Johnson. On the other hand, in 1972, President Nixon contemplated using nuclear bombs in Vietnam and was talked out of it by Henry Kissinger. In 2021, Washington's media and literary circles were speculating that a top US general had instructed the military hierarchy not to follow President Trump's orders should he launch a nuclear attack on China, and he also cautioned the Chinese military leadership of a nuclear threat from the White House. President Trump, who was out of power by the time the speculation surfaced in Washington's charmed circles, promptly denied having any thought of attacking China. We will never know the truth, but speculation of such nature raises the question of whether there can be smoke without a fire. These incidents reveal that the leaders of the US are not as rational as they are made out to be in decisions pertaining to the use of nuclear weapons.

There is speculation in the media that at times British Prime Ministers may have considered using nuclear weapons against China in the conflict over Hong Kong and against Argentina in the conflict over

the Falkland Islands. We do not even know what Russia's Vladimir
Putin or China's Xi Jinping think and if they, or their predecessors,
have ever contemplated any catastrophic decisions. But some of the
remarks made by the two leaders give us an inkling of their thought
processes. Addressing a meeting of top officials from the Central Military
Commission in January 2019, Xi Jinping said: 'China's armed forces
must prepare for a comprehensive military struggle from a new starting
point. Preparation for war and combat must be deepened to ensure an
efficient response in times of emergency.'[46] In June 2020, President
Putin signed an executive order stating, 'Russia could employ nuclear
weapons in the event of aggression against Russia using conventional
weapons that threaten the very existence of the state.'[47]

India and Pakistan do not seem to have come close to pushing the
nuclear button by accident or due to a wrong interpretation by radar
technicians. This is because the Indian and Pakistani nuclear weapons
are not in a deployed state. But General Pervez Musharraf, former
President of Pakistan, has disclosed that he considered deploying and
using nuclear weapons against India after the relations between the two
countries reached a nadir following a terrorist attack on the Indian
Parliament in 2001.[48] He has not clarified why he finally opted against
the nuclear option. Imran Khan, Pakistan's Prime Minister till as recently
as April 2022, openly speculated about the risk of a nuclear war in
the subcontinent in his address to the UN in September 2019: 'When
a nuclear-armed country fights to the end, it will have consequences
far beyond the borders. It will have consequences for the world.'[49]
He reiterated this message several times.[50] In 2020, Kim Jong-un, North
Korea's supreme leader, either directly or indirectly threatened nuclear
attack on the US in some of his statements.[51]

Abdicating Morality

India and China are the only two countries adhering to the No
First Use doctrine, which voluntarily commits them not to be the
first ones to use a nuclear weapon against an adversary. The Russian

position is ambiguous—eschewing a pre-emptive strike but allowing counterstrikes in response to an early warning of a possible attack on Russia. Other countries have not found it necessary to be bound by any self-restraint. They are abdicating whatever ethical constraints they had adopted over the years by terminating arms control treaties. Since the 1970s, the US and the USSR/Russia had willingly accepted some restrictions on the use of nuclear weapons in the greater interest of the survival of humankind, introducing barriers to any hurried use of such weapons. One of the most significant instruments was the Strategic Arms Reduction Treaty (START) signed in July 1991. It placed limits on deploying nuclear warheads to 6,000 by each side, and the delivery vehicles, such as missiles and bombers, to 1,600.[52] START 2 aimed to bring these limits further down, but consensus collapsed before it could come into force. It was replaced by New START, placing restrictions on deployment by each side,[53] but this has changed since the beginning of the twenty-first century.

President George Bush, Jr, was the first to begin the dismantling of the arms control agreements in 2002 by withdrawing from the Anti-Ballistic Missile (ABM) Treaty. The treaty, signed in 1972, had barred both the signatories—the US and the USSR/Russia—from deploying nationwide defences against ballistic missiles. The rationale was that a restrained defensive capability would deter the nations from developing and deploying more advanced offensive weapons. Russia reciprocated by withdrawing from START 2.[54]

Russia also rescinded the Conventional Forces in Europe (CEF) Treaty in 2007. It had been signed by NATO and World Trade Organization (WTO) members in 1990 to prevent a new arms race in the post–Cold War period. Russia continued to be a member of the consultative group to be able to negotiate another agreement constraining the spread of nuclear weapons but withdrew from it in 2015.[55]

In 2018, President Donald Trump took the US out of the Intermediate Nuclear Forces (INF) agreement, a move that was promptly reciprocated by Russia. The INF was signed by President Reagan and Soviet General Secretary Gorbachev in 1987, with the intention of eliminating all nuclear and conventional ground-launched ballistic and cruise missiles that had ranges from 500 km to 5,500 km.[56] It was the first time that an entire class of nuclear weapons was to be dismantled.

President Trump also took his country out of the Iran Nuclear Deal, technically known as JCPOA (Joint Comprehensive Plan of Action), between Iran and the P5 countries (France, Germany, the UK, China, Russia and the US), signed in July 2014, and endorsed by the UN Security Council (UNSC) in 2015. The agreement set forth conditions to ensure the verified compliance of Iran with regard to its nuclear programme. The verification was entrusted to the International Atomic Energy Agency (IAEA). In return, the accord provided for the lifting of economic sanctions against Iran. In May 2018, the US withdrew from the agreement unilaterally, and in November 2018, sanctions were reinstated.[57] Although the American withdrawal does not automatically call the agreement off as the other P5 states are still party to it, it does discourage Iran from complying with the agreement.

In the last quarter of 2020, the US and Russia abdicated the Open Skies Treaty. This allows any signatory country to undertake unarmed reconnaissance flights over the territories of other signatory countries with prior notice, and gather and share information on military issues. It was finalized in 1995 and entered into force in 2002 with thirty-five signatories from the former NATO and Warsaw Treaty countries. With the two main protagonists out of its coverage, the treaty is effectively dead.

The only remaining arms control treaty is New START, signed in 2010. It replaced START 2, which Russia had withdrawn from in 2002. New START limits the number of deployed strategic warheads to 1,550, and deployed strategic bombers and missiles to 700, by each of the two countries. Critics may argue that 1,550 for each side is too many, when 150 nuclear bombs are more than enough to annihilate the planet a few times over. Others may argue that a limit of 1,550 on deployment by each side is better than no limit at all. New START expired in February 2021.[58] The assumption of office by Joe Biden as President of the US in January 2021 saved it as Biden and Putin quickly agreed to extend it by five more years. President Trump's proclivity to end the treaty and President Biden's efforts at salvaging it shows how such agreements are vulnerable to the whims and facies of individual leaders. It proves that so long as leaders like Biden govern major countries, we can hope for stability, but a future Trump or a future Hitler can dismantle the arms control regime in a jiffy and invite Armageddon.

While a nuclear war will have damaging consequences for the world's population, nuclear powers have no moral compunction to respect the wishes of a large number of countries that want to abolish such weapons. In 2017, the UN approved the Treaty on the Prohibition of Nuclear Weapons (TPNW), prohibiting testing, production, development, storage, transfer, use and threat of nuclear weapons, with 122 countries supporting it. None of the nuclear weapon states or NATO members voted for it. The only country that officially voted against this was the Netherlands, which has not indicated any desire to produce nuclear weapons and which is a home for many peace organizations. The treaty entered into force in January 2021, but remains hollow so long as the nuclear powers and their allies do not sign it. As we can see, hypocrisy is often an honourable code of conduct in international diplomacy. The world now has a legal instrument to abolish nuclear weapons, but those possessing deadly arsenals and all their allies do not want to use it. This is a complete abdication of moral responsibility by a significant section of the international community.

As the arms control regime lies in tatters, people hope that deterrence will prevent calamity. The main premise of nuclear deterrence is that the fear of a massive retaliatory second strike removes the incentive for the first strike. Nuclear-armed countries invest in second-strike capabilities including mobile silos and SLBMs. The second strike need not wait for the first strike to materialize. If an incoming missile is identified, it would be deemed as the first strike and a response would be delivered.

In this case, the political masters would go by the technical judgement of the persons or inputs received from AI supporting the missile attack warning system. If the enemy actions are misinterpreted, on account of the technical failure or malfunctioning of the early warning system, a nuclear war would take place. For example, the US Nuclear Posture Review of 2018 states that a cyberattack on the nuclear command-and-control system would be construed as the first strike, even though it might not be nuclear, and the US would launch a retaliatory nuclear attack.[59]

Nuclear-armed countries persuade their citizens to believe that possessing such weapons can deter enemies from attacking them, and that the doctrine of deterrence based on the fear of the second strike thus prevents war. Will deterrence prevail across the spectrum of weapons—nuclear, autonomous, biological, chemical and some secret technology that is not yet known? How long will such faith last: ten, twenty or thirty years?

Advances in AI can make it possible for states to detect and target mobile missile launchers as well as submarines and underwater vehicles of the enemy. This would destroy the second-strike capability and make the deterrence theory totally redundant. Since Russia and China particularly depend on mobile missile launchers and nuclear submarines it would not be surprising if their defence planners spend sleepless nights worrying about the vulnerability of mobile systems to AI-driven capacity to detect and attack their assets. Also, AI can help countries to create a missile shield, preventing second-strike enemy missiles from entering their airspace. This is another way in which the deterrence theory becomes obsolete. With large nuclear-armed states developing AI at a fast speed in the 2020s, the concept of deterrence is nearing its demise.

Alexey Arbatov warns:

In the short term, this risk may grow significantly along with the development of military hardware. For example, space weapons and cyber warfare are likely to have the ability to disable early warning systems or trigger false alarms. The proliferation of sea-based nuclear missiles poses the risk of provocative 'anonymous' third-party attacks from underwater. The development of hypersonic systems will deprive ground-based radars of the ability to determine, in a timely manner, the trajectory of enemy missiles and their impact area, which means that a launch-on-warning response will have to be authorised immediately upon detection from satellites, which periodically signal false alarms.[60]

The risk is not confined to an accidental war. If deterrence implies a colossal second strike, a state launching the first strike is not going to limit it to a small scale. It will hit with full force to destroy the adversary's nuclear arsenals at different locations, its command-and-control structures, leaders and population. The deterrence theory is patently dishonest in the face of the refusal of most nuclear-armed countries to commit to the No First Use doctrine and the presence of 2,800 warheads on hair-trigger alert.

Deterrence inevitably creates a vicious cycle of an escalating arms race. Various media reports claim that China currently has about 300 nuclear warheads. Some American strategists speculate that China will double its stockpile to 600 warheads in the next few years. China would like to have ready a second-strike capacity in case the Americans destroy its 300 warheads in the first strike. If the Americans enhance their offensive capacity to destroy 600 Chinese warheads, China will want to have even more warheads for the second strike. The more warheads China adds to its stock, the greater lethality the Americans will add to threaten China in the form of long-range missiles and hypersonic gliders. And the more strike capacity the Americans add to their stock, the more warheads China will want to possess.

The competitive withdrawal of major powers from arms control treaties reveals a mindset that accepts the risk of a war involving nuclear and post-nuclear weapons. Deterrence may delay but not eliminate the probability of nuclear warfare; with the development of AI, in fact, there would be an incentive to expedite the first strike in a major war. With the continuous modernization of nuclear arsenal and its coupling with autonomous weapons and delivery systems, deterrence creates a deadly spiral, whereby the risk of human extinction goes up. If Truman dropped nuclear bombs in Japan and Nixon almost did it in Vietnam, if Thatcher threatened to launch a nuclear attack on Argentina, if Kim Jong-un made not-so-subtle threats of using his nuclear arsenal, and if Imran Khan could warn the UN General Assembly of a nuclear war, what is there to stop a future head of state of any nuclear-powered country to launch a nuclear strike against his adversaries? We may trust the current group of leaders despite their bellicose tendencies, but how can we believe that there will never, ever be any leaders who will be tempted to use their stockpile? Moreover, if the decision-making structure around the leader—where fast decisions must be taken— is managed by AI, can the most rational behaviour in the shortest period be guaranteed? And we have no clue about the nature of neXt Weapons, misuse of synthetic biology and other endeavours that are probably secretly being explored. In times of crisis, leaders act based on a narrow set of choices. As they lose the broader perspective, using nuclear weapons may seem inevitable. Particularly, the development of low-yield, high-impact tactical weapons would remove the taboo on the use of nuclear arms. Once a war is ignited with a tactical weapon, it is bound to cross the strategic threshold in a few hours.

The Dead of An Lushan

Despite the fearsome proof we have encountered in the previous sections, some people believe that the world has entered a peaceful era since the end of the Cold War. Steven Pinker, a professor of psychology at Harvard University, and the author of a 2011 book titled *The Better Angels of Our Nature*, is the cheerleader of the peace paradigm. His argument is based on a single strand of statistics, that the deaths in conflicts have been declining proportionately as compared to historical experience. He borrows information from Matthew White, a self-designated expert in atrocity statistics data on the deadliest events in the last 2,000 years. He and other scholars like him measure peace in relative terms by comparing the number of deaths per 1,00,000 population at two different points of time in history. The population of the world was 1 billion in 1800, 2.5 billion in 1950 and 7.7 billion in 2020. If, in a hypothetical conflict in the year 1800, 1 million people died, it should be considered equal to 2.5 million deaths in 1950 and 7.7 million deaths in 2020.[61]

Pinker uses the population of 1950 as the benchmark to compare deaths in the events listed by White on a pro rata basis. Such a statistical device enables him to conclude that the twentieth century, even after the two World Wars, was a relatively peaceful century. The most violent period according to him was the An Lushan rebellion in northern China from 755 to 763 CE, triggered by the revolt of a military general against the Tang dynasty. According to Pinker (drawing from White), 36 million people died during this period. Around that time, the world's population was 210 million. Pinker adjusts the death toll in Tang China to his benchmark year to conclude that it would have been equal to 429 million in 1950. Therefore, the An Lushan rebellion causing 429 million pro rata deaths was more violent than the Second World War, which killed only 55 million people as per his research.[62]

Let's present Pinker's argument even more starkly using 2021 as the benchmark year, when the adjusted death toll of the An Lushan rebellion would be 1.32 billion. Thus, if in 2021 a catastrophic event exterminates the population of 1.2 billion people in the entire African continent, or a similar number in North America and the European Union together, we would still be living in a comparatively peaceful era as these deaths would be less than the pro rata number for the An Lushan period in the current time.

Let's now consider the second most violent event as per data adjusted for the 1950 benchmark year. The Mongol invasions led by Genghis Khan killed 40 million people according to White's list. So, the total number of deaths was almost the same as the An Lushan rebellion; in fact, somewhat more. However, Genghis Khan's invasions took place from 1206 to 1227, when the world's population was around 360 million. Therefore, on a pro rata basis, the death toll in the benchmark year of 1950 would be 278 million. This makes Genghis Khan considerably kinder and gentler than An Lushan in Pinker's peace paradigm: the main reason for this being that Genghis Khan appeared some five centuries after An Lushan, by when the world population had increased from 210 million to 360 million. As every next century has more population than its previous century, the number of deaths in any given century on a pro rata basis is less than the same number of deaths in the previous century. Therefore, every next century is statistically more peaceful than the preceding one. As the world population has been increasing exponentially since it reached 1 billion in 1800, the same period has been producing a decreasing number of deaths in violent events on a pro rata basis. Unless a major war takes place that kills one-fifth of the world's population—which will be at least 1.5 billion today or 2 billion in 2050—our century will always be more peaceful than the An Lushan rebellion or Genghis Khan's invasions.

There are many other statistical tools to make the current period appear relatively peaceful and past incidents relatively violent. Almost every war has a wide range of estimates of fatalities. This is especially true as we go back in history, when measuring the body count was difficult. If we want to propose that the present wars are not so violent, we should use the lower end of the fatalities estimated for them. Conversely, we should use the higher end of the estimates for wars in the past so that they appear violent. Matthew White presents two death toll estimates in the An Lushan rebellion: 13 million and 36 million. Pinker chose to use 36 million for his table. On the other hand, Pinker mentions two estimates for death in the Iraq War of 2003–06 from two different sources. *The Lancet*, the medical journal, presents 6,00,000 as the likely number. The World Health Organization presents an estimate of 1,00,000 deaths. As the Iraq war took place in what he would like to claim to be the most peaceful quarter century in the history of humankind, Pinker accepts the lower estimate.

The scrutiny he applies to the sources presenting higher estimates in the Iraq War is missing in his examination of the sources and methods of determining the death toll in the An Lushan, Genghis Khan and other past episodes. In Tang China, a census conducted in 753 indicated 52.9 million inhabitants, and the one conducted in 764 indicated 16.9 million inhabitants for the purpose of tax assessment. The difference between the two censuses was 36 million. According to White, the difference was the death toll of the An Lushan rebellion, and this figure was accepted by Pinker without any questions. Several historical records show that the strength of the combatants together from both sides in the An Lushan conflict was 1 million. We are told to believe that 1 million soldiers slaughtered 36 million people without machine guns, tanks, air power or any other arms capable of inflicting mass fatalities. The only means of organizing large-scale extermination in the eighth century was arson. In order to kill two-thirds of China's population, almost all of China would be required to be set on fire. There is no mention in any history book that the parties in the An Lushan rebellion, a palace feud, intended to destroy the country, including every town and village, completely. Besides, the conflict was limited to northern China. We are expected to believe that one-sixth of the world's population died in one region of one country in one civil war.

Similarly, it is not clear how White reached the conclusion that Genghis Khan's invasions in twenty years from 1206 killed 40 million people. Genghis Khan initiated the Mongol invasions, which were then carried forward by his descendants throughout the thirteenth century. There was no single war, but several of them. The plunder of Baghdad took place in 1258, much after Genghis Khan's death. If 40 million people were butchered in the first twenty years of the century-long attacks, how many people would have been killed in the Mongol invasions throughout the century? What was the method of accounting for the dead in each of the wars so that historians could sum up casualties from all Mongol wars together and present a reliable gross estimate? If *The Lancet* could be faulted for exaggerating fatalities in Iraq at the beginning of this century, how reliable were methods and techniques for measuring fatalities 700 years ago? Or should we just accept huge death figures from historic episodes—even when they are unconvincing to common sense—so that the past centuries will appear more violent than our present times?

To measure peace or violence with a single indicator of the number of deaths, either proportionate to population or gross numbers, is misleading. The Global Peace Index measures peace as a product of twenty-three indicators in three categories: ongoing domestic and international conflicts; societal safety and security; and militarization.[63] Even if we disregard the societal safety group of indicators, there are thirteen indicators that characterize measurable peace. Out of them, only two are related to death in conflicts. Other indicators cover a broad range of facets of a country's peacefulness. They include military expenditure; arms trade; armed service personnel; nuclear weapons; participation in UN peacekeeping missions; presence of small arms; domestic and international conflicts; relations with neighbouring countries; and deaths in organized conflicts. If we understand the comprehensive nature of peace, we will find that the world has been anything but peaceful since 1945.

In the second half of the last century, violent conflicts erupted in different parts of the world. These included the Arab–Israeli wars, the India–Pakistan conflict, wars and civil wars in Lebanon, Iraq, Vietnam, Cambodia, the Korean peninsula, China, Burma (Myanmar), Indonesia, the Philippines, Morocco, Tunisia, Kenya, DR Congo (Zaire), Sudan, Uganda, Burundi, Rwanda, Angola, Somalia, Nigeria, Mauritania, Ghana, Gambia, Liberia, Sierra Leone, South Africa, Hungary, Czechoslovakia, the UK, Paraguay, Colombia, Honduras, Nicaragua, El Salvador and Peru. In the first half of the twentieth century, large-scale violence was concentrated in Europe. In the second half, it spread to almost all continents. The propaganda about our enjoying peaceful times since the

Second World War does not reveal the truth about the period from the 1950s to the 1990s, when conflicts occurred in multiple geographies of the world, millions died and the superpowers lived on the edge of extinction in a nuclear apocalypse.

When the Cold War ended in the 1990s, the world hoped that it would experience peace for a long time. However, the quarter century since 1994 has been one of the bloodiest periods. We have seen wars between India and Pakistan in the Kargil sector, Ethiopia and Eritrea, DR Congo and its neighbouring countries, North and South Sudan, Azerbaijan and Armenia, between constituents of the former Yugoslavia, and continuous violence between Israeli and Palestinian groups. We have seen the invasions of Afghanistan, Iraq, Syria and Libya. We have been witnesses to the civil wars and internal strife in DR Congo, Albania, Indonesia, Nigeria, Pakistan, India, Georgia, Guinea-Bissau, Ethiopia, Côte d'Ivoire, Mali, Somalia, Yemen, the Central African Republic, Afghanistan, Sudan, South Sudan, Turkey, Chad, Kenya, Russia, Kyrgyzstan, Ukraine, Egypt and the Philippines.

The advocates of the peace paradigm claim that the fatality rate in the first two decades of the twenty-first century has declined, which is statistically true. At the same time, humankind has doubled its arms expenditure and exponentially enhanced the lethal potential of arms. The intent to slaughter on a massive scale is supported by augmenting the exterminating potential of arsenals meant for the complete annihilation of humankind. If we take into consideration massive transfers of financial, scientific and technological resources to the cause of destroying humankind, without being fooled by the singular statistics of battle deaths, we will realize that the twenty-first century has ushered in the most militaristic mindset in the history of *Homo sapiens*.

More Dangerous Than Weapons

The mere presence of weapons of final destruction, with the potential to render the planet uninhabitable for several thousand years, is frightening. The willingness of our leaders, from Truman to Nixon and from Kim to Musharraf—and of others about whom we can only speculate—to detonate some of these weapons is even scarier. It means that humans in flesh and blood, occupying exalted positions, can ravage swathes of humanity with no compunction. Edward Teller, father of the hydrogen bomb, once said, 'The preservation of peace and the improvement of the lot of all people require us to have faith in the rationality of humans. Humanity in all its history has repeatedly escaped disaster by a hair's breadth.'[64]

It is most chilling to see that ordinary people desire to slaughter other ordinary people like them in other countries by the millions. In July 2019, Alida Howorth, Scott Sagan and Benjamin Valentino published the results of a survey of American attitudes on a preventive nuclear strike on North Korea.[65] About one-third of the respondents approved a strike that would kill a million Koreans (not to mention the damage to property and environment caused by nuclear weapons, and the long-term effects of radiation). It may be argued that for one-third of the respondents approving the attack, there were the two-thirds who did not support it. Nevertheless, the belligerent minority of a third of the American respondents shows how significant segments of the population in large countries are callous about the deaths of millions of people. They obviously seem to presume that North Korea would not launch a retaliatory attack. Would they accept Los Angeles turning into ashes in a few minutes if the North Koreans were to act in a similar way, with the nuclear cloud spreading across California and beyond? Obviously, those approving of the massacre of a million North Koreans have not given any thought to collateral damage in North and South Korea, parts of China and Japan, and the Pacific. Neither have they considered the possibility of retaliatory attacks on the US, the shadow of a nightmare across North America, and the annihilation of some of the most prosperous and beautiful parts of their own country, along with the end of the American advantage in technology. They do not seem to think that nuclear weapons delivery could be quickly passed on to the lethal autonomous systems and hypersonic missiles. They are not bothered that a preventive nuclear attack on North Korea to massacre a million people will, in fact, result in the termination of large pockets of the population, property and nature in East Asia and Western US.

In a similar survey conducted by Sagan and Valentino about a hypothetical nuclear attack on Iran in 2017, which would result in 2 million civilian deaths, 60 per cent of the Americans surveyed approved of a nuclear first strike on Iran.[66]

In a blog post on the Roper Center website in 2015, Carl Brown provides the summary of several opinion polls conducted since 1945 in the US on the use of nuclear weapons. He points out that at least 20 per cent of American respondents have always supported the first use of nuclear weapons, for preventive or other reasons, without being attacked. The percentage of Americans willing to use nuclear weapons on Russia reached 40 per cent at one stage during the Cold War. However, it has remained at a constant of 20 per cent since the end of the Cold War. But this is barely reason for any cheer as it means that one in every five Americans is comfortable with the idea of starting a nuclear war. In a situation of threat perception, dealing with a specific post-Cold War enemy such as North Korea or Iran, one in every three or even two Americans seems fine with their country using a nuclear weapon to slaughter several million civilians belonging to the adversary nation.[67]

If opinion polls are conducted in Israel and Iran, Saudi Arabia, Russia, India and Pakistan, would the results be any different? Whenever there is any crisis in India–Pakistan relations, highly educated television anchors and commentators in the two countries casually talk about the use of nuclear arms to destroy the other country. In the minds of many people, the extermination of people they hate is acceptable. Whether such warmongers are in a majority or a minority is a mathematical exercise. The mere fact that an articulate group of people in so many societies is willing to initiate a war using nuclear and other weapons is reason enough for us to worry about the prospect of a deadly war.

Our withdrawal from the precipice cannot be achieved only through arms control agreements. So long as there are people who want to annihilate large segments of humanity for the sake of their nation's pride, the pursuit of apocalyptic weapons will continue. If nuclear weapons, killer robots, hypersonic missiles and killer pathogens were to disappear with the wave of a magic wand, those who want to annihilate enemy nations will develop more lethal weapons. Of course, weapons by themselves do not kill. Nationalism breeds the killers. In the last few centuries, nationalism, including religious nationalism, has spread like a virus in many countries. But the strength of nationalism in the nine countries possessing nuclear, AI and neXt weapons is the most relevant to assess the prospects of the survival of humankind. In the next chapter, we will examine nationalism in these countries before we proceed to craft a way out to prevent the end of the human race.

2

Dark Times: Menace of Nationalism

The cobbled path of Andriyivskyy Descent in Kyiv tells the story of how easy it is for warmongers to fool us. It connects the baroque-style St Andrew's church at the top of the steep Zamkona Hora hill to Kontaktova Square below, winding down over 700 metres. This little path is known for its art galleries and small museums. It might also be the only street in the world that has a museum dedicated to itself.

Every Sunday morning, on the sidewalk of Andriyivskyy Descent, grandpas and grandmas exhibit their treasures and invite shoppers to buy their trinkets. The wrinkles on their faces invite empathy. On a wintry day, they wrap themselves in blankets. They seem to be the children and grandchildren of soldiers in the Second World War. They sell the insignia of military uniforms, mostly belonging to Stalin's forces, and some recovered from Nazi soldiers.

In the Second World War, young men had worn the insignia of their countries with great pride. That is what they fought for. They earned medals at the cost of their lives. Their pride in their nation ruined a continent. Their patriotism killed, maimed and raped hundreds of thousands of people. But the uniform justified it all.

Today, the insignia is on sale on bedsheets spread on the footpath. The symbols of honour that led to the murder of millions, obliterated trillions of dollars of economic assets and devoured humanity, are available for anyone to purchase in exchange for a few Euros.

One expects that the Ukrainians and Russians would learn a lesson about the futility of war after a casual visit to Andriyivskyy Descent. In fact, they seemed to have been faring well for the first few years after Ukraine's independence in 1991. The country gave up its nuclear weapons, feeling secure with Russian guarantees. But the good times did not last long: since April 2014, the two countries have been engaged in armed hostilities, and by early 2022, more than 14,000 people had been killed in conflict.[1] Finally in February 2022, Russia invaded Ukraine, killing thousands of people on both sides in a few months. A war that could not have been imagined in 2010 had broken up the country within a decade and ignited the most significant military confrontation in Europe since the Second World War. Patriotism, respect for the national flag and the honour for uniform remain intact. If we are to visit Andriyivskyy Descent a few decades from now, we will perhaps be able to buy insignia from Russian and Ukrainian uniforms of soldiers fighting in the current war for a few paltry coins.

Us and Them

Why are people willing to die and kill in the name of the nation, only to have their national pride be sold on the streets for cents and dimes by their grandchildren? Ever since human beings began to form social groups, they began to differentiate between 'us' and 'them'. 'Us' are the people bound to us by relation, caste, creed and ideology. 'Them' are the people who do not share our blood or beliefs. And the 'us' and 'them' keep varying. In the Second World War, the Ukrainians thought that the Russians were 'us' and the Germans were 'them', and the Ukrainians and the Russians shed blood together against their common enemy. In the twenty-first century, the Ukrainians and the Russians are no longer 'us'. The Russians hate the Ukrainians, who, in their view, deserve to be butchered. The Ukrainians feel that the Russians should be slayed. The Ukrainians and Russians loved a common nation in 1940. They were loyal to different nations in 2020. They want to sacrifice their lives in dedication to an esoteric illusion, the 'nation', that is not even permanent.

The divisions between 'us' and 'them' are spurious in many respects. When one sees himself as a Muslim, the Christians are 'them', and vice versa. However, when one sees himself as a Sunni, the Shi'as are 'them', even though both Sunnis and Shi'as are Muslims. Similarly, for Christian believers, another Christian is a part of 'us' and the Muslims are 'them'. But for Catholics, Protestants are 'them' even though both Catholics and the Protestants are Christians. For the Shi'as, all Shi'as are 'us', but for the Twelver Shi'as, the Bohras, Zaidis and Alawites are 'them'. Similarly, at one level, all Catholics are 'us' but at another level, the Roman Catholics are 'us' and the Anglicans, Orthodox Christians and Assyrians are 'them'. In India, the adherents of some other religions have imported the caste system from Hinduism. The Hindus consider themselves 'us', and Muslims and Christians 'them'. But once there are no Muslims and Christians around, the Hindus go on dividing themselves as 'us' and 'them' along the lines of caste, sub-caste and sub-sub-caste. With more than 3,000 castes and sub-castes, there are that many in-groups and out-groups. Moreover, there are 1,600 distinct languages in India, potentially providing scope for 1,600 linguistic identities. India's population is nearly 1.4 billion. Papua New Guinea, with 8 million inhabitants, has 800 languages and potentially 800 in-groups and out-groups. In Africa, for most people, the Blacks are 'us' and the Whites are 'them', but closer to home, a particular tribe is 'us' and another tribe is 'them'. The list is endless!

The greatest irony about dividing society between 'us' and 'them' is seen at a famous church in Jerusalem. The Church of the Holy Sepulchre is one of the holiest shrines for Christians around the world and pilgrims have been visiting it since the fourth century. It is in the Christian quarters of East Jerusalem. This is the place where Jesus Christ is believed to have been crucified, buried and resurrected. Jerusalem was also the cause of one of the greatest conflicts between two communities: the Israelis or Jews and the Palestinians or Muslims. As we enter the Church of the Holy Sepulchre, a different identity conflict plays out, where neither Jews nor Muslims are involved. Within the precinct of the church, the Roman Catholics, the Greek Orthodox and the Armenian Christians consider one another as 'them' and at times, tensions between different Christian groups run high. In fact, the key of the church is not with any Christian but has been entrusted to Joudeh, a Muslim family, for several centuries. Another Muslim family, Nusseibeh, has the task of opening and closing the doors of the church every day.[2] There is a historical reason for this. In contemporary Jerusalem, the fact that two Muslim families are given the responsibility for the keys and doors of the Church help reduce tensions between the rival Christian denominations. The Christians and Muslims have shed blood all over the world against each other, most notably in the Crusades, which were launched in the name of Jerusalem. Yet, at present, in that very city, in the holiest of holy churches of Christendom, where Catholics, the Greek Orthodox and Armenian Christians find it arduous to coexist with one another, Muslims are trusted with the most sacred functions.

Sociologists and psychologists have written about collective narcissism, social identity and in-group and out-group treatment. Clearly, the difference between 'us' and 'them' is a matter of choice. When we want it, there is unity of one race, and other races are enemies. When we want to, racial unity is discarded for tribal loyalty. When we want to, there is unity of one religion and other religions are repulsed. On other occasions, we may sacrifice the sanctity of a religion to advance a sect within it. The chasm between 'us' and 'them' has deepened with the increasing sophistication of the institutions of societal organization, which finally culminate into the nation. National pride represents the grandest expression of collective narcissism. When the nation we die for keeps changing every few decades, we need to examine if something so transient is real, or if it is a constructed myth for which we gladly allow someone to ask for our sacrifice.

For several centuries after the early states were formed, wars were fought to acquire neighbouring territories. They did not need any justification. Almost 1,300 years ago, beginning with the Battle of Badr, religion emerged as an eminent excuse for violent confrontation. Armies were raised, and people were ravaged in honour of this or that holy book for a millennium. For the last 300 years, nationalism has provided a raison d'être for a clash. Wars are waged in the name and for the honour of a flag. For about half a century, the spectre of communism loomed large, and then it was exorcised. Now, the spectre of nationalism has appeared on the global horizon. If it seizes the minds of nations that possess the weapons of final destruction, human survival will become uncertain.

Many scholars argue that the nation states came into being as a result of wars. Charles Tilly, American sociologist, famously said, 'Wars made states and states made wars.' He is known, among other works, for his analysis of state formation. Tilly discerns that the primary function of the state is to acquire means of warfare. On the other hand, war offers the state its administrative and institutional backbone. Thus, the state and war are intertwined. Tilly studied the rise of states from the days of the Roman empire to the present times. Where rulers could raise standing armies to obey their orders, nations were formed. This was the case with England and France, as compared to several agrarian societies and city states. He feels that recurrent hostilities motivate citizens to identify with the territory and national symbols, and help build national consciousness.[3]

Tilly draws his conclusions from the study of European experience. These are only half-truths. What he leaves out is that the Europeans invaded Latin American, Africa and Asia for colonization. These wars did not create any nations in the colonized landscape. The colonies were as far from being nation states as they could be. Back home, the European states already existed, and colonization merely expanded them. However, centuries later, liberation struggles established the postcolonial nation states.

Since the end of colonization, though war has been one of the factors that created nations, it has not been not an essential one. For instance, Bangladesh was born out of an independence movement, but a war between India and Pakistan expedited the birth of a new nation. On the other hand, the creation of Slovakia was the result of a friendly agreement between two elite groups in the former Czechoslovakia. Neither did the states carved out of the former Soviet Union result from wars. US military interventions in Indo-China, Iraq, Syria, Libya, Afghanistan and elsewhere, as well as the French interventions in Africa, have demolished states and fragmented nations. The wars between neighbours in Africa, Central America and South Asia have had similar outcomes. Therefore, the first part of Charles Tilly's dictum that wars make states is not universally true; it merely represents the experience of some countries in certain periods of history. The second part of Tilly's dictum that states make wars is generally true. In order to mobilize the resources of the state in their entirety, the state depends on national spirit. Thus, nationalism is an essential instrument in the warfare of the modern states.

Sir Michael Howard, Daniele Conversi, Sinisa Manesivic, Anthony Smith, Caroline Marvin, Derek Ingle and Andreas Wimmer are some of the authors who argue that there is a correlation between war and nationalism. Some, drawing from the European experience, ascribe it to the origin of states. Some attribute it to the deliberate creation of collective in-group sentiment using public rituals, festivals and symbols that are depicted as sacred. Some believe that regular wars are required to consolidate citizens' commitment to the nation. Some others believe that the nation is a moral community: one's own nation is on a higher moral ground and others are less moral and, therefore, need to be crushed. For example, the US regularly attacks many countries in the name of promoting the high moral value of democracy, whether in

Vietnam or Iraq. The former Soviet Union did the same to promote the great moral value of equality, whether in Angola or Afghanistan.

Hannah Arendt argues that warmongering is necessary for totalitarian regimes. She says, 'Evidence that totalitarian governments aspire to conquer the globe and bring all countries on earth under their domination can be found repeatedly in Nazi and Bolshevik literature. They consider every country as their potential territory.' Arendt argues that totalitarian regimes do not care for material objectives. They follow a sense of destiny defined by themselves. In order to realize the destiny, they need a machine capable of inflicting violence, both internally and externally. They can live without an industrial complex, but they cannot live without a disciplined, loyal and organized military force. Therefore, war machinery is integral to the survival of totalitarian states, and nationalism is the essential fuel to keep this machinery well oiled.[4]

The close interface between nationalism and war does not mean nationalism does not produce anything other than a military endeavour. The original purpose of nationalism was to awaken people to their history and destiny. Nationalism integrates society and polity, overcoming local differentiation. It enables people of diverse backgrounds, languages, cultures, ethnicity and religion to live together and commit to a common ideal. It can be effective in mobilizing the masses for economic development, building a corruption-free society, responding to natural disasters and contributing to good causes. There are many examples of people offering their services and resources to those who might have suffered in an earthquake, a flood or a fire.

Such camaraderie often even extends beyond national affiliation. People are benevolent when they hear of catastrophes anywhere in the country or in some hitherto unknown part of the world. Such empathy is the call of the human spirit that dwells in all of us; but that is not nationalism. Empathy is awakened in response to humanitarian crises, but it does not remove the national spirit that helps mobilize armies against real or perceived adversaries.

Columnist David Brooks distinguishes between positive and negative nationalism. He points out that if leaders do not offer uplifting nationalism to people, they will go for the nasty version of it.[5] However, Belarusian novelist Vasil Bykau says that there is no such thing as either good or bad nationalism. All nationalism is one day bound to degenerate into chauvinism and imperialism.[6] It would seem that he is right if we look at the competition between the US and China, or Saudi Arabia and Iran to expand their national influence.

World Wars

The modern history of nationalism began with the Treaty of Westphalia in 1648, which established the autonomy of the state from the church and gave birth to the idea of a nation. The French Revolution and the American War of Independence created early nations in the late eighteenth century. In the following century, independence movements led to the emergence of free nations in Central and South America, including Mexico, Bolivia, Chile, Brazil, Argentina, Guatemala, Costa Rica, Uruguay and Paraguay. The nationalist sentiment spread to different parts of Europe soon afterwards, including to Russia.

Czar Nicholas I emphasized Russian national pride during his long reign from 1825 to 1855, and used nationalism as a convenient doctrine to justify his imperial ambitions. Russian nationalism was underpinned by pan-Slavism or a desire for the unity of Slavic Orthodox Christian nations across Europe. In the twentieth century, the former Soviet Union transformed Russian Slavic nationalism into Soviet nationalism blended with communist internationalism. In the twenty-first century, Vladimir Putin transformed it into proud Russian nationalism. Despite the transition of the country from monarchy to communist authoritarianism to authoritarian democracy, nationalism has survived. Not only that, it has been fortified in every successive phase.

The Sino-Japanese war of 1894–1895 spurred nationalism in the two countries where resentment of foreign traders and priests had been growing since the beginning of the century. In Japan, the growth of nationalism was aggressive; in China, it was chaotic. When China and Japan went to war over controlling Korea in the 1890s, Japanese jingoism was beginning to come to the surface. There was a domestic movement to establish a unified nation and newspapers competed with each other to provide colourful and patriotic accounts of the war with China. As Japan emerged the winner in the war, victory processions were organized to whip up the nationalist spirit. Popular theatre, children's games, textbooks and war memorials were employed to build up national fervour, and in this heady atmosphere, the idea of war being necessary to protect the national ego became popular. Japanese victory over Russia a few years later consolidated the rise of nationalism in the country. At this time, China suffered defeat and humiliation not only at the hands of the Japanese but also from European powers. The accumulated humiliation of the Opium Wars, the Sino-Japanese war and the Boxer Rebellion did not help China promote a strong nationalistic image at that time. However, this experience did underpin much of China's drive for respect and security in the twenty-first century.

Around the same time as the rise of hyper-patriotism in Japan and China, momentous changes were taking place in Europe. Germany's victory over France in 1871 had an impact beyond the borders of the two states. In Britain, Sir George Chesney, an army general, published his novel titled *The Battle of Dorking: Reminiscences of a Volunteer* soon after the Franco-German war.[7] In his fictional account, a German-speaking nation engages Britain in a battle in Dorking, Surrey. Compared to the sophisticated German army, the British army is ill-prepared, lacks professional soldiers and equipment, and depends on the auxiliary units. Germany wins the war, breaks the British Empire into pieces and occupies and heavily taxes Britain, converting it into a German province.

Following the publication of Chesney's novel, a new genre of invasion novels became popular in Britain, France and the US. Several hundred war novels appeared between 1871 and 1914, the beginning of the First World War. H.G. Wells, one of the leading authors of the time, penned three invasion novels that became instant hits. Rudyard Kipling, the Nobel laureate in literature who was well-known for children's classics, wrote pamphlets and stories promoting militarist nationalism. He was a great advocate of Britain's participation in wars to protect and aggrandize national interest—whether it was the Boer War or the First World War.

The period around 1914 also saw poetry in praise of patriotism. Rupert Brooke's 'The Soldier' characterizes the mood in Britain at that time.[8] In this poem, a soldier asks his countrymen to treat his grave in a foreign land, where he might get killed in action, as a piece of England, because his life was made of the English dust.

> If I should die, think only this of me:
> That there's some corner of a foreign field
> That is for ever England.

Despite growing war literature, there was also an active peace movement in Europe in the two decades preceding the First World War. The International Peace Bureau was formed in 1891 to organize world peace congresses. With its initiative, two major peace conferences were held in the Hague in 1899 and 1907 to regulate future wars, advocate mediation and prohibit the use of certain types of weapons. A worldwide women's peace organization was formed soon after the First World War broke out. In the first few months after the beginning of that war, many peace marches were held in Europe, particularly in France, Britain and Germany, the three main war protagonists.[9] Although the working classes and peasants were not enthusiastic about military confrontation, the middle classes saw national glory in combat. Several thousands of students, educated at elite schools, offered themselves as cannon fodder in the name of their king and country.

In the contest of ideas between pacifists and nationalists, the latter won. The ruling elite in Britain, Germany, France and Russia believed that theirs was the militarily superior country that would win the war and create an international order on its own terms.

The British were proud of their imperial achievements, which also fuelled nationalist feelings. They presided over a network of colonies far and wide and had a modern navy. The French had dual feelings. On the one hand, they were proud of their colonial achievements in Africa and elsewhere. On the other hand, they felt humiliated by their defeat to the Germans in 1871. Karl Marx had predicted in 1871, in the midst of the Prussian–French war, that France would one day want to wage war with Germany, with Russian help, to recapture Alsace-Lorraine.[10] This was not a question of territory alone; the French equated the region with their identity and national ego.

On the other side, the Prussians were, for a long time, nursing the grievances of Napoleon's rule over German-speaking regions of Europe. Until 1870, there was Prussia and other disparate German states. In 1871, Germany was created by unifying twenty-six German-speaking states. In this new German state, nationalism was used as a glue to forge unity. Along with Goethe's literature and Wagner's music, the German rulers also fostered support for military prowess. Kaiser Wilhelm II, the German emperor, and Otto von Bismarck, the first Chancellor of the unified state, were very ambitious. They wanted to wage wars to expand German power. For this they had to mobilize people in the name of the nation's honour. German nationalism saw itself in competition with British, French and Russian nationalism. The Kaiser was related to the British royal family and was jealous of Britain's global empire and advanced navy. He wanted to take Germany to greater heights than Great Britain.

The nationalism of Germany and Austria clashed with the pan-Slavic nationalism of Serbia, supported by Russia. By this time, the confidence of the Serbs had been boosted by their victories in two Balkan wars—against the Ottoman Empire and Bulgaria. They began dreaming of a Greater Serbia. The Slavs living in Austria and Germany were fed up with being forced to speak German and follow the German way of life, and wanted the downfall of the German state. Moreover, the head of Serbian intelligence, who masterminded Serbia's victory in the two Balkan wars, also directed the plot to murder Archduke Ferdinand of the Austro-Hungarian Empire during a visit to Sarajevo. This triggered the First World War.

Italy was born as a nation state through the unification of the Italian-speaking regions in the nineteenth century, much like Germany. The Italian elite admired the strong rule in Austria and Germany, and felt a natural affinity towards Germany, inspired by its jingoistic rhetoric.

Nationalism generated natural fault lines in Europe in the second decade of the last century. Italy was drawn to Germany and Austria, which, in turn, hated Slavic nationalism, which was supported by the Russians. In another trajectory, Germany competed with the British and French, who considered it useful to enter into an alliance with the Russians. These competing alliances were bound to result in combat. Although there are many explanations for the breaking out of the First World War, including the competition to dominate the seas and the colonies in North Africa, it cannot be denied that nationalism, even if it was not the only factor, was certainly the core driver.

Historians have widely studied the causes of the two World Wars and established a linear relationship between them, and most agree that the First World War led to the Second World War. To put it in a counterfactual perspective, had there not been the First World War, Germany would not have been chastened and Hitler might not have risen to power.

The First World War concluded with the Treaty of Versailles, which held Germany responsible for the Great War. The treaty placed demeaning terms on Germany, including total demilitarization, prohibition on unity between Germany and German-speaking Austria, surrendering of overseas colonies and heavy financial reparations. With its hand forced, Germany had to accept these humiliating terms.

These conditions produced a feeling of shame among the Germans. Moreover, the recession of the 1930s resulted in the US stopping financial assistance to the country. Facing economic disaster, and living with national disgrace under the terms of the Versailles treaty, the Germans were looking for a strongman to lead them. They rallied behind Adolf Hitler and bought into his theories of 'pure' German nationalism, where minorities had no place and Germany was superior to other nations. They followed him in whatever he asked of them: they killed their neighbours and looted their houses. Emboldened by unconditional public support, Hitler attacked Czechoslovakia and got away with it. He then proceeded to attack Poland. This met with international resistance and resulted in the Second World War.

Alongside German nationalism, Italian jingoism rose to the zenith, hurtling the country towards war. Much like Hitler's desire to create a Greater Germany, Mussolini, the Italian dictator, wanted to establish a New Roman Empire. Italy's military victories against Ethiopia and Albania generated euphoria. At the same time, Italy faced an economic crisis. The strange combination of economic insecurity and military superiority made the Italians fall in line with the strongman approach of Mussolini. They supported him in the creation of an ideal fascist society.

At this time, Britain and France, unlike in the years leading to the First World War, were not suffering from the hyper-nationalistic fever that seemed to be engulfing much of Europe. Even when the two countries saw Hitler rising, their leaders tried to reason with him at the Munich conference and accepted his claim over the German-speaking region of Czechoslovakia. Many, in fact, saw this as an appeasement policy. But things came to a head as Hitler's attack on Poland was totally unacceptable, and as Britain had a security pact with that country. Whitehall, the seat of the British government, concluded that Hitler had crossed the limits of tolerance and plunged into the war.

In the Far East, the Japanese were also on an expansionist spree. They attacked China in 1937, ending the Western domination there, and managed to occupy large parts of the country, establishing their own rule. They inflicted vicious atrocities without any hesitation: they raped, looted and murdered the civilians of Nanjing for six weeks from December 1937 to January 1938 and massacred almost a quarter million innocent people.[11]

The expansionist drives of Germany, Italy and Japan needed strong armies. Thus, in the three countries, nationalism and imperialism forged a marriage with militarism. Such was the might of the military at this point that in Japan, the armed forces were accorded veto over the appointment of cabinet members.

Aggression by Germany, Italy and Japan was bound to be countered. The outcome of such counteraction found the most vivid expression at Bayeux, Le Cambe and Colleville-sur-Mer in the Normandy region of France, places that are strewn with mass graves of soldiers from both sides of the Second World War. The liberation of Normandy alone cost the lives of almost 50,000 American, British and Canadian young men,[12] besides 20,000 French citizens.[13] Overall, the killing of 80 million people during the Second World War is the dreadful evidence of the vicious cycle involving nationalism, occupation and the desire for liberation. There must be no compromise with those intending to conquer and dominate, in order to perpetuate national ego. There is no alternative to liberty. But the price of liberation is a lost son, a widowed daughter, an orphaned child, a maimed brother and a broken family.

Whether human beings will repeat the folly of the two World Wars is the biggest question of our time. There is enough evidence to show that nationalism tends to be belligerent, resulting in wars either to push imperial ambitions or to claim justice for humiliation that took place decades or even centuries earlier; a strong nationalist leader can drive a nation into war. If a conflict is confined to one region, it would be devastating but limited in its impact. However, if it involves any of the countries possessing the weapons of final destruction, it will not be limited to one corner of the planet. It will engulf much of the world in its fire.

Nine countries—Britain (the UK), France, China, Russia, the US, India, Pakistan, Israel and North Korea—have acquired nuclear weapons and some of them are producing killer robots, hypersonic missiles and cyberweapons. Of these nine countries, Britain and France have been known over centuries for their fierce nationalism. There are significant sections of the population in the two countries that reject the European Union, with the UK having already exited it. In both countries, there is disdain for overseas workers, though traditionally they have accepted large numbers of migrants from their former colonies. The nationalist leaders in the UK seem confused as they drove the country out of the European Union fearful of foreigners undermining their national identity, but very warmly invited migrants from Hong Kong the following year when it was politically expedient to do so. Both countries are known for their love of national symbols, heritage and traditions. Nevertheless, there is no indication of either contemporary Britain or France craving to annex territories to reclaim lost glory. There is no rhetoric of using nuclear bombs against perceived adversaries in France. British Prime Minister Boris Johnson's decision in March 2021 to increase its nuclear stockpile substantially has perplexed observers and attracted strong criticism in the country.[14] France and the UK appear to be tame nuclear tigers. But we can hardly foretell the future.

We will now assess the implications of nationalism in the other seven countries that possess weapons of final destruction.

God Bless America

The story of nationalism practically began with the foundation of the United States of America in 1776. It gave birth to the idea of a nation, though the idea of a sovereign nation had originated earlier in 1648 in the Treaty of Westphalia. In America, nationalism, unlike in many other countries, is not based on race or ethnicity. Though some groups have made an effort from time to time to equate it with White supremacist ideology, such arguments have had marginal impact. The average American, even today, does not define his or her identity in racial, ethnic, linguistic or religious terms. American nationalism is about advancing the interests of the US in the world and has clear militarist connotations.

A typical American is very much global in his outlook and yet absolutely American. This was beautifully explained by anthropologist Ralph Linton in his famous book *The Study of Man* in 1936:[15]

> Our solid American citizen awakens in a bed built on a pattern which originated in the Near East, but which was modified in Northern Europe before it was transmitted to America. He throws back covers made from cotton, domesticated in India, or linen, domesticated in the Near East, or wool from sheep, also domesticated in the Near East. He slips into his moccasins, invented by the Indians of the Eastern woodlands, and goes to the bathroom, whose fixtures are a mixture of European and American inventions, both of recent date. He takes off his pajamas, a garment invented in India, and washes with soap invented by the ancient Gauls. He then shaves, a masochistic rite which seems to have been derived from either Sumer or ancient Egypt.
>
> Returning to the bedroom, he removes his clothes from a chair of southern European type and proceeds to dress. He puts on garments whose form originally derived from the skin clothing of the nomads of the Asiatic steppes, puts on shoes made from skins tanned by a process invented in ancient Egypt and cut to a pattern derived from the classical civilizations of the Mediterranean, and ties around his neck a strip of bright-colored cloth which is a vestigial survival of the shoulder shawls worn by the seventeenth century Croatians. Before going out for breakfast he glances through the window, made of glass invented in Egypt, and if it is raining puts on overshoes made of rubber discovered by the Central American Indians and takes

an umbrella, invented in south-eastern Asia. Upon his head he puts a hat made of felt, a material invented in the Asiatic steppes.

On his way to breakfast he stops to buy a paper, paying for it with coins, an ancient Lydian invention. At the restaurant, a whole new series of borrowed elements confronts him. His plate is made of a form of pottery invented in China. His knife is of steel, an alloy first made in southern India, his fork a medieval Italian invention, and his spoon a derivative of a Roman original. He begins with an orange, from the eastern Mediterranean, a cantaloupe from Persia, or perhaps a piece of African watermelon. With this he has coffee, an Abyssinian plant, with cream and sugar. Both the domestication of cows and the idea of milking them originated in the Near East, while sugar was first made in India. After his fruit and first coffee he goes on to waffles, cakes made by a Scandinavian technique from wheat domesticated in Asia Minor. Over these he pours maple syrup, invented by the Indians of Eastern woodlands. As a side dish he may have the egg of a species of bird domesticated in Indo-China, or thin strips of the flesh of an animal domesticated in Eastern Asia which have been salted and smoked by a process developed in Northern Europe.

When our friend has finished eating, he settles back to smoke, an American–Indian habit, consuming a plant domesticated in Brazil in either a pipe, derived from the Indians of Virginia, or a cigarette, derived from Mexico. If he is hardy enough he may even attempt a cigar, transmitted to us from the Antilles by way of Spain. While smoking he reads the news of the day, imprinted in characters invented by the Semites upon a material invented in China by a process invented in Germany. As he absorbs the account of foreign troubles he will, if he is a good conservative citizen, thank a Hebrew deity in an Indo-European language that he is 100 percent American.

It can be argued that the same description applies to almost every urban dweller in many parts of the world in the twenty-first century. An 'average' American is therefore as global as an average German engineer or a Thai businesswoman.

The globalization of the American has continued in the last eighty-five years since Linton's book was published. Simultaneously, nationalism has also gained in strength in order to afford the common American the luxury of preserving her or his global lifestyle. Nationalism justifies the American aim of expanding control over resources around the world, but without annexing territories in an old-fashioned way.

The gradual rise of American nationalism is evident in the proliferation of a number of symbols and songs. US Presidents in recent years have been ending most of their speeches with 'God Bless the United States of America' or simply 'God Bless America'. President Richard Nixon used this term for the first time in 1973 to end an address to the nation on an emotional pitch, when he was trapped in the Watergate scandal. Since Ronald Reagan in the 1980s, the practice of ending speeches invoking god has become very popular among American politicians. Earlier, great Presidents such as George Washington, Abraham Lincoln, Woodrow Wilson and Franklin Roosevelt did not feel the need to call upon god to save America. With the silent march of nationalism since the 1980s, this has become a popular ritual.

Lee Greenwald's song of the same name was released in 1984 (from the album *You've Got a Good Love Comin'*) and made a sentimental appeal to defend the country. It invoked pride in America, reminding people of those who sacrificed their lives for the country, and underlined the duty to defend the nation: ''Cause there ain't no doubt I love this land, God Bless the USA.'

The song was so popular that people sang it at baseball games, political rallies and other events. One could argue that this represents patriotism rather than nationalism in people. But when the same people support the use of nuclear strikes on other countries, whether the former

Soviet Union, Iran or North Korea, the lines between patriotism and nationalism are blurred.

We have already seen how nationalism in major European countries led to a series of conflicts beginning with the Napoleonic wars and culminating in the two World Wars. At that time in the nineteenth century, the US was not much of a player in global politics. However, it did respond to calls from allies in the two World Wars to support the war effort. Since the Second World War, though, America's dominance has been on the ascent, and it has been driving the global geopolitical agenda. We see American leaders talking eloquently about their global objectives being inspired by the Declaration of Independence—life, liberty and the pursuit of happiness. What they really seem to be interested in is the pursuit of power.

The Cold War was made to appear as a competition between two ideologies. The Americans said that they were on the side of freedom and democracy, opposed to communism and dictatorship. The Russians, on their part, pretended to be on the side of equality and justice, opposed to capitalist exploitation. In truth, the Cold War was driven by the rivalry between American and Russian national interests.

A closer look at the American track record during the Cold War shows that they went out of their way to overthrow democracies in Iran, Chile, Guatemala, Congo, Brazil, Vietnam, Bolivia and Chad. In addition, the US supported militaries in Pakistan, Laos, Iraq, Indonesia, Syria and other countries in Latin America and the Middle East to fight the angels of democracy. The common motive behind prompting coups and attempted coups in these countries was to advance American national interests there so that Linton's global American citizen at home could preserve his lifestyle. During the Cold War, the Americans proclaimed their opposition to communism. But, when it served their national interest, they took the initiative to cross the Great Wall and cultivate the Chinese communists, much before Deng Xiaoping introduced his reforms. Over the years, America's partnership with communist China grew in spite of occasional tensions and America's support to Taiwan, which yearns for independence from China. The US and China entered into a cold war in the late 2010s, when nationalism experienced a new surge in both countries and their perceived national interests collided. Undoubtedly, American commitment to democracy *and* their opposition to communism were half-lies. The only truth was America's loyalty to its imperial ambitions and the aggrandizing of its national interests.

The epoch following the Cold War was described as the Clash of Civilizations by Harvard academic Professor Samuel P. Huntington, implying a religious conflict between the Western and Islamic countries.[16] The terrorist attacks by Al-Qaeda on key economic assets and the Pentagon, followed by the war on terror, seemed to prove this theory. America's steadfast support for regimes known to be supporting radical Jihadi groups, such as Saudi Arabia and Pakistan, while attacking Iraq, despite there being no evidence that it sponsored Al-Qaeda, showed its hypocrisy. As 2021 came to a close, the US handed over Afghanistan to the Taliban, which had sponsored Al-Qaeda, allowing proscribed terrorists to become ministers in the Taliban government and exposing America's love for crude national interest, devoid of any commitment to life, liberty and happiness.

Whether it was the Cold War or the civilizational clash, American justification of military adventures in the name of ideology and values has been hollow, most visibly depicted by the scenes of young Afghan people clinging to the wheels of American military aircraft, only to die minutes later. Values have only been a flimsy cover for the naked national expansionist ambitions of the US.

Constant military interventions in different parts of the world have necessitated the escalation of its defence and aerospace business. Some would argue that the presence of the military–industrial complex has been the cause, and not merely the result, of constant American military involvement, far and wide, on the pretext of promoting democracy and countering Jihadi terrorism.

The American habit of engaging militarily around the world can be expected to persist over the next few decades, since the evidence of past behaviour does not inspire confidence to believe otherwise. The critical question is whether American aspirations will now clash with Russian, Chinese and North Korean ambitions, resulting in a devastating confrontation. If these countries, with their nuclear and AI arsenal, fear an American aggression and panic, a war would be likely sooner rather than later. If the US is determined to prevent Russian expansion beyond Crimea and the Chinese takeover of Taiwan, it may one day find itself embroiled in battles, and then the nuclear threshold might be crossed in no time. In order to assess the risks of an impending Armageddon, we need to examine the rise of nationalism in other strategically armed countries, particularly China and Russia, which are America's rivals.

Russian President Vladimir Putin announced towards the end of 2019 that the Russian Federation had surpassed the US in the modernity of weapons with its deployment of hypersonic glided missiles.[17] Around the same time, China displayed similar missiles in its seventieth-anniversary military parade.[18] The two countries have the wherewithal to destroy the US. Whether they will want to use these weapons will depend on their nationalist visions.

Mother Russia

Throughout the nineteenth and twentieth centuries, pan–Slavic nationalism supported by Russia resulted in wars, culminating in the Second World War. The Cold War was presented as an ideological dispute. However, for the Russians as much as the Americans, it was national interest dressed in the garb of ideology that propelled that rivalry. If the Americans had affairs with dictatorships, the Russians flirted with multiparty democracies when it served their interest. If the Americans developed cosy relations with communist China, Russia slowly distanced itself from it. Since the end of the Cold War, the Russians have pursued crude nationalism, dropping any pretence of ideology.

Authoritarianism has been the common characteristic of Russian rule during the imperial era, communist rule and the contemporary period. Russia has not experienced a genuinely free multiparty democracy with regular changes of power through the ballot box. Whatever façade of democracy existed in the post-Soviet period in Russia, Vladimir Putin removed it with his constitutional amendments, claiming them to have been supposedly approved by three-quarters of the Russian electorate at the end of June 2020. Putin will now be President until 2036, completing four decades in power. This will make him the longest-serving leader of Russia, or the former Soviet Union, surpassing Stalin, who had ruled for three decades. In such a monopolistic political structure, ethnic and Slavic nationalism is subsumed and used by the reigning political ideology at any given time.

During the Soviet era, ethnic Russians constituted 50 per cent of the population, but with the separation of the former Soviet republics, the population was redistributed, with Russia getting the largest concentration of ethnic Russians. So, the ethnic Russians account for almost 80 per cent of Russia's population now. Tatar and the ethnic Ukrainians account for 5 per cent. The rest of the population is dispersed into tiny minorities, accounting for less than 1 per cent of each of the ethnic groups.[19]

Russian Slavic nationalism has given rise to the movement against migrants from the poorer Muslim regions in the former Soviet Union—the five Central Asian 'stans' and the Volga–Ural region in Russia. More than a decade ago, it had led to an anti-immigrant, ultra-right movement. Initially, under Vladimir Putin's gaze, the Russian state quietly encouraged far-right activism. There used to be an annual march of violent far-right nationalist groups, with a few thousand people participating in it. Now, the state wants to crush the far right. The leaders of the movement have gone into self-exile and the march has been reduced to a trickle.

With the abandonment of the violent far-right movement, Russian nationalism currently displays three characteristics. First, it is very much led by the state. When the state found it useful to have far-right groups on the ground around 2005–08 in response to the colour revolutions in Europe, it allowed them to gather strength. When the state found them to be of no use—after the separation of Crimea from Ukraine due to differing views in the far-right movement on the Crimea issue—it applied various tactics to squeeze them. Criminal investigations were launched by the state under a new 'anti-extremism' law, accusing the far-right nationalists of money-laundering and other illegal activities as well as extremism. The state arrested some of these nationalists and forced the rest to flee abroad and go into exile. Second, nationalism in Russia is based on the idea of recovering Russia's respect. The dissolution of the grand Soviet state and Russia's perceived degradation in the Yeltsin years have generated a desire for Russia to be treated with respect by other nations. Thus, when President Putin annexed Crimea to Russia, he received popular support for his act as he projected it as an exercise in restoring Russia's place in the world. The Russians feel that there is a need for strong leadership to retrieve its honour and so support Russian authoritarianism, which is both bottom-up and top-down. It feeds nationalism and nationalism drives the centralization of power.

The third feature of Russian nationalism is its affinity with Russian minorities in other countries, who are known as compatriots. With the dissolution of the former Soviet Union, almost 25 million ethnic Russians presently reside in other republics.[20] Russia feels close linguistic and cultural camaraderie with them and treats them as part of a Greater Russian Nation, even though they are legally residents and citizens of other countries. Russia even considers it essential to include them in its emotional frontiers.

When Russia decides to convert its psychological map of a Greater Russian Nation into an actual map to include compatriots, it will go on an expansionist spree. We have already seen that during the imperial era, Russia had an ambition of becoming the Third Rome, bringing together all Slavic people and the Orthodox Church under its umbrella. There are subtle hints of the revival of this sentiment in twenty-first century Russia as well.

Over the years, Russia has been pursuing its expansionist agenda through cultural and peaceful means as well as by militarist ways. In 2007, Putin articulated the need to set up a foundation to promote Russian language, culture and heritage. Accordingly, a few government departments came together to establish the Russkiy Mir Foundation. Its task is to spread knowledge of the Russian language in nearby countries, such as Ukraine and Estonia, as well as countries as far as Australia and Canada. In its efforts, it uses a poem by Anna Akhmatova, the legendary Russian poet of the last century who narrowly missed the Nobel Prize for literature in 1965.[21] The poem promises the preservation and flourishing of the Russian language.

> And we will preserve you, Russian speech
> The great Russian word.
> We will keep you free and pure,
> And pass you on to our grandchildren,
> Free from bondage
> Forever!

In addition to promoting the language, the foundation has several programmes to establish linkages between the Russian diaspora and the homeland. It opens up spaces for Russian culture around the world by sponsoring the visits of Russian artists for performances in different countries. It donates funds to civil society institutions around the world for cultural activities. The foundation is a peaceful way of expanding Russian identity. The other method is militarist, the implementation of which is mostly visible in Russia's extended neighbourhood.

The first major militarist project of new Russian expansionism has been Ukraine. Russia has conquered Crimea and broken the eastern provinces of Donetsk and Luhansk. To what extent and in what form Russia might replicate the Ukraine model of expansion in other countries in its neighbourhood remains to be seen.

Russia's expanding aspirations need the support of weapons. Like the US, Russia has been increasing its military expenditure since the beginning of the century, after its reduction in the years following the dissolution of the former Soviet Union. It is also increasing the lethality of its weapons. Russia still possesses the largest nuclear bomb, the Tsar Bomba, with a TNT capacity of 50 megatons.[22] It has killer robots and hypersonic missiles, and advanced capabilities in cyber technology and AI in international security and political affairs. In the recent past, there has been huge speculation in the US about Russians using cyber technology and AI to influence the outcome of American elections.

It is quite evident that Russian nationalism has been marching on the twin path of peaceful cultural expansion and violent militarist aggression. Whether its imperial ambitions will directly clash with American nationalist ambitions remains an open question. Russia is certainly preparing for such a conflict by modernizing and deploying weapons that can hit the American mainland.

The state of peace between the Russian Federation and the US currently rests (uneasily) on nuclear deterrence. A summit between Presidents Biden and Putin in June 2021 resulted in creating a strategic stability mechanism to preserve the deterrence. But it is important to realize that nuclear deterrence is dictated by the political environment, which with every passing day is being polluted by hyper-nationalism in both countries. There is only so much pollution that any ecosystem can tolerate. Once its limits are crossed, a catastrophe is inevitable. If there is a war between a nationalist Russia and a nationalist US, hundreds of missiles will leave silos and bombard their destination in less than an hour. The clash of competing nationalisms can lead to a devastating war between the two countries. All it needs is a trigger, which will be unknown until it is pulled.

George Beebe, a former US intelligence officer who has served in the White House, fears a nuclear war between the US and Russia. In his latest book, *The Russian Trap*, he argues, '[A] war that no one wants is frighteningly plausible due to a combustive mixture of clashing ambitions, new technologies, misplaced fears, entangled alliances and commitments, domestic political pressures and mistaken assumptions about how adversaries might react.'[23]

The Chinese Conundrum

If one American scholar warns against a bear trap that could lead to a devastating war with Russia, another American scholar warns about a Thucydides trap that could lead to an equally devastating war with China. Thucydides was a Greek historian and military general who lived in the fifth century BCE. He wrote the history of the Peloponnesian Wars in ancient Greece, and concluded that an established power would not be comfortable with a rising power, leading to a confrontation between the two. Harvard's Graham Allison argues (echoing Thucydides) that when a rising power such as China challenges an established one such as the US, the most likely outcome is a war.[24] This would depend on what China sees as its role in the world in the twenty-first century.

Beijing's Tiananmen Square is the birthplace of China's modern nationalism. It is also a popular venue for its military parades. One of the most notable parades with 25,000 military personnel took place on the seventieth anniversary of the foundation of communist rule on 1 October 2019. It was held on Chang'an Avenue, Beijing's main thoroughfare. Thousands of people gathered at Tiananmen Square, waving red flags while their national leaders addressed them from a rostrum. The ceremony began with the hoisting of a huge red flag in the square. The Central Military Band, with 1,321 musicians, played twenty-eight pieces of music, including the national anthem, military anthem, 'Steel Torrent March', 'Blue March' and 'Victory Is Upon Us'. Besides disciplined performances by men and women in uniform, there were dances by women in white, blue, green and pink skirts.[25] Music, songs and dances evoked patriotic sentiment.

The most prominent part of the parade was the exhibition of Chinese military equipment. There were DF-41 ICBMs in different shades of green. This road-mobile nuclear-capable missile can hit any part of the world, with its ten warheads and multiple independent re-entry vehicles (MIRV) technology. It can hit the US within half an hour of being launched.

There were DF-100 hypersonic glided missiles; H6N bombers capable of inflight refuelling and carrying ballistic missiles; and black HSU-001 underwater drones capable of hitting ships.[26] The names of all missiles were written in English, and not in Chinese, in a clear signal to the world.

The Chinese military parades on its national days and special occasions are designed to deliver a message: that pride in the nation is the same as the pride in its military, guns, drones and missiles. The parades subtly prepare people for an invisible war that will become visible one day.

Before we examine the modern avatar of Chinese nationalism, it will be useful to understand its roots. China was not a nation state until the last century. However, it has been a civilizational nation for several thousand years. It traditionally sees itself as Chung-Kuo, or the middle kingdom at the centre of the universe. Chinese emperors attacked Korea, Vietnam and Japan, and exacted tributes for hundreds of years. The Chinese believed that their emperor had a heavenly mandate, while the rulers of the rest of the countries were mere kings. A similar Sino-centrism formed the core of Chinese nationalism. Although it collapsed when China was defeated by the Western countries and Japan in the nineteenth century, it has not disappeared from the collective Chinese subconscious. Chinese strategists argue that the country has not been a hegemonic power, but Chinese philosophers believe that China's place is at the centre of the world.

China was shocked to experience defeat at the hands of the British and accepted humiliating terms in the Opium Wars of the mid-nineteenth century. It was infuriated that the Germans had established supremacy over its Shandong province. So, in the First World War, it sided with the Allies. Yet, the victors of the war granted the rights over the Shandong province to China's arch-enemy, Japan.

Together with the deeply held belief of being at the centre of the universe, and the disgrace inflicted by the Western powers and Japan, the loss of Shandong in the Treaty of Versailles enraged the Chinese youth. On 4 May 1919, thousands of students in Beijing protested in Tiananmen Square, giving birth to a nationalist movement. They were opposed to the Shandong concessions given to the Japanese and, indeed, everything Japanese. They burnt Japanese goods on the streets. They were critical of their own government for being weak and longed for a strong one,[27] and they were opposed to imperialism. The protests spread from Tiananmen Square to ten corners of China, involving workers and merchants in addition to students. A strong wave of nationalism swept the country.

The movement that began on 4 May—the May Fourth Movement—with its antipathy to imperialism on the one hand and a weak national government on the other, gave way to nationalist and communist forces promising a strong state. Eventually, forcing the nationalists to flee to Taiwan in 1949, the communists adopted the mantel of nationalism. That is why, in order to keep alive the flames of nationalism, China's leaders organized an annual parade every year for the first ten years after the establishment of communist rule.

Modern Chinese nationalism, born in 1919, eventually fathered the establishment of communism in 1949. The gradual transformation of communism into an elitist political system, operating in a controlled society with an open economy, has given way to reinvigorated nationalism in the twenty-first century. President Xi Jinping has harnessed the new brand of nationalism with great skill. Using China's sense of its national worth—which is deeply ingrained in its belief of having a place at the centre of the world—and rejecting a language denominating the past, President Xi has coined a futuristic term: Chinese Dream.

China's controlled nationalism is very evident in manifold ways. China has restricted the use of the internet and banned many Western search engines and social media channels. It has set up a sophisticated surveillance system, not only to monitor potential troublemakers but also to evaluate whether the Chinese are being 'good' citizens. The state also exercises control over Chinese students abroad. They demonstrate, when required, to support the government and criticize its enemies. Chinese artists and intellectuals who are not considered adequately nationalistic are trolled. Thus, from social media to a robust surveillance framework, China aggressively uses new technology to promote its nationalism.

The nationalism embodied in the Chinese Dream yearns for respect from the world. In the first few years of the twenty-first century, Chinese experts participating in various international seminars and colloquia did not hide the Chinese thirst for respect. This yearning is gradually being turned into an exuberance of national confidence. China wants the world to accept its supremacy in its geographical turf, which includes Central Asia, Tibet, Taiwan, Hong Kong and the South China Sea. The concept of China's turf is also expanding with its Belt and Road Initiative. China is extending its network geographically across Asia and Africa, and is making entries into Latin America, where it has proposed a grand canal in Nicaragua, parallel to the Panama Canal.

The new Chinese policy of expansion reminds us of Zheng He, a fifteenth-century admiral and commander of Nanjing. He led seven naval expeditions in the first half of the fifteenth century to ports in Asia and Africa. As his influence strengthened the merchant class, the bureaucrats became jealous, and towards the end of his career, China withdrew from seafaring. Moreover, soon after Zheng He's death, the Mongols attacked the country from the north. This required China to protect its land and expand the Great Wall, diverting resources away from activities on the ocean.[28] Several factors combined to reduce China's naval expansion. Had it not been curtailed, the Chinese explorers might have discovered the American continent before Christopher Columbus and conquered the world. We would be forced to read this book in Chinese, which would have been the prime language of the world for the last half-millennium.

China's Belt and Road Initiative reinvents Zheng He's glorious endeavours. It is a great Chinese expedition over land and sea, to spread Chinese interests and influence across half the world. It is charted along with a new international financial architecture. Thus, the Asian Infrastructure Investment Bank in Beijing has vice presidents from different parts of the world. The New Development Bank in Shanghai has an Indian founding president. China has managed to co-opt the global elite in its new financial framework.

In addition to its economic might, China is also active in spreading its cultural influence. The country hosted the most spectacular Olympic Games in Beijing in 2008. The opening ceremony at the Bird's Nest Stadium had almost 15,000 performers and an exceptional show of fireworks. Over eighty heads of state graced the occasion along with Hu Jintao, then President of China. The ceremony began with the thunderous clap of 2008 'fou drums', a traditional Chinese instrument made of bronze. The Olympics ended with China winning the highest number of medals. Similarly, the Chinese contingent returns with one of the highest tallies from most international tournaments. China is busy establishing a network of Confucius Institutes around the world to spread the study of the Chinese language and culture. The maximum number of institutes have been established in the US and Japan (China's two main competitors), and hundreds of others in selected countries in different parts of the world. In another approach, international organizations are cajoled into praising Chinese traditional medicine.

With a clearly defined immediate turf around it on all sides, a tactical alliance with Russia, growing exploration of new territories such as the Arctic, new international financial infrastructure, the Belt and Road initiative, investments across continents and the widening network of Confucius Institutes, China is emerging as the new magnate of the world. This has made American strategic thinkers nervous.

China has almost secured its place at the centre of the world. It has proved its dominance after being subjugated and defeated by others for a century. It now needs to consolidate its gains and expand its national influence, and has therefore spared no effort to build its military strength.

Since the end of the Cold War, China has emerged as the second-highest spender on arms, only behind the US. Its focus on its military strength is qualitative. China sends dangerous signals to its rivals, such as using English labels on its deadliest missiles and weapons that are exhibited in national parades. In 2007, it destroyed its own satellite in the lower geosynchronous orbit, the lowest orbit of the earth with an altitude below 2,000 km, to test its anti-satellite missile capability. It landed a probe on the far end of the moon in 2019 in a civilian scientific endeavour, while simultaneously signalling its technological prowess. The far end of the moon is also known as the dark side, and is never visible from the earth. It is considered an extremely rare endeavour to attempt a landing on the far side—a feat only China has achieved. It landed a rover on Mars in May 2021, establishing communication with the Martian surface. China has the largest number of petaflop computers in the world—a machine capable of simulating nuclear tests—followed by the US and Japan. China has some of the most ambitious genomics and chimaera production programmes, blending the human genome with animal genes, with the potential to develop viruses capable of exterminating large chunks of humanity and unprecedented biological weapons.

China's celebration of its military strength is as much a message to its own population as to its external competitors and rivals. One of the key concerns of the demonstrators of the May Fourth Movement was a weak government in the last days of the Qing dynasty, and in the immediate aftermath of its collapse. Since then, the Chinese have longed for a militarily strong government. The Xi government in

Beijing understands the deeply felt need of the Chinese population and goes out of its way to demonstrate its muscle power. At the same time, it announces its arrival to the world by showcasing its ICBMs, which can hit the American homeland, and other specialized missiles that can target the US navy. Finally, the exhibition of China's military power is a signal to Taiwan. There is no secret about China's intention to acquire the territories that it considers the historical property of the Chinese civilization. It began with Tibet in the 1950s, when it did not have many of today's strengths. Then it secured Hong Kong in a peaceful transition. It would now like to incorporate Taiwan, allowing it to maintain its free economic area, but under China's suzerainty. China is more than irked by the arming of Taiwan by the US, which makes a takeover difficult.

It would be naive to believe that massive investments, research and exhibition of the most sophisticated and dangerous weapons of the nuclear and post-nuclear generation by China are only for show. It would be foolish to believe that China's destruction of its own satellites in outer space and deployment of hypersonic cruise missiles in its armed forces are actions taken with no ulterior motive. Such actions are, in fact, aimed at achieving and sustaining China's position at the centre of the universe. There can only be one nation at the centre. Two would be an unmanageable crowd, bound to result in a quarrel. China does not consider that it has almost secured its place in the world. It believes that it is reclaiming its lawful place of honour that was temporarily lost.

When Chinese strategic affairs experts participate in international conferences, they make humble assertions about China's place in the world as a developing country in their formal speeches. However, while talking informally during coffee breaks at the conferences, the same experts assert that China is merely retrieving its rightful place at the centre of the universe after a century of humiliation, not securing a new one. China will go to any extent to preserve its newly found respect, secure its unity and expand its national sphere. It can be expected to counter any obstacles standing in the path of its unity. But treaty obligations between the US and China's neighbours, including Taiwan, may require the US to accentuate its pivot in Asia. In the dynamic web of obligations, with China's promise to its supreme nationalism and America's promise to its allies and friends, the casus belli of a dangerous war might be hidden.

Juche and Songun

A war between the US and North Korea, however blunt it may sound, is plausible if North Korea does not compromise on its present nationalist philosophy. The Juche calendar that North Korea uses is perhaps the most vivid symbol of its nationalism. In most parts of the world, including Islamic countries, the Gregorian calendar is used for civil purposes. Iran and Afghanistan are the only exceptions. India has a Hindu calendar, but it is only used to identify religious days. North Korea uses the Juche calendar, beginning with the birth of its founder, Kim Il Sung, in 1912, which is the first year of Juche. Gregorian 2022 CE is Juche 111. There are also Juche songs, festivals and a tall Juche tower in Pyongyang.

Juche is the official North Korean philosophy, which means that man is in command of his destiny. North Korea rejects Marxist communism, which places the movement of material forces at the centre. The Juche philosophy believes that people are at the centre of progress and the supreme leader is at the centre of people. The general body of people are supposed to think and articulate through the supreme leader.[29] North Korea's supreme leader has all-encompassing powers including political, quasi-religious, economic, moral and those related to security.

Nationalism was born in North Korea in a similar way to China. Japan had occupied Korea after defeating China and Russia in wars around the turn of the century. The Koreans hoped that they would be offered independence by the victorious powers of the First World War in the Treaty of Versailles, since the right of self-determination was recognized in some parts of Europe. But they were destined to be disappointed. Realizing that the allied powers did not care for their aspirations, the Koreans organized themselves in various groups to launch a struggle against imperialism and occupation. Their March First Movement ignited protests in 1919, which subsequently transformed into a liberation struggle.[30] In China, the May Fourth Movement was the spark for similar agitation against imperialism in the same year. It is possible that the Korean March First Movement inspired China's May Fourth Movement. The Korean liberation groups split into two branches in the 1920s: one group formed a government in exile, which provided the base for the South Korean state; the other group chose guerrilla tactics, under Kim Il Sung's leadership, and formed the North Korean state in the 1940s.

Kim Il Sung introduced the Juche philosophy as an improvisation of communism, to put people before materials in the process of development, and to emphasize self-reliance and independence from foreign influence. The hatred of the Japanese was at the core of the concept of self-reliance, which was later expanded to include the hatred of the US. One of the ways the Kims still manage to stoke nationalistic fervour among people, despite dire economic conditions and the famines of the 1990s, is by promoting a jingoistic and xenophobic mindset by appealing to Juche.

Ever since the birth of the nation, North Korea's national identity has remained inextricably linked with Kim Il Sung, who is deified as more than just a national hero. North Korea shares the anti-Japanese sentiment with South Korea, but it is distinct from its southern neighbour in leadership worship. Kim Il Sung's deification and demi-god status have been carefully cultivated over the seven decades of North Korea's existence. The level of devotion and adulation enjoyed by him has been passed on to his successors, Kim Jong-il and Kim Jong-un. One of the many stories that are purportedly believed by the people, which further exalts the Kims in their imagination, is the claim in Kim Jong-il's official biography that his birth atop a sacred mountain was marked by the emergence of a new star that transformed winter to springtime.[31] Other strategies include the crushing of religions, particularly Christianity, in order to perpetuate the belief that Kim Il Sung is the only real god, and his descendants are divine beings.

North Korea's nationalism is advanced through a combination of social control and a cultivated fear of foreign powers. The bellicosity that the regime displays towards Japan and the US is also aimed at the domestic audience. The regime uses the temptation of favours, deception and intimidation to subsume opposition rather than repress it. The intellectual class comprises professionals and bureaucrats who are loyal to the Kim dynasty. Military and administrative elites' loyalty is won by fulfilling their needs. All student activities are acutely monitored to control and prevent dissent. A deep network of informants helps the regime track any seeds of dissatisfaction or disgruntlement among citizens. Minor offences are detected and dealt with in a manner that aims to 'reform' and 're-educate', projecting a soft, accommodating and benign side of the regime. All major transgressions, and any real threat of coups against the dictatorship, are nipped in the bud through executions or incarcerations—of not just the offender, but also their family members. The fate of two of Kim Jong-un's closest relatives comes up in this context, about which there has been wide coverage in the international media.

Jang Song Thaek, one of the most prominent figures in the North Korean government, was married to Kim Kyong-hui, the only daughter of North Korean supreme leader Kim Il Sung and only sister of North Korean General Secretary Kim Jong-il. Jang Song Thaek was, therefore, the uncle (by marriage) of the current supreme leader, Kim Jong-un. Media reports indicate that he had assumed a central leadership role when Kim Jong-il's health was declining. Jang was also considered a 'key policy adviser' to Kim Jong-un. In December 2013, Jang was abruptly accused of being a counter-revolutionary and stripped of all his posts and expelled from the ruling Workers' Party of Korea (WPK).[32] One day, in the same month, North Korean state media announced he had been executed. It is possible that, along with Jang, some of his close family members and advisers were also killed.

Kim Jong-nam, the eldest son of North Korean leader Kim Jong-il, was considered the heir apparent to his father before the present ruler was appointed. He was thought to have fallen out of favour after embarrassing the regime in 2001 with a failed attempt to visit Disneyland Tokyo on a false passport. Another reason for the fallout could be the reports of his criticism of the Kim family. Kim Jong-nam was exiled from North Korea in 2003, and thereafter became more vocal with his criticism. He died on 13 February 2017 at the Kuala Lumpur International Airport in Malaysia as the result of an apparent assassination by North Korean agents using the VX nerve agent, which took less than twenty minutes to accomplish.[33] There have been reports from time to time of the Kim Jong-un regime executing top military officials, but such reports are impossible to verify because of lack of freedom of information in the country. They could be rumours, but they instil fear in the public mind nonetheless.

The reigning supreme leader, Kim Jong-un, has introduced a new edition of Juche, known as 'byungjin'. He wants to balance the modernization of the economy with the advancement of military objectives.[34] There are indications that Kim Jong-un wants to transform the economy by carefully introducing economic reforms. Many visitors and observers of Pyongyang have noticed a steady, if gradual, change in the culture-scape. Notable among these are the growing fashion-consciousness of people, increased vehicular traffic and the growth of mobile phone users.

Since Juche is based on the suspicion of foreigners, despite the recent adoption of byungjin, it requires military preparedness. North Korea has, since the beginning, been developing its capacities in science and technology in the service of the military. This strategy has enabled it to produce nuclear bombs and ballistic missiles, despite failures in managing hunger and famine. North Korea today boasts of one of the largest conventional military forces in the world, although it is one of the poorest countries. Estimates of the country's nuclear stockpile vary from thirty to sixty, and the country has ICBMs capable of attacking the US mainland with nuclear weapons.[35] The state policy of ceaseless militarization is fed to the domestic population by harking back to Juche, which praises self-reliance but blurs the line between self-reliance and isolation.

The ideological justification of militarism has its roots in Kim Jong-il's ideology of Songun. Under Songun, it is essential to choose guns over butter, lest the Korean people lose both.[36] The discourse that was made popular was that the Japanese and the Americans were waiting for the North to let their guard down. This would invariably lead to recolonization, which was to be avoided at all costs. Now, North Korea's security interests are intimately tied to its nuclear weapons, which are described as 'swords of Juche'.[37] Since inheriting power in 2010, Kim Jong-un has enhanced the scope and speed of the nuclear weapons and missiles programme. The nuclear weapons are considered by the leadership as a part of the country's deterrence to prevent a US attack, and North Korea has indicated that it will consider a nuclear attack on Guam, if not the US mainland. The US, on its part, has hinted at a pre-emptive attack to hold North Korea in check. It might also be possible that North Korea will emerge as a factor in a potential US–China war. As is evident, the risk of future brinksmanship leading to a war is very real. So long as North Korea depends on its nationalism defined by Juche and Songun, which inherently requires an enemy and military preparedness to deal with the enemy, it is going to be a bellicose state. No country can live in a permanent state of belligerence. Either it must withdraw from its combative mindset, which for North Korea is giving up the core of its nationhood, or slide into a war sooner rather than later.

If North Korea has its indigenous brand of nationalism in East Asia, Israel has its own nationalism in West Asia. However, Israel's identity and nationalism are not only in conflict with the nationalism of its rivals in the Middle East, but they are also enmeshed with religion, energy politics and international geopolitical competition. Any risk of war in the Middle East cannot be assessed only through the lens of Israeli nationalism. However, the remaining two nuclear-powered countries in Asia—India and Pakistan—function in a strong ideological framework. It is necessary to examine if competitive nationalism between South Asia's two belligerent neighbours could one day lead to nuclear mayhem, risking the lives of the 1.5 billion people inhabiting the region.

Most Dangerous Place

US President Bill Clinton once described the line of control between India and Pakistan as the world's most dangerous place.[38] Since then, scary theories of a nuclear war between the two neighbours have surfaced from time to time. Whether such a war, with an impact much beyond the South Asian landmass, will take place in the twenty-first century is a pertinent question.

The Indian subcontinent, much like China, has been home to an integrating civilization for a few thousand years. Ancient India experienced a renaissance around 400–600 BCE when Takshashila University became the fountain of wisdom and invention in different spheres; Emperor Chandragupta prevented the Macedonian ruler Alexander from entering India, and Emperor Ashoka spread Buddhism to different parts of Asia. It experienced a golden age under the Gupta Empire around 400–600 CE, when the northern and western parts of today's India were united under one rule. Since then and until 1947, the Indian landmass has never been governed as a unified state under indigenous rulers. The only exception was in the eighteenth century, when India was united under the indigenous Maratha Empire. Once the Maratha Empire fell apart, the British ruled the Indian landmass. Even under the British Raj, India in the twentieth century was a conglomeration of a few hundred princely states. The formation of modern India, after the British left in 1947, led to the birth of a new nation. At the same time, sections of the Muslim population established their own nation on a religious premise and named it Pakistan. India and Pakistan may be young nations, but together they represent an old civilization.

Pakistan's founder, Mohammed Ali Jinnah, earlier a stalwart of the Indian liberation movement, proposed the two-nation theory. He claimed that Hindus and Muslims could only exist as two separate nations because of cultural and religious differences. He envisioned Pakistan as a Muslim country, but not as a theocratic state. Within two years of Pakistan's birth, the country's first Prime Minister, Liaquat Ali Khan, moved the Objectives Resolution in the Constituent Assembly, proposing Pakistan be made an Islamic state, which would also safeguard the interests of the minorities. It sought to establish Pakistan's legitimacy as an expression of the will of Allah.[39] In 1971, East Pakistan—which had a significant presence of Hindu minorities and a distinct Bengali identity—separated from West Pakistan to form Bangladesh, as an independent nation. In the 1980s, under General Zia ul Haq's military rule, the process of the total Islamization of Pakistan began, which continues to date. The country now seeks a lead role in the Organisation of Islamic Cooperation (OIC), and its nuclear bomb has been sometimes described as an Islamic bomb. Leading Islamic countries, such as Saudi Arabia and Turkey, cultivate good relations with Pakistan for various reasons, including Pakistan's nuclear weapons programme, from which they might benefit sometime in future.

Pakistan's religious nationalism has an ethnic dimension internally and an anti-India obsession externally. From the ethnic point of view, the state is dominated by the Punjabi people, with the Sindhis, the Baloch, the Pathans and others living as Muslim ethnic minorities. Externally, the anti-India rhetoric has led to the country's military taking on major political importance. Pakistan has effectively, though not always formally, been ruled by the military, its predominant role being justified in withstanding the perceived Indian threat. In fact, Pakistan's existence is defined in terms of mistrust and denunciation of India; its institutions are arranged mainly to deter India. Thus, anti-India sentiment is very much at the core of Pakistan's national identity.

The centrality of the army in Pakistan's political life has made it a saviour of the nation, not only from external threats, whether India or otherwise, but also from internal schisms and weaknesses. While most of Pakistan remains bureaucratically chaotic, the army is a cohesive and well-disciplined organization. It takes over popularly elected governments without any opposition from civil society. In fact, Pakistan's white-collar urban middle class seems to be an active supporter of the army's omnipotent presence, though sometimes they may meekly complain about its excesses. They applaud the army's discipline over the real, and perceived, incompetence of civilian governments. Moreover, civilian politics is dominated by influential families and religious groups, which makes the apparently meritocratic army an attractive choice for the masses.

Pakistan and India have already fought two full-scale wars in 1965 and 1971. They have also been involved in major military confrontations in 1948 and 1999, and skirmishes near the line of control in Jammu and Kashmir are almost a daily occurrence.

If Pakistan's nationalism at its core revolves around 'not being India' and in nurturing an Islamic theocratic state, Indian nationalism also began as 'not being Pakistan' and developing as a secular nation. The latter's nationalism was rooted in the anti-imperial, anti-colonial philosophy of struggle against the colonial British rule of about 300 years, especially from the war of independence in 1857 to freedom from the British Raj in 1947.

India has pursued secularism as the defining feature of the nation state for six decades since Independence. In the twenty-first century, this fundamental building block has been challenged by the electoral victories and preponderance of the Bharatiya Janata Party (BJP), a political party that believes in the idea of a Hindu nation. However, one thing has remained constant: the secular political forces as well as the recently ascending nationalist forces in India equally despise the hostility of Pakistan's Islamic state.

A Pakistan that is forever apprehensive of India needs a strong military. An India that is perpetually mistrustful of Pakistan sees the value of strong defence forces. But India does not define its national aspirations vis-à-vis Pakistan alone. The Indian elite dream of reviving

India's golden age of 400–600 CE, when the Gupta dynasty had established an expansive empire. They see India as an emerging global power soon to be in the league of the US and Russia. They see India as an honorary member of the Western industrialized group of nations and China as a strategic competitor. A rising India requires a strong and effective army to establish its place in the world, restrain China and deal with Pakistan as an irritant in India's ambitions. As a result, arms and wars are valorized every day by using television programmes, movies, songs, art exhibitions, sports and school activities, which are promoted to glorify the armed forces. The military, being a disciplined institution, is often seen to be coming to the aid of people at times of natural disasters and terrorist attacks, and has always enjoyed a unique place of respect in the minds of the masses since India's Independence in 1947. With the rise of Hindu nationalism and the advocacy of a strong state, the military's popularity is soaring, and most people in India support the idea that the armed forces must be properly equipped to give it the strength it needs.

The arms race between India and Pakistan has formally crossed the nuclear threshold, as each country has a huge supply of nuclear warheads and missiles. Before long, they will be in the race to acquire post-nuclear weapons such as killer robots and hypersonic missiles. Adding fuel to the fire of this incessant rivalry is the frequent habit of both countries to escalate psychological and rhetorical warfare with each other. As mentioned earlier, former Pakistan Prime Minister Imran Khan already made his intentions clear when he speculated about the risk of a nuclear war while speaking at the UN General Assembly in 2019; he had made similar pronouncements in other fora too.[40] His stance is a reiteration of the position his country's erstwhile governments have held and advocated in public. Not to be outdone by political leaders, the television anchors of twenty-four-hour news channels in the two countries have taken up the cudgel of nationalism, and these self-appointed nationalist crusaders routinely outshout each other in the advocacy of a devastating war, always presuming that the other side would lose. In the media and social media, and at times in political rallies, a future nuclear war is not a taboo topic but a distinct reality.

There is a strong push from sections of the population in both countries, mesmerized by the glory of war, to attack the other side and finish it forever. For the time being, sanity prevails at the top levels of political and military decision-making, which has prevented the outbreak of more conflicts, though leaders cannot be absolved of their responsibility in stoking the burgeoning fire of popular hyper-nationalist sentiment. The international community hastens to pressure the two countries to return to normalcy whenever tempers cross dangerous limits. But we must remember that despite the track record of restraint and persuasion of the major powers to dissuade India and Pakistan from committing nuclear suicide, there is no guarantee that the constant bellicose pressure from religious nationalist forces will not result in a military confrontation one day. There is no certainty that a repeat of the ghastly terrorist attacks in the past, such as the one on the Indian Parliament in 2001 and Mumbai's economic centres in 2008, will not lead to a swift conventional war. There is no assurance either that a conventional military conflict will not quickly transform into a nuclear war.

Betrayal of Patriotism

It is now clear that seven out of the nine nuclear-armed states, and some of the aspiring ones, pose the hazard of starting hugely devastating wars—not only because of the weapons they have, but also because of the strength of bellicose nationalism they all brandish. The powerful ruling elites in these countries confuse patriotism with nationalism. These two terms are often used interchangeably, but they represent two very different notions. To French President Emmanuel Macron, 'nationalism is a betrayal of patriotism'.[41] Patriotism denotes love for one's country in a positive spirit; nationalism is aggrandizing the identity and interests of the nation at any cost, especially to the detriment of the interests of humankind.

American author Sydney Harris explains the difference thus: 'The difference between patriotism and nationalism is that the patriot is proud of his country for what it does, and the nationalist is proud of his country no matter what it does; the first attitude creates a feeling of responsibility, but the second a feeling of blind arrogance that leads to war.'[42] Similarly, German sociologist Erich Fromm, writing in *The Sane Society* (1955), declared that he abhorred nationalism that put one's nation above the principles of truth and justice. He denounced nationalism that aimed to exercise power over other nations. He said, 'Love for one's country which is not part of one's love for humanity is not love, but idolatrous worship.'[43]

Voltaire lived several decades before the French Revolution and the rise of nationalism. But he foresaw the dangers of nationalism in treating 'the greatness of one's fatherland to wish evil to one's neighbours'. Once nationalism is accepted as a doctrine of aggrandizing national identity and interest, beyond mere love for the nation embodied in patriotism, it follows that force might be required to achieve national objectives. Thus, nationalism is invariably associated with the ability and willingness to use military force.

Albert Einstein described nationalism as a disease. He said, 'It is the measles of mankind.'[44] His analogy with measles is difficult to understand today, but in the 1920s, when Einstein made the comment in an interview, millions of children used to die every year due to this infectious disease. In a modern comparison, nationalism would be equated to the COVID-19 virus. Einstein was then living in Germany. It was four years before Hitler became Chancellor, but he could foresee what was going to happen.

Another great thinker of the last century who rejected nationalism was Rabindranath Tagore, an Indian poet, educationist and artist, who was awarded the Nobel Prize in Literature in 1913. Irish poet

W.B. Yeats had lobbied for Tagore getting this prize. The story behind the awarding of the Nobel Prize is a subject of speculation. One version, circulated in Europe, is that Peter Rosegger, an Austrian poet, was a top contender that year. Rosegger was a staunch German nationalist. He was associated with many cultural initiatives to promote German nationalism, including Schulverein Südmark, which advanced the Germanization of Slovenian schools. It was the year before the First World War. The forces of nationalism were in ascendance across Europe. Some authors and poets, including Yeats, looked at Tagore's humanism as a counter to the nationalism in Europe and wanted to raise his profile, thus lobbying for a Nobel Prize for him. There are other speculations as well, which suggest that Yeats wanted the West to recognize the Indian talent. We will never know the truth. But there is no doubt that Tagore was a strong opponent of nationalism. His lectures on nationalism, which he describes as a menace, were published in a volume titled *Nationalism*. It is worth quoting from it.

> The idea of the Nation is one of the most powerful anaesthetics that man has invented. Under the influence of its fumes the whole people can carry out its systematic programme of the most virulent self-seeking without being in the least aware of its moral perversion—in fact feeling dangerously resentful if it is pointed out . . .
>
> There is only one history—the history of man. All national histories are merely chapters in the larger one. The call has come to every individual in the present age to prepare himself and his surroundings for this dawn of a new era, when man shall discover his soul in the spiritual unity of all human beings.[45]

Tagore's warning that the cult of nationalism can cause a sudden and violent death of nations is as relevant today as it was a hundred years ago when he issued it. However, there is one substantial variance. Tagore was talking about the lonely death of a nation that drank the poison of nationalism. In the present times, the destiny of any such nation, if it has the weapons of final destruction, cannot be separated from the fate of the world. With competitive nationalism blending with militarism, all the nations that possess such weapons risk the obliteration of the human civilization.

So long as our mental frameworks, national pride and institutional arrangements are organized in such a way that a nuclear and post-nuclear war is a reality—involving any two of the nine countries possessing such weapons—we will continue to live in the shadow of an apocalypse. What gives us hope, though, is the evidence that war is a matter of choice. Just as it is possible to choose a war, it is also possible to not choose a war. It should be possible not merely to postpone the surety of human extinction by war, but to eliminate the risk altogether. This, of course, will require humankind to consider a new direction for its journey. The beginning of such a difficult and challenging sojourn must begin with our examination of whether indeed war is a matter of choice, a question we will explore in the next chapter.

3

In Twilight Hours: War, a Choice

'War is not foisted on us by forces beyond our control, whether inner male aggression, competition for scarce resources, or entrenched cultural attitudes. Wars begin with human decisions. Choices!'

—John Horgan, author[1]

Whether some leaders will one day make a wilful choice to launch an apocalyptic global war is an existential question. We cannot ignore the answer merely because it is inconvenient and infuriating. If we want to ensure our species' survival, we must realize that war and peace are choices we ourselves make. We should not allow those wielding power to fool us into believing that wars simply have to be waged to secure national interest, and that they are a fait accompli.

Those who want to wage wars excel in inventing emotive excuses. Consider the case of the Crusades. In 1095 CE, Pope Urban II proclaimed the First Crusade at the Council of Claremont, with an ostensible objective of capturing Jerusalem, which had fallen to the Muslims in 638 CE. The Pope was clearly looking for a cause that would unite Christendom, and initiating a ferocious feud seemed to be the need of the hour. In his times, Christian knights and lords were constantly involved in bloody fights with one another. The Pope conceived of the brilliant idea of a religious war to bring together Christian combatants on one side. He claimed that his call to arms was about recapturing Jerusalem in the name of Christ; but that was not the only reason. The real purpose was to ravage other religious communities. Pope Urban's crusading armies slaughtered Jews in Rhineland, today's Köln and Frankfurt, killing them in large numbers and with the same viciousness that they did Muslims when they conquered Jerusalem. All this only to lose the holy city to Saladdin, an Egyptian prince, a few decades later in the Third Crusade!

Pope Urban dredged up a 450-year-old episode—the loss of Jerusalem to Muslims—to wage bloody war, which just goes to show that there is no death of pretexts if one wants to ignite a conflict. If we all start looking back hundreds of years to justify present invasions, the world will soon be devoured by revenge and anarchy.

Pope Urban's legacy inspired Pope Innocent III to launch the Fourth Crusade, a hundred years later, to once again retrieve Jerusalem from the Muslims. His armies borrowed ships from Venice for 85,000 silver marks; however, the crusaders could only repay part of the amount. They were, therefore, persuaded by Doge Enrico Dandolo, the cagey chieftain of Venice, to invade, annexe and pillage Zara, a Catholic city on the Adriatic coast, to compensate the Venetians for their financial investment. While in Zara, the Crusaders met emissaries of Prince Alexius, who had been deposed by his uncle in Constantinople. The shrewd Doge convinced the Crusaders to attack Constantinople, the Orthodox Christian capital, ostensibly to restore Prince Alexius to the throne but essentially to loot the treasures stored in the ancient city at the centre of the Christian civilization.

Constantinople, now known as Istanbul, stands testimony to the fact that every war is someone's choice. It is located at the confluence of Asia and Europe, with the Bosphorus Strait separating the two continents. Very close to the southern entrance of the Bosphorus Strait stands the 1,500-year-old Hagia Sophia. For almost a century, since the formation of the Turkish Republic in 1923 until the decision by President Erdogan to convert it into a mosque in 2020, it had been a museum. In the distant past, the Hagia Sophia had served both as a church and a mosque. It was an Eastern Orthodox Cathedral from its construction in the year 537 until 1204, at which time the armies of Pope Innocent III seized it and converted it into a Roman Catholic Cathedral. In 1204, the invaders were wrapping up the Fourth Crusade, originally aimed at recapturing Jerusalem. They consciously decided to sack Constantinople, desecrate the Hagia Sophia, steal priceless artefacts, break open tombs of ancient kings and rape nuns. They tore the high altar and pulpit into pieces, distributing precious metals and stones embedded in them among soldiers. They brought mules and horses into the church to carry away the treasures.

Soon after sacking Constantinople, a special branch of the Crusaders attacked the Cathars, a Christian sect in southern France, to empower Pope Innocent III so that he could extend his influence. The Cathars were a puritanical sect, steadfastly against the opulence and materialism of the Catholic clergy. They posed a challenge to the Catholic establishment, as well as the French crown, with their independent philosophy, and so a Crusade was launched to annihilate them. It began with setting on fire the city of Beziers in southern France, which killed not only the Cathars, but also Catholics. Emboldened by this demonic victory, the Crusaders marched on, carrying out genocides in town after town in France's southern province.[2]

The massacres of Christians in Zara, Constantinople and Beziers by the Christian Crusaders of the Roman Catholic Church in the early thirteenth century prove that these religious wars, purportedly against Muslims, were nothing but wars of acquisition aimed at pillaging

Muslims, Jews, Catholics and Cathars alike. They were deliberately undertaken for looting, raping and conquering using a divine ruse. Just as Pope Urban's Crusaders planned to plunder and kill Jews, Pope Innocent's forces, and their Venetian allies, intended to sack Constantinople and violate the nuns of the Hagia Sophia. The holy wars were choices made, in the name of god, to serve the interests of priests and princes.

Within decades of Constantinople being razed and divided by the Roman Catholic armies, Baghdad was sacked by the Mongol forces in 1258. This city was the centre of the rich and thriving Islamic civilization under the Abbasid reign. Mongke Khan, Genghis Khan's descendant, wanted to conquer it for no reason other than satisfying his ego, greed and desire. The Mongols had long wanted to establish themselves across what is Iraq and Iran today. Not satisfied with the tribute that the Caliph of Baghdad, Al-Musta'sim, used to send to them, the Mongols demanded that he should submit the tribute personally. Moreover, they ordered him to offer a military detachment to aid the Mongol campaign in Persia. As the Caliph refused to accept these humiliating terms, the Mongols decided to seize Baghdad. Under the leadership of Hulegu Khan, Mongke Khan's brother, the Mongol forces massacred the ordinary people of Baghdad, destroyed palaces and libraries, tore up books, and burnt hospitals and other public buildings. The Mongols arrested Caliph Al-Musta'sim and forced him to watch the mass murder of his citizens before he was wrapped in a rug and trampled under horses. There was no natural, economic or religious reason for the Mongol invasions of Baghdad; it was caused by nothing more than someone's longing for blood and treasure.[3]

This was not the only occasion when Baghdad had been raided. Timur, who described himself as the Sword of Islam, raided it in 1393 and again in 1401 because he wanted to establish his dominance over the region. He ensured the massacre of most of the Muslim residents of the city, except theologians and dervishes. The Islamic empire of Persia invaded Baghdad several times between the sixteenth and nineteenth centuries. If prosperous Christian settlements in Christendom were destroyed by Christian armies, the centre of the Islamic golden age was ruined by Mongols—who came to eventually embrace Islam—and the Persian Islamic armies.[4]

The destructions of Constantinople and Baghdad were great losses for humanity. The Romans came from the West. The Mongols and the Persians came from the East. They spoke different languages, followed different faiths, had different cultures, looked different from each other and enjoyed different cuisines. What they had in common was a penchant for warfare.

It wasn't only in the medieval period that priests and princes started wars to amuse their egos and fill their treasuries. Baghdad offers a testimony to how war often depends on nothing more than an intruder's vagaries. Just as Pope Urban II conceived of the Crusades to divert attention from a sluggish economy, forge internal unity and establish dominance, President George Bush, Jr, of the US wanted to initiate a modern crusade against any feeble nation as a message of American domination to the world. His city of choice for an invasion, following the legacy of Hulegu Khan, Timur and the Safavids of Persia, was Baghdad.

In the winter of 2002–03, a scholar from the American Democratic Party visited Mumbai as a part of his campaign to galvanize international support for the Republican plot to attack Iraq. He met scholars and researchers behind closed doors at the Nehru Centre in Mumbai and advocated assaulting Baghdad on the suspicion that the dictatorial Iraqi regime possessed nuclear arms. Someone asked him if the US also planned to attack Pakistan and North Korea, which were both dictatorships and possessed nuclear weapons beyond any suspicion. The American had no answer. He could not openly admit that the US did not want to risk a war with a real nuclear power. The US had made a calibrated choice to target a regime that was weak, unpopular and incapable of retaliation, as it did not, in fact, have nuclear weapons.

A few weeks later, Colin Powell, US Secretary of State, addressed the annual meeting of the World Economic Forum in Davos, a charming Swiss village where the world's business elite gather every year as a part of the summit that takes place in the last week of January.[5] There were some 3,000 people in the audience at the Congress Hall in Davos that year. In his speech, Powell tried to justify the plan to ravage Iraq. When he finished his address, about 800–900 Americans in the room offered him a standing ovation. All the others held on to their seats, refusing to applaud. Powell had failed to convince anyone except his American compatriots.

Eventually, the US raided Baghdad, arrested its dictator Saddam Hussein, and hanged him. They bombed the country, slaughtering women and children, ruining homes, destroying schools and libraries, and giving birth to new terrorist groups. According to calculations made by Professor Joseph Stiglitz in 2007, Iraq's economy suffered a loss of $3 trillion. The Strategic Foresight Group's report titled *Cost of Conflict in the Middle East* estimates that by 2008, a quarter of a million Iraqis were killed in the war. Almost 70,000 Iraqis joined various insurgency groups in 2007, as compared to 3,000–5,000 in 2004. About 7,60,000 children were out of school; the National Library lost half a million books; and archaeological sites equivalent to 3,000 football fields were plundered. The Americans built their bases in Ur and Babylon, the earliest cities of human civilization, damaging everything from walls to pavements. The US military deployed 2,22,888 troops in Iraq by 2008, which was an increase of a hundredfold from 2,200 in 1993.[6] The Americans did not find any nuclear weapons. It became clear that Iraq was chosen as a target precisely because it had none.

Whether it was Xerxes burning Athens and Dao attacking Yue almost 2,500 years ago, or whether it was the Russians capturing Crimea and the Americans ransacking Syria in this century, every war has resulted from someone's preference for violence. Sometimes it may be for an apparently obvious reason, and at other times, it may be because of an invented excuse. The common characteristic of all wars across five continents, through five millennia, is that each one of them was the result of a choice someone consciously made to start a conflict.

Robbers' Cave

Our historical affinity for wars is reflected in some of the known social and psychological experiments conducted by researchers. In 1954, Muzafer Sherif, an American psychologist of Turkish origin, undertook an experiment at Robbers' Cave State Park in Oklahoma, which is still studied by professionals. Students of psychology all over the world are familiar with it even now.

In 1954, in a project funded by the Rockefeller Foundation, Sherif and his wife brought together twenty-two fifth-grade boys from stable Protestant families for a Boy Scouts' camp. The boys were divided into two groups but were not made aware of the existence of the other group. In the first phase of the experiment, the facilitators promoted solidarity within each group and encouraged them to play games to build team spirit. For example, a treasure hunt would attract a cash prize for the whole group, which the group could decide how to spend. Within a short time, each group developed separately, and an internal organization and hierarchies became apparent, along with the emergence of certain individuals as leaders. The groups were allowed to choose a name for themselves: one chose 'Eagles', while the other chose 'Rattlers'. Once the groups evolved, Sherif arranged for each to have a glimpse of the other. As each group became aware of the existence of the other, in-group solidarity increased and the boys developed feelings of 'us' versus 'them'.

In the second phase, Sherif and his team arranged competitive games between the two groups. They offered a big trophy for a tournament, which only one group would win. There were also other competitive prizes. The rivalry between the two groups increased, with name-calling and fisticuffs. Finally, the groups prepared for a gang war, which could have resulted in broken bones. The facilitators intervened just in time.

In the third phase, Sherif's team tried to encourage the two groups to mingle at common lunches, movie shows and picnics. But the Eagles and Rattlers kept to their own teams, showing no inclination of making friends from the other camp. At this stage, new challenges were introduced. The water supply from the top of a hill was disrupted and the boys had to form a chain to remove stones from the hill to fix the water supply. They also had to restart a stalled food truck. They had to decide on one movie that they could all go to. With such goals to achieve, the two teams began to work together. The camp ended with boys from both groups becoming pals and sharing sweets.

Several social psychologists have studied this case for over fifty years and drawn many conclusions from it. Although some of the inferences have been debated, one basic fact is clear. It was not in the inherent nature of the boys to fight with one another: to fight or not to fight was their conscious decision. In the first phase, when they had opportunities to cooperate, they made friends with each other. In the second phase, when they faced the rival group, they chose to get into a conflict to establish or oppose domination. In the third phase, boys from both groups chose to overcome their differences when their water and food supplies were in peril, or when there was an incentive to see a movie that they would all like. In each phase, the boys *chose* either conflict or cooperation.

A decade later, Lutfy Diab, a professor of psychology at the American University of Beirut, decided to replicate the experiment in a Lebanese setting. Lebanon is a kaleidoscope of religions: coexistence and conflict characterize the relations between Christians, Sunni Muslims and Shi'a Muslims, and sectarian violence is not uncommon. At present, political power is shared between the three religious groups, with the President being a Christian, the Prime Minister being a Sunni Muslim and the Speaker of Parliament being a Shi'a Muslim. The parliamentary constituencies are organized along religious lines. Diab had a long stint at the American university as a senior academic, once serving as the president of the university, and by 1963, he was already known as a creative young professional. To replicate Sherif's experiment, he organized a camp for eighteen students from fiercely religious schools. He split them into two groups: Blue Ghosts and Red Genies. Diab did not organize his groups based on religion, and each of the two groups had five Muslim and four Christian students.[7]

The boys developed close in-group identities as Ghosts or Genies, not as Christians or Muslims. When a fight broke out over some verbal disagreements between the two groups, the Red Genies attacked the Blue Ghosts with a kitchen knife. Both the attackers and the victims happened to be Christians. Professor Diab, a neutral observer, saw that the boys felt committed to their Red and Blue affiliations, artificially created in a controlled environment, and not to their religious identities. In the external world of Lebanon's complex social milieu, the boys might get embroiled in violence between communal groups, but in Diab's setting, the Muslim and Christian boys in each group bonded and supported each other against the enemies from the rival group. The boys obviously chose their enemies depending on the circumstances they found themselves in.

In the 1990s, worried about growing tensions between India and Pakistan, two nuclear-armed neighbours, many American and German foundations organized workshops and summer schools for young professionals from the two countries to come together in neutral and serene locations. Initially, the participants displayed a strong identification with their national positions on various issues and engaged in verbal fights. But later, personal and social bonds developed in the summer school, and soon the members were taking sides based on these connections.

Many psychological experiments undertaken in the last few decades prove that entering into organized conflict is a matter of choice. However, such tests do not necessarily tell us much about wars between nations and how individuals behave as a representative of his or her nation. An air force pilot may feel proud of murdering hundreds of innocent people in an enemy country, although he avoids brawls at the local pub. Similarly, many military men become peaceniks after retirement. For example, during the Cold War, a new concept of parallel diplomacy, also known as 'track-two diplomacy', was conceived of by retired American diplomats. As per this practice, retired ambassadors as well as retired generals and admirals of the US and the former Soviet Union met privately, without the media's knowledge, and often in a relaxed and informal atmosphere, to explore solutions to bilateral problems. The governments were kept informed about the discussions of the dialogues. At times, the governments asked their friends in the parallel diplomacy process to test certain ideas with the rival groups in an informal and non-committal manner. This practice of parallel diplomacy was eventually imitated in other strife-torn regions, particularly the Middle East and South Asia, and continues even today. Retired officers from the armed forces, intelligence agencies and foreign ministries from rival countries meet in scenic places. They advocate their respective national positions during the day; they enjoy drinks and delicacies in the evening. Neemrana, a fort in the desert state of Rajasthan in India, and Murree, a quaint hill station in Pakistan, used to be the favourites for track-two meetings between the former officials of the Indian and Pakistani armed forces and diplomatic services. Now, more elegant venues in Asia and Europe are preferred. The amity between generals and ambassadors from rival countries in these retreats proves that the psychology of the individual soldier has little to do with inter-country warfare. The armed forces follow orders when someone makes a choice to wage war.

The psychology of individual leaders does not automatically produce military conflict in most cases. Timur, Bloody Mary, Pol Pot, Idi Amin and Hitler might have been psychopaths, but they were exceptions. US President George Bush, Jr, enjoyed the company of his family, holidays on ranches, Sunday visits to the church and a glass of wine at dinner, neither did he suffer from any mental illness. As President of the USA, he made a calculated choice to invade Iraq when he realized that there was no threat of a nuclear counterattack. Most heads of warring states are regular men who love their families and neighbours. If psychoanalysts had examined them as young adults, they would have seemed like the boys next door, not as future leaders who would organize massacres in foreign lands. As borne out by countless examples, personal or group behaviour is different from how individuals behave as part of armies in a war between nations. War is a multidisciplinary and complex undertaking that requires sophisticated management techniques. Preparations for it involve nukes, pathogens, killer robots and cyberweapons, and neXt weapons require a particularly high degree of organization. War is thus a dispassionate, critical and considered choice made by leaders.

Ambitious Dozen

Not every nation chooses war. Some nations choose to renounce weapons and violence. Some only prepare for self-defence, but do not intend to conquer others. Some others, though, love to invade, strike and intervene, pretending to protect lofty principles. Those nations with high military spending and nuclear as well as post-nuclear weapons seem quite ready for war. These are the US, Russia, China, the UK (Britain), France, India, Pakistan, Israel and North Korea. Then, there are three other countries that splurge on conventional weapons, and hope to acquire nuclear and other deadly weapons if they can obtain the technology and raw materials: South Korea, Iran and Saudi Arabia. These dozen countries have placed war at the heart of their strategic thought. This is not a static list of a dozen ambitious countries. Australia seems desperate to militarize itself, as proven by its decision to acquire technology for nuclear submarines in September 2021 from the UK and the US and build the third-largest fleet of nuclear submarines in the world, bypassing the Nuclear Non-proliferation Treaty.

There are 195 countries on the rolls of the UN. However, the ambitious dozen mentioned above account for two-thirds of the global military expenditure. The remaining 183 countries are responsible only for one-third of such expenditure. Table A5 in Appendix 1 reveals the countries that contribute most to global militarism.

The US's military expenditure alone has accounted for around one-third of the world's for several years, even though it declined from 2010 to 2017, only to rise again starting 2018. During the same period, the expenditure of ten countries of the ambitious dozen (excluding the US and North Korea, for which data is not available) leapt from $476 billion to $624 billion. The combined expenditure of the other 183 countries increased from $447 billion to $483 billion. Germany, Japan, Italy, Brazil, Canada and Australia together currently spend about $200 billion on arms, though Australia's military expenditure may go up steeply in future. The remaining 177 countries in the world account for $275 billion. Thus, the twelve most militarist countries spend more than four times what 177 countries together spend on the instruments of mass violence. This data reveals that most countries in the world—177 out of 195—are not a threat to human survival. They barely spend little more than a billion dollars each for their defence. The militarily ambitious dozen countries that are accumulating arms—especially nuclear weapons, AI and robotics-driven arms, and neXt weapons—are also the ones that are often involved in a hot or cold war.

China, Korea, India, Pakistan and Israel justify acquiring military wherewithal by citing threats posed by their neighbours. Take the case of China. It fought a war with India in 1962, one with Vietnam in 1979 and had a border skirmish with India in 2020. China does not rule out armed conflicts with these two neighbours in future either. It also faces tensions with Taiwan and its other neighbours in the South China Sea. Moreover, it is always suspicious of Japan, its historic tormentor. As Australia builds a fleet of nuclear submarines in the 2020s, a Chinese clash with Australia, by either design or accident, in the Pacific Ocean is a real possibility. With the US persuading its allies to declare China a strategic rival in 2021, China is also expected to be wary of a possible armed conflict with the US in the 2020s.

India and Pakistan have been engaged in continuous hostilities from the time the two nations became independent, with wars fought in 1948, 1965, 1971 and 1999. With ever-simmering tensions and hostile public opinion on both sides, the countries always seem to be preparing for an all-out confrontation. It is not as if collaborations between the two countries don't exist: several Pakistani movie stars have gained fame and glory in Bollywood and India's elite enjoy attending weddings in Karachi and Lahore. But most people gleefully support bombing the other when election rallies and television debates call for blood in times of turmoil.

Looking at the Israelis, one would think that their country is always on the brink of yet another war. Just as Israel's birth took place amidst warfare, its growth is also mired in conflict as the country continues to have bellicose relations with all its neighbours. In 1948, the neighbouring Arab states decided to invade Israel: not only did the Jewish nation repel the attack, but it also acquired Arab territories by the time the intense hostilities came to an end. In subsequent years, Israel has fought with its neighbours several times: In the Yom Kippur war of 1973, Israel encountered an invasion from combined Arab forces. In the early 1990s, and again in 2006, it fought with forces in Lebanon. Not to mention the violent clashes Israel and Palestinian groups have been involved in for decades.

Israel has increasingly come to consider Iran as its Enemy Number One, though the two countries have not faced each other on a battleground. On the other hand, Israel had a cordial partnership with Turkey until the Israeli invasion of Gaza around Christmas of 2008. A spat between Israeli President Simon Peres and Turkey's Prime Minister (now President) Recep Tayyip Erdogan at Davos in January 2009 set off a downturn in their relations. Israel went out of its way to establish relationships with Arab states in the Gulf such as Saudi Arabia, the UAE and Bahrain in 2020, including fostering cooperation in high technology and security, while its relations with Turkey reached a nadir. Israel's relations with Turkey and the Gulf states in the last thirty to forty years offer evidence of how the same nations, and particularly their armed forces, can become friends when they want and foes when they wish.

North Korea has fought only one major war with its southern neighbour from 1950 to 1953. However, it has spent more than the next half a century anticipating the resumption of hostilities—not only with South Korea but also with the US. Maintaining a 'blow hot, blow cold' relationship since 2018 with the US, North Korea has proudly built missiles that can hit targets in its rival country. Meanwhile, preparations for the next war are on in full swing, with North Korea having tested ballistic missiles in November 2019, March 2020, March 2021, and a long-range cruise missile in September 2021.[8]

France is another country that has been involved in one battle or another for the last fifty to sixty years. In the period immediately after the Second World War, France was engaged in conflicts in Algeria and Indo-China. Since the beginning of this century, it has joined the Western campaigns in the Middle East, Afghanistan and Libya. It has also been involved in military conflicts in its former colonies in West Africa—Chad, Mali, Côte d'Ivoire and the Central African Republic.

Similarly, the UK has been involved in the Western campaigns in the Middle East, Afghanistan and Libya. It began its post–Second World War career with the Suez Canal crisis in 1956. Then it fought against Argentina for control of the Falkland Islands in 1982 and intervened in the civil war in Sierra Leone in 2000. It has proved to be America's great ally in desolating Iraq for the last two decades.

The US and the Russian Federation are the fountainheads of the ambitious dozen nations and they have made war a habit. Their lust for lethal weapons provides inspiration and justification for others to acquire the same deadly arsenal. Only when the US and Russia sincerely agree to disarm will it be possible to motivate the UK, France, China, India, Pakistan and Israel to renounce their weapons of final destruction, and discourage new aspirants wanting to acquire such arms.

Since the Second World War, neither the US nor the USSR/Russia has had a long spell without engagement in a war somewhere in the world. Proxy wars in different parts of the world were common during the Cold War. In the early 1990s, after the Cold War ended, 'hot' wars continued. In fact, there is not any continent, except Australia, where American or Russian bombs have not ravaged towns. The countries seem to be itching to wage one war or another all the time. Besides these direct engagements, they have been involved in many conflicts indirectly by selling weapons to help their client states to kill and maim. After assuming office, Donald Trump, whose presidential election campaign was partly based on his anti-Islamist rhetoric, made his first overseas visit to Saudi Arabia in 2017. During this visit, he sold the Saudis billions of dollars of weapons, at a time when they were involved in a war in Yemen and a conflict with Qatar and Iran. When the Qataris complained, the Trump administration sold arms worth a few billion dollars to them as well. President Biden refused to sell arms to Saudi Arabia to attack Yemen, but his decision to bomb Syria within a few weeks of his inauguration demonstrated that the American penchant for wars was very much alive.

The constant engagement in war by the US and the Russian Federation—either directly, indirectly or through arms sales—gives the impression that violence, hostilities and destruction are the oxygen of their political economy. Their methods and instruments are sophisticated when compared to those of the Crusaders and Mongols, but their mindset is no different.

The other ten countries possessing and aspiring for deadly weapons constantly try to imitate the two big powers. With their growing desire for dominance and unending appetite for arms, they constantly wait for the next war.

The majority of countries in the world do not want to acquire the weapons of final destruction. Their national ego, their sense of insecurity and their pride do not exceed their common sense. But the twelve lethally armed countries and potentially a thirteenth one (Australia) have made our continued existence dependent on the priorities of a handful of leaders when evidence shows that it is the political masters in these countries who have been continuously involved in violent military confrontations over the last several years. A hundred years ago, a different set of countries, including Italy, Germany, Austria and Japan, along with Britain, France, Russia and the US, held the promise of becoming the most dangerous threats to humankind. They redeemed their promise in two wars, turning humans into killing machines, ripping apart countries and destroying families.

Thus, the tragedy of human civilization has become that there are always some hyper-belligerent states in the world, even though most countries prefer to live in peace and harmony.

Since pursuing war and peace are choices that nations make, their positions change from time to time. Those who are preparing for a mega-war today were once willing to agree on limiting lethality, just as those professing peace today once sabotaged initiatives for worldwide disarmament. Therefore, those who are following a bellicose trajectory today can, in theory, choose to shift their position in future.

In 1932, the League of Nations (the precursor to the UN) had convened a World Disarmament Conference to lower the intensity of warfare in Geneva. Sixty countries sent delegates to the meeting to consider reducing the accumulation of offensive arms. Even though the US was not a member of the League, it participated.

In April 1932, the General Commission of the conference agreed on the principle of a phased reduction of armaments. Already in the previous conferences in Washington and London, major powers had decided on limiting the number of battleships. Previously, in the Washington Naval Treaty, signed by the five victors of the First World War in 1922, it was decided to limit the construction of battleships, battlecruisers and aircraft carriers.[9] Moreover, tonnage restrictions were placed on the destroyers and submarines. A subsequent conference in London in 1930 extended the treaty. Great Britain and the US would have liked to extend the limits further, but Japan and Italy, two of the original five signatories of the Washington Naval Treaty, opposed the extension.

In July 1932, the General Commission of the League of Nations' Disarmament Conference unanimously adopted the Benes Resolution.[10] This resolution emphasized the prohibition of aerial bombardment on the civilian population, quantitative limitations on certain categories of heavy artillery, and an absolute ban on chemical and biological warfare.

Britain and the US were positively inclined to downgrade offensive arms in the conference, but Germany and France were opposed to it. Germany wanted others to disarm to their level, failing which it threatened to fortify its military. France wanted an international police force to be set up before it could agree to disarm. Stuck in a deadlock, the conference was adjourned in the summer of 1932. It reconvened in February 1933, only days after Adolf Hitler had assumed power in Germany. Determined to re-arm itself, Germany rejected all proposals that did not accord it immediate military parity with the Western powers. Finally, on 23 October 1933, Germany announced its withdrawal from the Disarmament Conference as well as the League of Nations. Now, a little less than a century later, we find that the hawks of the 1930s have now become doves, and those willing to compromise then are currently the world's most aggressive and armed nations.

Germany's variable position in global politics in the last 150 years is a study in how one nation can believe in multiple truths at different times. In the late nineteenth century, Bismarck's Prussia, later Germany, invited war by manipulating, threatening or directly attacking its adversaries. Again, in Hitler's Germany, extreme antagonism surfaced. However, by the time of the Cold War, we find Chancellor Willy Brandt making every effort to prevent the conflict from turning into a full-blown war. All his successors have shown preference for diplomacy over conflict and even kept military expenditure under check, relative to other big powers, until politically forced by the Trump administration to increase it. It is important to underline that this same Germany had opted for war at times and peace otherwise under the leadership of different heads of state.

Opting Out

Indeed, the hope for humankind's survival stems from the evidence that both war and peace are choices.

If we turn our attention to Africa, we find that since the end of colonization until the beginning of this century, feuds ravaged the continent. Several regional conflicts had erupted, and civil strife and enmity between neighbours had engulfed the region. Such was the scale and impact of hostilities that the landscape was strewn with refugee camps. In the international media, Africa was portrayed as a continent without hope.

But things have started to change now. Since the beginning of the twenty-first century, African leaders have resolved to end wars. It is true that the continent is plagued by brutal games of thrones within countries, ethnic clashes and skirmishes between herders and shepherds, not to mention terrorism. However, Africa has chosen to liberate itself from wars between countries. One of the grandest successes in this direction was achieved when in 2019, Ethiopia and Eritrea agreed to end their schism, earning Ethiopian Prime Minister Abiy Ahmed the coveted Nobel Peace Prize, despite ongoing brutal strife within his own country. It was the last active interstate conflict in the huge continent, Western Sahara being the only frozen conflict. Morocco had a military confrontation with the Polisario Front of the Sahrawi people involved in a struggle for the independence of their region from Moroccan control in the last century. There is an uneasy ceasefire in force; since Algeria supports the Polisario, it is the only international conflict remaining in Africa.

On the other side of the Atlantic, we have the examples of Uruguay, Chile and Mexico, which did not wage any war in the whole of the twentieth century. Although these countries were not ideal models of good governance—Chile had ruthless dictatorships for long durations, as did Uruguay for a brief spell—they did not engage in fights with nations across their borders.

In Europe, Iceland, Switzerland and Lichtenstein have chosen not to participate in any war for several centuries. In fact, there is no record of warfare involving Iceland for at least the last 600 to 700 years. Even if it is argued that Iceland is an exception as it is an isolated island nation, we still have to explain the cases of Switzerland and Lichtenstein. The two countries are surrounded by Germany, France, Italy and Austria, which were the main protagonists in the two World Wars. Switzerland's last battle was at Marignano in 1515. At the beginning of the nineteenth century, it was a theatre of a military confrontation between France and other European powers over control of the Alpine routes.[11] But by 1815, in the Paris Agreement, the European countries endorsed Swiss neutrality. In the Hague Convention of 1907, the laws of neutrality were laid down, which assured the territorial integrity of a country in response to its non-participation in wars.[12] Thus, the Swiss ensured their country's integrity and security by rejecting war. A choice against war was a choice in favour of the nation's security.

The Swiss are no different from the Germans, French, Italians or Austrians. Most of the population is Christian, whether Roman Catholic or Protestant. They speak slightly adapted dialects of German, French and Italian. They have the same pride, love, hatred, ego, generosity, jealousy and ambition that their neighbours have. Switzerland has actively rejected war even when other European countries embraced death and devastation over the last half a millennium.

Since Switzerland chooses not to initiate wars, it uses its army for peaceful and humanitarian activities. Its navy acts like a police force, mainly preventing crime on international lakes. The Swiss constitution does not allow the country to join military alliances.

The now-famous Swiss neutrality has given the citizens of the country very high dividends. Switzerland is one of the three richest countries in the world according to the UN, the World Bank and the

International Monetary Fund. It has moved far ahead in scientific research, infrastructure development and international diplomatic presence compared to other European countries.

In 1955, Austria decided to follow the Swiss example and embrace neutrality,[13] even though, till then, it had one of the most violent histories in the world; it is common knowledge that the Habsburg monarchy and the Austro-Hungarian Empire had aggressively launched several military campaigns for almost 400 years. Post the World Wars, though, Austria did not feel nostalgia for its imperial glory. Instead, it saw value in the pacific behaviour that had accrued many gains for Switzerland by then.

Considered superficially, there is apparently nothing in common between Switzerland and Uruguay, two countries separated by 11,000 km. They are as different as can be economically and in terms of technological advancement. Switzerland is landlocked, while Uruguay has gorgeous beaches. Switzerland practises democracy by referendum, and Uruguay relies on representational democracy. But the two countries do have something very important in common: their determination to reject war for the last several years.

If similar countries can make contrasting choices and vastly different countries can make the same choices on the acceptance or rejection of war, there is only one conclusion to be drawn. Countries wage wars only because they want to. Geography, history, economy and other such factors can provide legitimacy once the choice is made. But pretext is not the same as cause. Choice—mostly a calculated and conscious one—is the sole cause of war.

A decade ago, many experts had advised Ukraine to learn from Switzerland and declare for itself an impartial status. If Ukraine had indeed done so, it would have provided better livelihoods and respect for its citizens. Currently, it ranks below 100 on the per capita income index of all international organizations. It would not have lost Crimea and the affection of the people in Donbas. It would not have deprived several thousand mothers of their sons by sending them off to fight in conflicts. Ukraine has chosen war; Switzerland has chosen peace. Thus, it is that in the old town of Kyiv, old men and women sell the military insignia of their family members to eke out a living, but in the old town of Bern, young men and women enjoy romance over fondue, wine and chocolate mousse.

However, there is an irony concerning Switzerland, Sweden, Norway and some other countries that have eschewed wars: these nations have no hesitation in exporting arms. Switzerland has been exporting armaments to neighbouring European countries. It has also exported small quantities of arms to Saudi Arabia and the UAE, which have been involved in military conflicts in the Middle East. Sweden has not gone to war for over 200 years. That has not stopped it from exporting weapons, mostly to its European partners, the US, Brazil, India and to Saudi Arabia and the UAE. Another country that keeps out of war but exports arms to others is Norway. Its defence products include rocket engines and ammunition. Finland, too, behaves in a similar way, like its Scandinavian neighbours. It chooses not to wage wars, but it exports war-related materials to others. Such duplicity in the policies of neutral countries raises moral questions. However, the fact that these countries choose not to engage in wars themselves remains valid. Our aim here is not to examine the moral code of countries; we are only trying to assess if war anywhere is indeed a matter of conscious choice.

Next, we come to the countries that are bidding farewell to arms altogether. They not only want to avoid military confrontation, but they also do not even want to have access to the instruments of warfare. Over twenty such countries in different parts of the world have abolished their military as they are confident of ensuring their security through diplomacy rather than armed defence.[14] They are Andorra, Costa Rica, Dominica, Grenada, Iceland, Kiribati, Lichtenstein, the Marshall Islands, Mauritius, Micronesia, Monaco, Nauru, Palau, Panama, St Lucia, St Vincent and the Grenadines, Samoa, Solomon Islands, Tuvalu and Vanuatu.

In some cases, such as Andorra and Panama, the armed forces of another country provide protection. But in most cases, countries do not see any need for a standing army of their own because they do not plan to wage war. Such is their confidence in their own statesmanship that they do not seem to be worried about invasion.

Critics might contend that these are small countries and, therefore, they do not need armies. This is not true. Singapore and the Maldives are also small, but they have decided that they require their military. In fact, one can convincingly argue that a tiny country has a much greater need for its own armed forces. For example, Panama had several excuses to continue maintaining its armed forces. It is home to the Panama Canal, a strategic waterway linking the Atlantic to the Pacific, which channels almost half of the trade between the Americas and Asia. The existence of this trade route can be threatened if Panama is attacked. But the country chooses to manage its foreign relations with discretion, averting any combat. Until a few decades ago, Panama had a vicious military, which even toppled a democratically elected government in 1968. General Manuel Noriega, Panama's strongman, was a favourite pawn of the US though, eventually, his luck ran out with them and he was overthrown in an American military invasion. Since 1994, when Panama decided to dissolve its armed forces, it has diplomatically rejected US moves to set up an American military base on its soil. For Panama, 'no means no' to the military, whether local or imported.

Panama's neighbour Costa Rica dissolved its armed forces in 1948. Costa Rica does not even have a military alliance with any country. In the 1980s, the country found itself in the middle of a violent region where all its neighbours were involved in savage wars.[15] Rival Central American nations had become pawns in the hands of the US and the former Soviet Union. Only Costa Rica remained neutral. It had not had an army for more than three decades by then. The leaders of the country had learnt the art of protecting their nation with diplomacy and statesmanship rather than guns and bombs. Had it felt insecure because of the violent conflicts raging all around just outside its borders, it would have established its own armed forces. Instead, its response to the regional mayhem was to craft the Central American Peace Plan. In recognition of this initiative, Costa Rica's president, Oscar Arias Sanchez, was awarded the Nobel Peace Prize.[16]

Among the nations that have abdicated armies is Nauru, the smallest island country in the world. It is also one of the richest, thanks to its mineral wealth. It is in the central Pacific Ocean, east of Papua New Guinea. With only a 21 sq. km area, it can be easily annexed by a foreign power. Indeed, Nauru was occupied by the Germans, Japanese and Australians at different times. When it became independent in 1968, it chose not to have a military despite its vulnerability.[17]

The decision to retain armed forces to deter aggression is a philosophical one. A small country with vital assets, such as a trade route or phosphates, may feel vulnerable and, therefore, seek a sense of security by establishing a military. But a small country can also resolve to depend upon diplomacy while eschewing feuds, and use its resources for the social and economic well-being of its people.

The size of the country has nothing to do with the choice to wage or prepare for war. Costa Rica, with an area of 50,000 sq. km, has a much larger territory than Bahrain, Lebanon and Qatar, but the latter are constantly busy arming themselves to the last dollar. It is therefore supercilious to argue that a small country can live without an army and a large one cannot. Those who have abolished armies have chosen to do so not because they are small or large, poor or rich, an island or landlocked, but because they do not want the tools of war to shape their destiny. Those countries that have given up weapons enjoy confidence in themselves. The countries that lack faith in their own statesmanship need the implements of violence. History has shown us that invaders do not often fear those with stockpiles of guns and bombs. There are examples aplenty of countries with big bombs that have been assaulted and countries without armies that have been spared. Weapons do not prevent an invasion. Statesmanship does.

Philosopher's Burden

While some countries renounce violence in their statecraft, others embrace it as if it were a part of the human condition. We must therefore examine the age-old discourse to determine if war can be forsaken or if it is innate to our nature.

Thucydides in Greece, Kautilya in India and Xunzi in China initiated this debate about 2,500 years ago. We have already met Thucydides in the previous chapter while examining the tensions between China and the US. He wrote a detailed chronological account of the Peloponnesian Wars between Sparta and Athens describing the battle, its main characters, and a speech made by Pericles. Nevertheless, his purpose was not to narrate the story of one war but to infer the laws of politics that would stand the test of time in the centuries to come. He concluded that war was inevitable since all societies are driven by three impulses—fear, honour and (self-)interest—and that war was a part of the human condition that would continue recurring in future. He, therefore, did not believe war to be a matter of choice or a calculated decision but something that happened naturally as a result of interactions between the three primal societal impulses.

An important episode in Thucydides's narrative is the Melian Dialogue. The envoys of invading Athens meet the representatives of Melos, a small island state, which wants to be neutral in the war between Athens and Sparta. Assuming that it is inevitable for a powerful state to crush a small state like Melos, the Athenians ignore their pleas and attack them. However, our experiences of war in modern times do not bear out Thucydides's claims. For example, we have already seen how Switzerland safeguarded its people and territory by remaining neutral in the two World Wars. After being involved in bloodshed for centuries, Austria declared neutrality in the 1950s, and since then nobody has dared to invade it. We cannot follow Thucydides in claiming that a strong state must automatically assault a weak one. It may choose to do so at its peril—just as Athens did in the Peloponnesian War and ultimately met its end or as Germany did in the two World Wars, and ended up being ravaged and beaten.

Thucydides explains that Archidamus, the ruler of Sparta, and Pericles, the leader of Athens, were each in favour of restraint. However, both were opposed by the youth of the two nations who were yearning for a contest. The rulers were guided by reason but the youth were driven by emotion.[18] When finally emotion triumphed over reason, war became inevitable. Thucydides implies that leaders have their hands tied and play no role in constraining popular outbursts. If this is true, war is our fate. We must accept that in an era of nuclear, hypersonic and autonomous weapons, human extinction is preordained by the victory of emotions over reason. But is Thucydides justified in portraying that a mob has command over leaders? Or should we question if leaders manipulate the minds of the mob? Did Adolf Hitler, Slobodan Milošević and Xi Jinping manipulate the public mind, or were they manipulated by the mob? We will examine this later in this chapter.

Mencius, who lived and taught philosophy in China between 372 BCE and 279 BCE, was Thucydides's contemporary. Mencius believed that human nature was compassionate and, therefore, it could be inferred that a regular person would not want war. However, Mencius did not discuss war in great detail, much like his guru, Confucius. A hundred years later, Xunzi, alias Hsun Tzu, lived in China from 300 BCE to 215 BCE. He taught philosophy and introduced the discussion on war to the ordinary Chinese people during the warring-states period when various kingdoms in China viciously fought with one another for three centuries until the Qin state unified the country. Xunzi argued in support of just war, which according to him is waged with an objective to end violence and injustice. He believed that ego and resentment caused human nature to become evil. Man always looked for ways to make selfish gains and so he was bound to be in conflict with others, as everyone else too sought their own advancement. He opposed war that was fought for territorial benefits, but he supported it for self-defence and justice. Xunzi suggested that the people of a conquered state should be treated with a certain fairness in order to win their affection as repressive measures would make them resentful and rebellious. His other views on war were also pragmatic: he thought that a state should only fight a war with an equal or weaker state. If there was any possibility of defeat, it would be better to avert a combat. He obviously determined that war was not an automatic phenomenon. It involved careful consideration and he thought it should be avoided if it were possible to quell the enemy without violence.[19]

Let us now turn to Kautilya, also known to us as Chanakya, a strategist who lived in Pataliputra in eastern India from 371 BCE to 283 BCE. He was the Prime Minister of Chandragupta Maurya, the first king to unify the Indian empire and stop Alexander's invading army at the border. In his well-known thesis, *Arthashastra*, Kautilya has provided a detailed account of effective military strategy. He proclaimed that the king must protect his subjects and therefore be prepared to wage war against the enemy. The king should also try to augment his power to be superior to others. This might result in expanding his interests and territory and bring him into conflict with others. He also proposed opportunistic invasion when the enemy was in trouble due to internal turmoil or weakness. The story of colonialism, American invasions in the Arab countries, French invasions in the West African countries, and a proxy war in Libya in the 2010s, seemed to have followed on the lines of Kautilya's strategy of taking advantage of weak and internally eroded countries. Kautilya believed in the pursuit of power like the later strategists such as Machiavelli and Hobbes. He was a strong votary of self-interest in the conduct of affairs of the state and believed that it was in the interest of states to aggrandize themselves. Altruism had no place in his philosophy of statecraft.

In modern India, Kautilya's obsession with power is confused with his preference for war, and he is often quoted in that regard in public discourses on political, diplomatic and military issues. But Kautilya was not a crude warmonger. His preferred strategy for dealing with enemy states was diplomatic negotiations. But where there was no peaceful option, he did recommend a well-planned battle.

Kautilya has earned a permanent place in Indian history for his four-step strategy of *saam, daam, dand, bhed* while dealing with any conflict—whether at a personal, societal or interstate level. The following is the strategy he proposes with regard to relations between states: saam means diplomatic persuasion. Kautilya suggests that in any conflict, the king should first try to convince the enemy of his own perspective through dialogue and constructive argument, persuading them to avoid war. If he fails in this, he can take recourse to daam, which is to offer material gains to the enemy. The king can try to win over the enemy by bribing him with a share of wealth or land. The third step, dand, indicates a punitive approach to deter the enemy from posing any opposition to the king when daam yields no results. If nothing else works out, Kautilya advises the use of bhed or war to annihilate the enemy state. Thus, for the master strategist, war, in effect, was the option of last resort.[20]

If we take a short detour and move a few centuries ahead, we will find that Edward Teller, who made the hydrogen bomb a reality, was like Xunzi or Kautilya, a pragmatist who believed that force should be used only when an agreement was no longer possible to restore peace between nations.[21]

It took a few centuries after Thucydides, Xunzi and Kautilya to revive a debate on the idea of war. Marcus Cicero, a Roman statesman who lived from 106 BCE to 43 BCE, believed that the nature of man was peaceful, and wars were an aberration. He is credited as the founder of the 'just war' theory and held that war was a matter of choice. In his opinion, there were two ways of resolving a conflict: The first was peaceful settlement through discussion and negotiation. The second option was war which should be chosen as an exception. Cicero believed that war was only desirable when it would help to establish durable peace.[22]

St Augustine revived the debate regarding the choice of war in the fourth century CE. He was a philosopher and theologian and the bishop of Hippo Regius in North Africa. When the Western Roman Empire began to disintegrate, he developed the idea of the City of God to draw people to the Church and ignore the attractions of material life. At the same time, he wanted to justify war to protect Rome. So, he suggested that war was a sacred duty if ordered by the sovereign for a good cause. Participating in conflict was a choice made in support of a good reason.[23]

St Thomas Aquinas further developed St Augustine's theory in *Summa Theologica*, where he specified three conditions for any war to be considered just. First, the war had to be waged by the authority of the sovereign. Second, it had to be for a just cause. Third, the belligerents should have peace as their objective, even though war was the means to achieve it.[24]

Ibn Khaldun carried the debate ahead. He emerged as a leading Arab philosopher in Tunisia, a century after Aquinas. He perceived war in Islamic terms. In his thesis *The Muqaddimah*, Ibn Khaldun says that conflict has been present since the origin of humankind and is bolstered by people differentiating between 'us' and 'them'.[25]

He believed that revenge was the motivation for war. The reasons for revenge could be envy, hostility, ambition or religious conviction. We can see that his diagnosis for the cause of war was close to the one offered by Thucydides. Just as Thucydides, he also suggested that war was natural to the human condition and that it was difficult for any society to escape warfare.

Thomas Hobbes completed the circle of discourse initiated by Thucydides. He was a seventeenth-century British philosopher known for his legendary book *Leviathan*. He believed that humans were arrogant and constantly sought power to dominate others. Mankind's natural condition, according to him, was that of a state of war. On an individual level, it was a 'war of all against all'. Hobbes identified three causes of war: competitiveness, diffidence and glory, which reflect the three impulses identified by Thucydides—(self-)interest, fear and honour. Hobbes wrote in *Leviathan* (1651):

> So that in the nature of man, we find three principal causes of quarrel. First, competition; secondly, diffidence; thirdly, glory. The first maketh men invade for gain; the second for safety; and the third for reputation. The first use violence to make themselves masters of other men's persons, wives, children and cattle; the second, to defend them; the third, for trifles, as a word, a smile, a different opinion, and any other sign of undervalue, either direct in their persons or by reflection in their kindred, their friends, their nation, their profession, or their name.[26]

Of Human Nature

The debate on whether war is innate to human nature or a choice has been confused with a more fundamental discourse on human nature. The discord between Hobbes and Rousseau has occupied central place in this debate.

Thomas Hobbes argued that human nature was evil and that humans were involved in the ceaseless pursuit of power. In the state of nature, humans were driven by physical traits much like animals. And therefore, he argued that every man was constantly in a state of war of one against all. On the other hand, Jean-Jacques Rousseau, an eighteenth-century Genevan philosopher, believed that human beings are innately good in their original state, with a natural sense of compassion, but are gradually corrupted by civilization.[27]

Although Hobbes and Rousseau presented unitary visions of human nature, we will do well to remember that a human being is neither in a state of perpetual peace nor in a state of constant war. A person is a part of a community from the moment of birth: he or she has parents, family, friends and is a part of a complex web of relationships from the very beginning. A person is bound to have cooperative relationships with some people and conflictual relationships with others, cooperative dynamics at certain times as well as conflicts with the same person at other times. From birth, a human being grows up within a family, and thus there is no alternative to social conditioning.

Of course, when human beings quarrel among themselves, it cannot be compared to a war. Individual, group and tribal conflicts, even the most violent ones, are different from clashes between countries. Even if our scientists try to throw light on the individual inclination for violence by studying the behaviour of chimpanzees, baboons and other primates, or even people living in isolated tribal societies, that shall not help us comprehend the complex phenomenon of organized effort involving thousands of men and machines called war. The squabbles between chimpanzees have nothing in common with a nuclear contest between China and the US or India and Pakistan.

Philosopher Anthony Grayling describes war as 'armed conflict between states and nations, or between identified and organised groups of significant size and character'. He argues that fighting between armed groups does not count as a war 'until such factors as the number of combatants, and the nature of their organisation and practices as fighting forces, places their conflict above what has been called the military horizon'.[28] The formal definition of war in international humanitarian law emphasizes the role of states and armed conflict between them. The Geneva Convention IV of 1949 defines war to be 'any difference arising between two states and leading to the intervention of members of the armed forces'.[29] Thus, the state is at the core of the legal definition of war. Clearly, clashes between tribes and groups before the formation of states were incidents of violence, but in the absence of states or the participation of other organized forces, they could not be considered wars.

Sigmund Freud, the founder of psychoanalysis, joined the debate in the second half of the nineteenth century. He explained why sometimes war appears to be innate to human nature even though it is not.

According to him, the phenomenon could be explained through the 'recovered memory syndrome', by which people recover memories of past abuse, violence and injustice from their subconscious and react. He tested this theory on individuals.

The validity of this theory is now being explored at the community level. The Centre for the Resolution of Intractable Conflicts (CRIC) at Oxford University leads international reflection on the psychology of violent conflicts. Researchers in its network have identified that a phenomenon similar to the recovered memory syndrome can also be seen at the collective level in a society. Moreover, the memory so recovered may actually be from another generation. Thus, memories of violence, even of acts committed hundreds of years ago, can create an impulse for revenge in present times.

Lord Alderdice, founding director of the CRIC, suggests that intergenerational collective memory recovery represents the collapse of complexity in our thinking. A regular person distinguishes between here and there, and now and then. With the collapse of complexity, space and time differentiation is lost. An impulse for war, driven by past grievances of the community or the nation or perceived injustice committed in a faraway geography, is generated. The Serbs justified attacks on Bosnians in the 1990s on the grounds of the Ottoman Turks lording over the Serbs several centuries earlier. Moroccan-origin youth in Belgium and the UK justified joining the ISIS (or Daesh or the Islamic State) terrorist organization due to what they considered injustice in faraway Iraq and Syria.

The memory of historical injustices or the perception of distant grievances need not be proven or real. They are planted, with convenient distortions, by a leader interested in waging war. Pope Urban II called for the Crusades to recover Jerusalem, lost to the Muslims 450 years earlier. Slobodan Milošević incited Serbs to launch sniper attacks on Sarajevo's children with stories of centuries-old repression. The spread of extremist Jihadi ideology that has produced many terrorist groups such as the Al-Qaeda, ISIS, Lashkar-e-Taiba, among a large network of terror organizations around the world is often presented as a spontaneous phenomenon in the absence of clearly delineated command-and-control structures. The extremist youth are motivated to violence by reading and seeing instigating material on the internet. But what we have to remember is that somebody deliberately uploads such propaganda material on the internet in an anonymous fashion. The terrorist groups have created extremely organized secretive structures using the internet, social media and video games. Whether it is legitimate political parties in democracy, or terrorist and extremist organizations mobilizing young people for different types of warfare, the collapse of complexity leading to the collective recovered memory syndrome is a process that can lead to vicious outcomes. It is engineered by forces or individuals with vested interests in igniting violence.

It is, therefore, questionable if we can accept Thucydides's description of the leaders of Sparta and Athens wanting restraint but being overpowered by the warlike emotion of young men. As we do not have the details of what transpired, it is difficult for us to assume that the youth of the two city-states were to blame for the devastating war. Were there any forces secretly inciting the youth? Were the leaders pretending to advocate restraint but using subtle propaganda to provoke, as many current leaders do? In the twenty-first century, some leaders pretend to be saintly devotees of peace, but they use their political cadres and social media to provoke violent emotions. They use a double-edged sword to break down the complexity of thought of ordinary people to create a simple dichotomy between 'us and them' with calls to annihilate the other.

Albert Einstein, greatly disturbed by the phenomenon of war, asked Freud if there was a psychological solution to it. On the surface, he seemed to believe that war was natural. He inquired in his letter to Freud, written in 1932:

How is it these devices succeed so well in rousing men to such wild enthusiasm, even to sacrifice their lives? Only one answer is possible. Because man has within him a lust for hatred and destruction. In normal times this passion exists in a latent state, it emerges only in unusual circumstances, but it is a comparatively easy task to call it into play and raise it to the power of a collective psychosis. Here lies, perhaps, the crux of all the complex factors we are considering, an enigma that only the expert in the lore of human instincts can resolve.[30]

As a response, Freud explains how the violent instinct of one person can be managed by the force of community action.

We know that in the course of evolution this state of things was modified, a path was traced that led away from violence to law. But what was this path? Surely it issued from a single verity; that the superiority of one strong man can be overborne by an alliance of many weaklings, that l'union fait la force. Brute force is overcome by union, the allied might of scattered units makes good its right against the isolated giant. Thus, we may define 'right' (i.e. law) as the might of a community.[31]

Eventually, Einstein concluded that war could be abolished through human action. In the Russell–Einstein Manifesto, signed by him just before his death in 1955, he called for the legal abolition of war.

According to the realist theory of international relations or political realism, the anarchic nature of the international system makes war a natural continuous phenomenon. Hobbes's observation of the permanent state of war against all is also applied to the relations between nation states. Hans Morgenthau is the most prominent modern proponent of political realism, or the realist theory of international relations. He traces the behaviour of states in the international system to selfish human nature, with a core belief that it is in the nature of states to aggrandize themselves and, for doing so, they define the concept of national interest in terms of power. When national interest is not backed by power, it only exists in theory without any practical value in the real world. Abstract moral principles are not relevant in real politics. This theory assumes that there is always anarchy in the international system. In such a situation, every nation must protect its interest and for that purpose acquire and use power.[32] Morgenthau's observations are apt to describe the behaviour of the countries that are constantly engaged in warfare, such as the US and Russia/USSR. But they do not stand the test of empirical evidence across the world. They are futile considering that 177 out of 195 countries in the world spend marginal amounts on armaments, and 122 of them voted to abolish nuclear weapons in 2017.

Mahatma Gandhi turned the realist theory on its head. He suggested that the international system was indeed characterized by anarchy. However, it was not essential and inevitable for all nations to compete with one another to increase anarchy. The nation states could consciously prefer coexistence and non-violence that would lead to cooperation— it was for them to *choose* between anarchy and coexistence.

American philosopher Lou Marinoff, a professor of philosophy at the City College of New York and the author of many books, revived the 2,500-year-old debate on whether war is innate to human nature in his book *On Human Conflict* in 2019. He begins his inquiry by asking, 'Can humankind end war before war ends humankind?' It was a question President John Kennedy had asked on the floor of the UN General Assembly in September 1961, but it has been generally avoided in policy and academic discourse.[33]

Marinoff presents detailed analyses of hundreds of tomes on war and peace in his treatise. He rejects the notion that war is inevitable based on the initial conditions found at the time of the inception of the universe. He concludes that there are no necessary causes of war, only sufficient ones.

> In terms of the causes of war, it means that we cannot construct a list of the necessary conditions for war because there are no necessary causes for the occurrence of war. If a war breaks out, then its causal antecedents, however we choose to identify them,

were unquestionably sufficient for, but were not and cannot
have been necessary to, the outbreak.

After surveying a vast amount of literature from philosophy, psychology
and sociology, he argues:

> Neither the outcome of battles nor the outbreaks are pre-
> determinable. There is no periodicity in the occurrence of
> war. Neither the beginnings nor the endings of wars can be
> probabilistically distributed. Since wars are not amenable to
> mathematical modelling as discrete entities, it follows that they
> must admit of continuous properties.
>
> We find no analytical truth, no mathematical rule, no natural
> philosophical deduction, no etiological necessity, no biological
> imperative, no cultural predestination, and no systemic
> inevitability which dictate that war must be; hence, we conclude
> that peace can be.
>
> The possibility of humankind ending war is conditional upon
> its collective willingness to find and implement one or more of
> the existing solutions [to war].[34]

Lou Marinoff has ignited the debate on whether war is innate to human
nature or a matter of choice at the theoretical level. The evidence from
the real world weighs in favour of determinism over fatalism. If Iceland
and Switzerland could avoid the battleground for over 500 years and
Uruguay and Mexico for over a century, while the US and Russia are
fighting every year and some other countries every decade, there is no
uniform global behaviour pertaining to war. If more than twenty nations
abolish armies, confident of not encountering military confrontation,
while a dozen nations accumulate increasingly lethal arsenals, it becomes
obvious that there is no universal pattern pertaining to the acquisition
of the instruments of destruction. If some countries fought wars until

a certain stage in their history and preferred diplomatic solutions in another phase of their life as a nation, there is no permanent human trait pertaining to wars. The evidence proves that some countries choose to go to war and prepare for it, and others choose not to go to war and do not even prepare for one. If war were innate to human nature, how would we explain the behaviour of people in Switzerland, Iceland and Uruguay? How could we explain the differentiated behaviour of people in Germany under different leaders and different circumstances? All wars, whether the Crusades a millennium ago or the invasions of Iraq and Ukraine in this century, were decisions made by someone.

The choice to engage in war can be exercised by any nation. If two countries with conventional weapons ravage a country or a region, it will be devastating. It will be an unpardonable shame as innocent men, women and children will be victims of the avarice and ego of their leaders. But in a limited war, with conventional weapons, humankind will not become extinct. However, if some of the states armed with nuclear and post-nuclear weapons go on the warpath, we will have to begin counting our species' last days. If we wish to come out of the shadow of collective death, we need to reorient our approach to the way we manage the world. We need to shift from confrontation to cooperation and compassion. Such a transformation will involve immense political, economic and psychological adjustments, where we will have to give up old habits and accept new truths. There is no doubt that we will find such changes prohibitive. However, it will be nothing compared to the benefits we shall accrue: the survival of humankind and the advancement of human civilization.

4

Dawn on the Horizon: Where Peace Dares

Professor Joe Huxley is a science teacher at Kansas University in Kansas City when a nuclear war begins between the US and the former Soviet Union, the latter mainly targeting the mid-western states of America. At the end of the war, a ceasefire is announced without either side gaining anything. The only result is all-round destruction of vast regions of the two countries. Kansas City is divided between the Kansas and Missouri states by a river and an invisible state line. The eastern side of the city is in Missouri, where Professor Huxley finds himself after he survives the nuclear attack. He builds a makeshift radio at the university and asks on it, 'Hello? Is anybody there? Anybody at all?'

There is no response.

This is the last scene from *The Day After*, a television film released in the US in 1983. It was viewed by more than 100 million people in its initial broadcast, setting a record as the highest-rated television film in history (which was surpassed only in 2009).

If a new edition of the film is made today, it will have to be revised in substantial ways to account for developments of the twenty-first century. America's enemy in the movie could still be Russia. Or it could be China or North Korea. The epicentre of the attacks would still be in the mid-western states. Instead of Kansas, it would be more realistic to locate it in Wyoming, Montana or North Dakota. Why these states will likely be chosen as the main theatre of conflict is a question that will be addressed elsewhere in this chapter. But the devastation will not be confined to a small geographical area. The new movie will have to show the entire western US and large parts of the enemy territory completely obliterated. It will also have to depict a nuclear winter damaging the rest of the world. And there will be no Professor Huxley to make a radio broadcast; in fact, there will be no survivors and no infrastructure. The movie screen will be filled with fire, clouds and smoke. In the backdrop, there will be sounds reiterating, 'megadeath, megadeath'.

Another popular movie that will have to undergo drastic revision if it were to be remade with events set in the present time is *Darkest Hour*, which tells the story of Prime Minister Winston Churchill of the UK. The film was released in 2017, and revealed how the legendary politician and leader managed a world war from an underground bunker. The cabinet war rooms from where Churchill directed the war effort were fortified with a 5-foot thick slab of concrete. Above ground, the Luftwaffe bombed London day and night, killing thousands of people. Churchill's cabinet survived to triumph in the war because the Germans did not have nuclear bombs to drop on London. There were also no cyber-weapons, sophisticated missiles or lethal autonomous weapons to penetrate the bunker. From the Cabinet War Rooms Churchill and his military generals could direct the war and call the White House for vital consultations. Today, these bunkers have been converted into a museum located underground near the Treasury and the Foreign Office.

Now, leaders in London, Washington, DC, Moscow or Beijing will find it impossible to lead a global war from a bunker. A realistic film on a future British Prime Minister joining a global war will have to show him dead with his cabinet colleagues and senior civil servants in the initial few minutes. A 20-kiloton earth-penetrating weapon, on a missile from China or Russia, which is especially designed to explode underground, will penetrate 5 metres beneath the surface, converting the bomb's yield to 400 kilotons. It will instantly obliterate the British leadership, along with the entire Whitehall, right at the beginning of the battle. The Thames will be full of poison. The Big Ben, Westminster Abbey and the Houses of Parliament will disappear, and the movie screen will be filled with the image of a huge mushroom cloud. This is how the movie must begin because this is how a real war will begin. Even if it is set elsewhere—say, in Beijing, where the Chinese leaders would operate from one of the underground tunnels where they have stationed the mobile missiles—it will probably not be any different. However, it is difficult to say how the story will unfold.

Minimum Assured Destruction

In 2011, experts from Lawrence Livermore Laboratory, Sandia National Laboratory and Applied Research produced a report on behalf of several US government agencies on the impact of a hypothetical detonation of a 10-kiloton nuclear device in downtown Washington, DC.[1] The size of the bomb mentioned in the study is smaller than the one used in Hiroshima and Nagasaki. Such small bombs began to be mass-produced under the Trump administration's policy of deploying low-yield nuclear weapons in large numbers, and there is no guarantee that the Biden administration will stop their production. On certain matters, there is bipartisan consensus in Washington, DC.

In the first minute after the explosion of such a device, almost all physical structures within a half-mile radius would collapse, killing all people in the area. If the attack is in downtown Washington, DC, key federal buildings such as the White House, the Treasury and

Capitol Hill would be vaporized and the national leadership would be eliminated. The underground shock waves would damage subways, water mains, power conduits and telecommunications. The impact of the fallout would depend on the speed and direction of the winds. The area within a 10-mile radius can be expected to experience mass destruction and death.

The assessment made by the leading nuclear laboratories assumed a terrorist attack at ground level involving a low-yield device. But, if Washington is hit with a 100-kiloton weapon by a missile detonated above the surface, the impact will be manifold. If more than one weapon is used in a state of war, the national capital region will vanish from the map of the earth.

There is no way to prepare for such a nuclear attack that will dismantle society as we know it. The US may destroy an enemy state several times over, but the minimum assured destruction in terms of the devastation of its capital would be beyond compensation. The chain of command would be broken—unless the top leaders have already escaped to a space station. Even a much larger revengeful second strike by the US on the enemy states would not bring Washington, DC, back to life. Nuclear weapons demolish society beyond any hope of recovery. When the US attacked Japan in the Second World War, it did not target Tokyo because it wanted the Japanese leaders to be alive to negotiate the surrender as the World War was expected to end. Besides, the bombs dropped on Hiroshima and Nagasaki were experimental. In the future, nuclear powers are quite likely to target the capital cities of their enemies.

Moscow, Beijing, Delhi and Paris would face the same fate if 100 kiloton nuclear bombs were dropped on them. Not even the ruins of the world's most powerful capitals would remain for posterity. Instead, there would be poisonous ash, so that nobody would dare go near them for several decades.

The possibility of attacks on capital cities and other main decision centres is very high. In a conflict, once deterrence fails, it is possible to pursue one of two pathways. One possibility is that there may be the temptation to use bombs of 5–10 kilotons, known as low-yield nuclear weapons, to force the enemy to surrender. If the enemy has nuclear weapons with hypersonic missiles that fly at several times the speed of sound and lethal autonomous weapons, he may escalate the warfare to a higher level using large warheads carried in multiple quantities by different types of missiles. Another possibility is to launch a massive attack to finish the enemy's strike capability. This can lead to a full-scale exchange of missiles in minutes.

After the instigator decides to press the nuclear button, it will take ten to fifteen minutes for the missiles to take off from the silos loaded with nuclear warheads. All further decisions will be expedited by AI-controlled systems. Cyberweapons will be used to attack the command, control and communication centres of the enemy. Speed will be of the essence, and therefore, the first offensive will be on the political and military command chains of the enemy state: this makes Washington, Moscow, Beijing, Delhi, Rawalpindi, Tel Aviv, London, Paris and Pyongyang the most vulnerable sites in the nuclear age. There will be attacks on communication satellite networks in the lower geosynchronous orbit as well as key economic clusters on earth. With algorithms guiding military decisions, there will be no scope to reverse a future confrontation.

Besides the physical impact of a nuclear explosion, there will be extremely hazardous long-term environmental consequences. Even if a nuclear war takes place in South Asia or the Middle East, without the direct involvement of the US, China and Russia, agriculture in North America, Europe and parts of China will be ruined. The toxic soot that will be thrown up due to a nuclear detonation of any sort would have shocking effects on the atmosphere. A nuclear winter may engulf the earth, annihilating almost all vegetation. The degree of devastation would depend on the quantities of smoke as well as the time of year that the nuclear detonation occurred, with plant life being affected much more if it takes place in winter.

Detonation of nuclear bombs above ground can inject radioactive particles that reach all the way to the stratosphere. The fallout in such a case would be huge. In a 2012 article published in the *Bulletin of the Atomic Scientists*, authors Alan Robock and O.B. Toon warned that the dense smoke from a nuclear war would block sunlight to the extent of plunging the world into darkness and hindering photosynthesis. This, in turn, would disrupt the food chain, triggering gradual mass starvation. The authors also pointed out that it may lead to a short growing season, leading to further food shortages.[2]

Several factors associated with a nuclear winter would have a significant impact on agriculture. For instance, nuclear war in growing seasons could bring about sudden episodes of low temperature (minus 10 degrees Celsius or more) for days or weeks, ruining crops. In 1816, known as the 'year without a summer', there were episodes of a sudden drop in temperature due to the eruption of Mount Tambora, a volcano in Indonesia. This volcanic activity in one corner of Asia had severe climatic consequences as far as Western Europe and North America. It caused heavy rains, flooding and a longer winter than normal from China to Ireland.[3] There was dry fog in the US. These weather abnormalities destroyed a large quantity of crops, and soon there were food riots. People were begging for food in many countries. Social scientists have been using the experience of 1816 to structure models of the likely impact of a future nuclear war.

Alan Robock and others estimate that even a regional nuclear war between India and Pakistan would substantially reduce the warm growing season in the northern and southern hemispheres for several years and severely reduce agricultural produce. The impact of a nuclear conflagration between the two countries would cause global climate effects that would last longer than a decade. These effects could include marked changes in seasonal crop patterns, a 10 per cent average decline in rainfall around the world and a cooling of several degrees over large areas of North America and Eurasia, including most of the grain-growing regions.

An immediate worldwide impact on agriculture and food supply systems would include the devastation of food crops and stores, radioactive contamination, uncontrollable fires, reduced fuel supplies, paralysis of major ports and disruption of the global food distribution network. The US and Canada are major food exporters that would suffer severe and widespread farmland damage. As they may not be able to grow enough food for their own population, they will ban exports. Other exporting countries would encounter similar dilemmas. As a result, large food shipments would be reduced, food prices would skyrocket, and there would be food riots in most countries in the world. The US, Britain and France would have their missiles in silos, but no food in their markets. They would starve even if they were not directly involved in a war in a faraway region.

A related 2012 study assimilated a dynamic system model to predict the agricultural effects of an India–Pakistan war.[4] The model, in this case, showed that a regional nuclear war in Asia could lead to a significant drop in yields for both corn and soybeans in the American Midwest, with the greatest crop losses occurring for the five years following the event. Over ten years following the event, corn production was predicted to decline by an average of 10 per cent and soybean production by an average of 6–12 per cent, depending on location. Year-to-year variability was expected to be high, and could be affected by anomalies in temperature, rainfall and sunlight. China's production of wheat, maize and rice would decline by 25–50 per cent. As there would be no food for humans, it would be difficult to feed animals, resulting in a severe decline in meat production.

Almost a billion people in the world who are chronically malnourished consume less than the minimum 1,750 calories required per day for healthy life. Even a 10 per cent decline in their food consumption would expose this entire segment of the population to grave risks. The bottom of the pyramid is not the only one that will be hit by global food crises. The suspension of exports from grain-growing countries would threaten the food supplies of several hundred million additional people who have adequate nutrition today but who live in countries that are highly dependent on food imports. The tally of the affected people would run into billions.

For Whom the Bell Tolls

If a nuclear war is limited in its scale, the main targets of instigating nations are likely to be American farmlands, Russian farmlands and Asian urban centres, besides the capital cities of the nuclear power states (depending on the enemy). In the US, the most vulnerable states are Wyoming, Montana and North Dakota, which are the sites of missile silos. America's enemies shall first want to neutralize these sites, along with the command-and-control structure in the national capital region. The three states are home to vast rural areas where agriculture will be destroyed. Similarly, Dombarovsky in Orenburb Oblast and Uzhur in Krasnoyarsk Krai in south-east Russia, which are also rural areas, are likely to be targets in the first round of a nuclear war, as they host missile silos. Since China's missile silos are in underground tunnels, the locations of which are often shifted, all of China will be subjected to a massive attack. In the case of China, India and Israel, urban centres will be particularly susceptible as they have key strategic and economic assets.

Thus, there is no doubt that the people living in these geographies need to lead the movements against nuclear and post-nuclear weapons. This would mean turning back on hyper-nationalism and militarism since nuclear weapons are only the topmost layers of the military–industrial pyramid.

It is not clear to what extent American farmers in the Midwestern states, Russian farmers in the south-east districts of the country, Chinese businessmen and Indian professionals are aware of the risk of their own suffering, the extinction of their families and neighbours and the obliteration of their farms and properties that will arise from weaponized hyper-nationalism. They should be the vanguard in opposing nuclear weapons and cautious of not falling into the trap of hyper-nationalism that could lead to a war involving the weapons of final destruction—a war that would begin with the ravaging of their immediate neighbourhood and end with the painful, brutal death of their families and friends, all in a matter of moments. Instead of understanding the danger to their own lives, powerful lobbyists of the hyper-nationalist cause get carried away by a rhetoric of hatred and foolishly engage in efforts to instil a fear of minorities. They support hollow ideas of national ego that place the world on a self-destructive path and are fooled by the artificially magnified differences between communities. It does not occur to them that a nuclear war can only guarantee the humiliation of their nation—what national honour is there in obliteration?

It is possible to mobilize popular support for a war machine in the national interest, for the restoration of past glory, the establishment of justice to correct perceived historical wrongs and for the illusion of creating a great nation. As we have seen in the last chapter, Pope Urban II did exactly that a millennium ago. Machiavelli advocated it in the Middle Ages; Hitler practised it in the last century; and Milošević used it in the 1990s. Several leaders in the twenty-first century are adopting elements of this tactic to boost national ego to perpetuate their place on the throne. Their supporters from among the American farmers, European working classes, Indian professionals, Russian and Chinese business groups and Pakistani middle classes are swayed by the need to support a strongman with strong weapons in the name of a strong nation. Those who are most likely to perish in a nuclear war are, ironically, at the forefront of promoting the kind of politics that can eventually lead to such a tragedy, beginning with their own slaughter.

The greatest challenge for us is to open our eyes to the reality that we are being led on a path of terminating the human race. In order to change our course, it is essential to wake from our slumber.

The strongman–strong nation–strong weapons syndrome hides certain realities. No nation is immune to an enemy attack. North Korea can obliterate Silicon Valley with a few nuclear warheads if it believes that it is likely to face an American attack. Or it may choose Wyoming and North Dakota to destroy the missile silos. The US can, in return, destroy the entirety of North Korea—but at the risk of spreading radiation to its allies, such as South Korea and Japan, as well as parts of China and Russia. This may force the Chinese and Russians to counter–attack the US. Pakistan can destroy Delhi and Mumbai in two simultaneous nuclear attacks if it fears dismemberment by the more powerful Indian army in a conventional war. India can exterminate the whole of Pakistan, but at the cost of radiation damaging vast swathes of its own territory and some parts of Central and West Asia. North Korea and Pakistan are economically crippled: large segments of their population live in poverty. Yet they have managed to build stockpiles of missiles and nuclear arms. Economic, technological and social limitations have not deterred them. Even though they are weak when compared to their rivals, they have the capacity to cause the minimum assured destruction. Therefore, it would be naive for nationalist groups in the larger countries to live under the illusion of invincibility from their enemies. No nuclear state enjoys unlimited capability to counter its nuclear rival without critical damage being caused to its own interests. In the Middle East, Israel is the only nuclear power, though there are some aspiring ones. But that does not make the Jewish nation impregnable. In an advanced stage of battle, Hezbollah can target its nuclear plants and desalination facilities with over 1,00,000 missiles and rockets and destroy Israel's population. Britain and France currently do not have hostile rivals, but having suffered in the Second World War, their people can imagine the devastation of yet another mega war. If they are obliged to support the US against Russia, they are likely to be the victims of Russian missiles before the latter hit the American mainland.

Mikhail Gorbachev and Ronald Reagan once said that nuclear wars could not be won and therefore should not be fought.[5] In the era of cyberweapons, hypersonic missiles and lethal autonomous weapons, it is a certainty that a nuclear war will be lost by all parties, however strong or weak, within a few minutes of its beginning. It may be sparked by intent or an unintentional series of incidents or an accident. The only safeguard from such a risk is the abolition of all nuclear weapons in the world, under vigorous supervision of an international organization.

The demand for nuclear zero must come loudly from American and Russian farmers, Indian professionals, Chinese businessmen and Israeli citizens, who are likely to be the biggest losers in an attack from a much weaker rival. Their love for a strong nation and strong weapons is the ultimate liability for humankind. It is an invitation to Armageddon.

Evidence shows that the idea of a great nation is an illusion. No empire has lasted forever. China, India, Japan, Europe and Egypt have survived as continuations of ancient civilizations, but all states and empires embodied by them have been destroyed. The Roman Republic and Empire together lasted for a thousand years as part of a great drama consisting of constant wars, murder and brutality, featuring Agrippina, Nero, Caesar and other characters. Finally, small tribes attacked the vast empire and broke it into pieces. All the Roman kings and their men could not put the realm back together again.

A similar fate awaited the Mongol Empire. It seemed powerful once upon a time, but collapsed within 150 years of being founded. Each Chinese dynastic rule, each Egyptian pharaonic regime, each Arab kingdom has been ruined within a few hundred years. The Habsburg, Ottoman and British Empires collapsed as the First World War played out. The Soviet Union lasted less than a century. When history has provided testimony time and again to the fact that no empire, no state, lasts forever—however grandiose be the arsenal it may possess—it would be naive to believe that nuclear and hypersonic weapons can help any state of the present times to prolong its survival or its glory.

The great powers are now also susceptible to cyber and biological attacks from weaker powers and even terrorist groups. In 2020–21, all the great nations of the world were exposed in their failure to handle the COVID-19 pandemic caused by a coronavirus. If big powers could not manage a pandemic, how would they ever handle a fast-spreading vicious killer pathogen deliberately used in warfare, or nuclear radiation, or cyberattacks on critical infrastructure? The proliferation of cyberweapons and killer viruses, much like the proliferation of nuclear weapons and missiles, is bound to take place in the next few decades. One option to counter such advancements in new weapons technology would be to pursue the ever-escalating arms race, with a growing commitment of resources and talent to bolster and sustain this endeavour. The other option is to reverse the competitive threats to our civilization's survival and liberate the world from the grip of all weapons of final destruction.

The military–industrial complex and nationalist leaders can be expected to prefer the belligerent option. They hope to acquire money and power by following the militarist path. But the proud followers of such leaders can gain nothing except vacuous national ego and an empty sense of greatness. While pursuing the illusion of great power status, they live in the real shadow of human extinction, devastation of their capital cities and farmlands, and famine and hunger. They may end up being obliterated by nuclear flames if there is a big war involving their own country, or as beggars on the streets if there is a small nuclear war in another part of the planet, but one that damages the environment and food supply. They may cease to exist without water, food and medical aid if vicious pathogens are spread infecting all people or if new bacteria are created to absorb oxygen from the atmosphere. If they care for self-respect, national honour and, most of all, their own survival, they must abandon their support for militarist nationalism.

It is natural that defence contractors, lobbyists, certain media moguls and bureaucracies in different parts of the world would find security in ignoring the old idea of deterrence by developing autonomous cataclysmic weapons. There are huge stakes involved in expanding the size of the defence pie. It is up to the common people, who do not benefit from such deals, to open their eyes to this deception being perpetrated in the interest of a handful of powerful individuals. Their support is now needed to promote policies for their own survival, respect and progress and not to encourage hyper-nationalism.

We must be circumspect while considering the ability of our leaders, and particularly the managers of our national security, to protect us.

Most of the nuclear power states have been attacked by terrorist groups from the ravaged battlegrounds of Iraq, the caves of Afghanistan or the wasteland of Chechnya. Nuclear weapons, missiles, cyberweapons, killer robots, killer pathogens and whatever else one can think of have not been able to prevent deadly terrorist attacks. The world's powerful militaries and police forces have been humbled by terror groups. It is true that they have in turn taken ruthless revenge on the terrorists and their supporters, but it must be reiterated that they have not been able to prevent the attacks. Yet, our leaders assure us that we should trust them to protect us from the weapons of final destruction launched by well-organized rival military forces!

We have seen in the previous chapter that war is a matter of human choice; it is not divinely ordained. Although the history of the world is strewn with thousands of wars, there are courageous examples of nations which made the choice of abdicating warfare, armies and armaments, which have been living in peace and prosperity for centuries or decades. That gives us promise that those who have been supporting an elusive suicidal nationalist path so far can still choose to change their course rather than risk the lives of their future generations. If they are secular, they can use scientific rationale to examine their choices. If they are religious, they must already know that god is against ending all life on the planet earth.

God's Mind

People of all religions who believe in god must rescind their support for leaders who promote nuclear and other deadly weapons. It is the pious duty of every religious person to support the politics of peace and disarmament. According to all religious texts, nowhere does god support the extinction of humankind. Each religion has its version of the End Times, which results in a catastrophe leading to the victory of good over evil—not in turning the world's people, animals, birds, trees and plants into smoke and vapour. Supporting nationalist leaders who promote militarism is deceiving god. The people in the Christian belts of the US and Russia who care for their faith must demand the abolition of all weapons of final destruction, including nuclear, chemical, biological and lethal autonomous weapons. Similarly, people in India who believe in Hinduism must be sincerely faithful to the age-old Hindu precept of *vasudhaiva kutumbakam*, which means the world should be treated as one family. The sincere following of these teachings would require calling for the abolition of all lethal weapons from all parts of the earth. The first verse of the Isha Upanishad is considered of utmost significance in Hindu religious texts: *Isha vaasyam idamsarvam yatkinchha jagatyaam jagat*. It means that everything that is there in the world belongs to god. Since it does not belong to us, we cannot covet it. By the same token, we have no right to destroy god's belongings which are everything pervading the earth.

Swami Vivekananda is considered the greatest modern sage and philosopher of Hinduism. Addressing the first Parliament of the World's Religions in 1893, he appealed for assimilation and rejected division.[6] There were no nuclear, chemical, biological or lethal autonomous weapons in his time. If he were living today, he would campaign against the weapons of final destruction. The real followers of Swami Vivekananda would believe in mutual respect of religions, tolerance and peaceful coexistence as his message from the rostrum in Chicago was to eliminate hatred and violence.

Buddhist teachings appeal for the alleviation of the suffering of all people. Even though extremist mobs in Thailand, Myanmar and Sri Lanka have at times inflicted brutality against minorities in their own countries, their selfish aberration does not invalidate the Buddhist philosophy of non-violence.

Many rabbis have spoken against weapons of mass destruction, and some of them have joined anti-war movements. Islamic scholars have said that nuclear weapons are not sanctioned by Islam. Ayatollah Khamenei has issued a fatwa against weapons of mass destruction on religious grounds,[7] though the West believes that Iran is clandestinely pursuing the development of nuclear weapons.

It is about time that people all over the world realize that nuclear and post-nuclear weapons are a fraud on all religions. They are against the will of god to preserve humankind. The seventh Parliament of the World's Religions brought together 10,000 persons of all faiths in November 2018. It declared:

> The destructive capacity of nuclear weapons is beyond imagination, poisoning the Earth forever. These horrific devices place before us every day the decision whether we will be the last human generation. The power to unleash this destruction is in the hands of a small number of people. No one should be holding such power over the very creation, which we regard as a sacred gift for all today and for future generations.
>
> The possession of nuclear weapons is immoral, illegal, and must be rectified by prompt action ... *Such a posture is unworthy of civilization, insults the dignity of life, is an impediment to all ethical and moral norms of all the world's religions. To ignore the humanitarian consequences of nuclear weapons by exalting nationalism as a higher principle raises moral corrosion to unprecedented levels.*
>
> We thus make a passionate plea to the leaders of all religions, all people of good will, and all leaders of nations both with and without nuclear weapons to commit to work to eliminate these horrific devices forever.[8]

In January 2020, Religions for Peace held its tenth World Assembly. Almost a thousand delegates from all religions unanimously condemned the existence of nuclear weapons and called for general disarmament covering several different types of lethal weapons.[9]

The Christian Campaign for Nuclear Disarmament has issued a document titled 'Biblical Case against Nuclear Weapons'. It begins with the following words:

> As Christians, our main reason for opposing nuclear weapons is: we believe they are counter to the teachings of Jesus and the

Bible. Jesus often spoke of the need for peace, as did Paul in many of his New Testament letters. Nuclear weapons also pose a threat to the very existence of God's creation and everything in it.

The statement issued by the organization quotes from verses in the Bible, which proves that any support for politics that enables nuclear and other weapons of mass destruction is against Biblical preaching. Here are a few examples from the statement:

When Jesus was asked about the greatest commandment, He replied: 'You shall love the Lord your God with all your heart and with all your soul and with all your mind.' This is the great and first commandment. And a second is like it: 'You shall love your neighbour as yourself' (Matthew 22:37–39). Loving God must mean loving His creation. If we are to love others as ourselves, then we must surely do all we can to remove the threat of death and catastrophic destruction from innocent people around the world.

God's creation is one of his many gifts to us. Writing to the Colossians, Paul reaffirms that all creation was made by God through Jesus—all 'things in heaven and on earth, visible and invisible' (1:16). When God saw what He created He said it was 'very good' (Genesis 1:31). Humans are entrusted with God's creation not to use and abuse it, but to be stewards of what actually belongs to God. David wrote: 'the earth is the Lord's, and everything in it, the world, and all who live in it' (Psalm 24:1). This stewardship goes back to the Garden of Eden when 'The Lord God took the man and put him in the Garden of Eden to till it and keep it' (Genesis 2:15). Nuclear weapons are the only weapons known to have the capacity to end life on earth, as we know it. Every day that nuclear weapons are armed, humanity runs the risk of a nuclear catastrophe, either through their use or an accident. Living alongside this threat is not being a good steward of creation.[10]

The declaration has quoted many other Biblical verses that explain god wants an end to war and not an end to humankind.

Pope Francis has emerged as a forceful advocate of nuclear disarmament. During a visit to Nagasaki in November 2019, he condemned the horrors of nuclear weapons. He reminded us that St John XXIII had urged the prohibition of atomic weapons in 1963. He passionately called for a world free of nuclear weapons and appealed to all individuals, religious communities and civil society organizations to come together to counter the nuclear threat. He said:

> Convinced as I am that a world without nuclear weapons is possible and necessary, I ask political leaders not to forget that these weapons cannot protect us from current threats to national and international security. We need to ponder the catastrophic impact of their deployment, especially from a humanitarian and environmental standpoint, and reject heightening a climate of fear, mistrust and hostility fomented by nuclear doctrines.[11]

The Christian support for nuclear disarmament goes back to the 1980s, when all churches rallied behind the Nuclear Freeze campaign in the US. These included the National Council of Churches, United Presbyterian Church, Catholic Church, Methodist Church and the Lutheran Church. In addition, the Synagogue Council of America supported the coalition of all main Christian churches in campaigning for immediately halting the testing, production and deployment of nuclear weapons.

The clear rejection of weapons of final destruction in the Parliaments of the World's Religions from 1893 to 2018, the World Assemblies of Religions for Peace, and the teachings of Pope Francis, Swami Vivekananda and other sages demonstrate that the seers do not find god's sanction for the obliteration of life on the earth. The weapons that threaten to do so are against god's will and the politicians and strategists who justify them do not care for either god or human beings. It would be a sin for believers to support them. There is no doubt that religion has been a cause for hundreds of wars over centuries. Several wars, including the Crusades and wars within Islam and within Christianity, as observed earlier in this book, have been waged in the name of religion for power and greed. But the manipulation of religion for destructive self-aggrandizement does not take away the fact that the sacred texts and their interpretation by institutions such as the Parliaments of the World's Religions do not sanction the use of lethal weapons to exterminate humankind. The leaders who want humanity to survive, both religious and secular, have sought to free the world from weapons of mass destruction, hatred and violence. In the last few decades, there have been a few such courageous and transformative leaders.

Reagan, Gorbachev and Brandt

Among those who expedited disarmament in the Cold War, American president Ronald Reagan and Soviet leader Mikhail Gorbachev stand out. Ronald Reagan was President of the US from 1981 to 1988 and was one of the most conservative leaders of the country. He reduced taxes, withdrew budgetary allocation for non-military public expenditure and increased defence spending during his first term. In fact, a quantum jump in the US military outlay was one of the highest in the Cold War period. In response to the Soviet deployment of SS-20 missiles, he ordered the deployment of Pershing missiles in Western Europe. Describing the Soviet Union as 'an evil empire',[12] he supported movements opposed to communism by overt and covert means.

President Reagan had an ambitious plan to station space-based missiles to counter ballistic missiles aimed at the US. It was known as the Star Wars programme or the Strategic Defence Initiative. Many experts were doubtful of its efficacy, but Reagan believed that it would create a protective missile defence shield around the US and render the Soviet nuclear weapons and missiles useless.

With such a conservative background, deep mistrust of the Soviet Union and commitment to strengthening the US, Ronald Reagan was not a liberal or a paragon of peace by any measure. Yet, he dreamt of abolishing nuclear weapons. On one occasion, he and Gorbachev agreed on a plan to free the world of nuclear weapons, but it failed because Gorbachev wanted Reagan to drop the Star Wars initiative, which Reagan was not willing to do. In subsequent interactions, they agreed on partial nuclear disarmament, which has made it possible to reduce the number of nuclear warheads from over 60,000 during their time to almost 10,000 now.

American public opinion played an important role in diluting President Reagan's hawkish stand exhibited during the first two years of his presidency. As people seemed to develop fatigue for military aggression, the US House of Representatives endorsed a freeze on the production of nuclear weapons. Two of Reagan's trusted advisers— Chief of Staff James Baker and Secretary of State George Shultz— found that rapprochement with the Soviet Union would be electorally advantageous.

At the same time, Ronald Reagan was heavily influenced by films and cinematic experiences which advocated an end to nuclear armament. Movies had been an important part of his life for several years before he became the President; he was a Hollywood actor before being elected as the governor of California, which ultimately led him on the path to the White House. He was also active in the politics of movie industry workers. Reagan was particularly influenced by three movies. One was *The Day Earth Stood Still*, in which space aliens warned people on earth of the planet's destruction unless they gave up their habit of warmongering between countries. The movie was made in 1951, when nuclear weapons were rudimentary. Julian Blaustein, producer, was so concerned about the atmosphere of mutual suspicion that he proposed the project to 20th Century Fox. The second movie that influenced President Reagan was *War Games*, featuring a high-school computer hacker who gained access to a supercomputer at NORAD and almost plunged the world into a thermonuclear war. The third was *The Day After*, the ABC film that has been discussed at the beginning of this chapter.[13]

The psychological impact of movies, combined with a perceived change in the public mood in support of peace and disarmament, shifted Reagan's stance on nuclear weapons. His new thinking was reflected in his address to the UN General Assembly in September 1984. He said:

> Deterrence is necessary, but not sufficient. We are ready for constructive negotiations with the Soviet Union. Our task must be to find ways to reduce the vast stockpiles of armaments in the world. Today, to the great end of lifting the dread of nuclear war from the peoples of the earth, I invite the leaders of the world to join in a new beginning. We recognize that there is no sane alternative to negotiations on arms control and other issues between our two nations, which have the capacity to destroy civilization as we know it.[14]

Soon afterwards, he invited Andrei Gromyko, the Soviet foreign minister, to the White House amidst fanfare and told him that he wanted to eliminate nuclear weapons.

At the beginning of President Reagan's second term, Mikhail Gorbachev became the General Secretary of the Communist Party of the Soviet Union (CPSU) in March 1985. He was known for introducing glasnost (openness) and perestroika (reforms) in the former Soviet Union, which eventually led to the collapse of communism. He also showed commitment to disarmament. During the famous Reykjavik Summit in October 1986, Gorbachev put forward a proposal for the phased elimination of nuclear weapons to Ronald Reagan. Proposing a window of ten years, Reagan seemed to be on board with the idea. However, the summit was not successful as a consensus could not be reached because the two parties did not see eye to eye on American plans for space-based weapons. Thus, in 1986, no treaty was signed between the two Cold War rivals. Even so, the summit was widely regarded as a step forward. Happily, after the disagreements in Reykjavik, the personal equation between Reagan and Gorbachev improved. Both leaders trusted each other more than before and spoke more respectfully in private of each other after the summit.[15]

This was followed by the historic Intermediate Nuclear Forces (INF) Treaty at the Washington summit in December 1987. This is considered a great achievement of Gorbachev in transforming the world and inching it closer to peace. The summary of the 127-page treaty is the following: 'Each side would, during the next three years, destroy all of its intermediate- and shorter-range land-based missiles and their launchers.'[16] So it came to be that together the US and the former Soviet Union destroyed over 2,500 missiles by 1991.

The Washington summit showed that the former Soviet Union was serious about arms reduction and that Gorbachev was willing to negotiate with the US. The new thinking in the Russian military sphere was real. Moreover, the two countries were able to reach an agreement on such an important issue, while the INF Treaty gave hope for further cuts in arms in the future. Gorbachev expressed his belief to dispel the image of the Soviet Union as an 'enemy' of the US and to show the Soviets' genuine commitment to peace. These developments created the ground for the START I Treaty, which was signed by General Secretary Mikhail Gorbachev and President George Bush in 1991. It was a very ambitious arms control agreement, resulting in the removal of almost 80 per cent of the two countries' nuclear arsenal over the next twenty years.

The success at the Washington summit in December 1987 added greatly to Gorbachev's popularity in the West. Domestically, however, his image was suffering.[17] His reforms were not received well, and political rivals criticized him for being too slow and piecemeal or being too hasty and impatient, depending on their political leaning. On the other hand, Reagan was all praises for his Soviet counterpart and even redacted his previous statement of the Soviet Union being an evil empire. He claimed that Gorbachev was a man interested in real reforms, who was serious about extending an olive branch to America. While Gorbachev's stature and achievements have been a matter of debate among his supporters and detractors in the former Soviet Union, his contribution to envisioning an alternative trajectory to global conflict cannot be discounted.

The détente pursued by Ronald Reagan and Mikhail Gorbachev had been started much earlier by Willy Brandt, who served as Chancellor of the Federal Republic of Germany from 1969 to 1974.

Willy Brandt formulated the policy of Ostpolitik and tried to balance it with Westpolitik. During the Cold War, when the world was divided into two blocs, Germany was bifurcated between East and West. At this time, Willy Brandt pioneered a new approach to German foreign policy. Ostpolitik was envisioned to secure peace, support cohesion of the German nation and to bring about the reconciliation of the Germans with their Eastern European neighbours. Brandt aimed to craft one destiny for Europe at a time when the continent was being pulled apart in two different political directions. He suggested that the security of Europe was indivisible and could not be fractured into two alliances led by the US and the former Soviet Union. In the times of divisive politics of 'with us or against us', he attempted to use soft power as a means to improve relations between the rivals.[18]

Even before reaching the highest echelon of power, Willy Brandt had been a staunch supporter of détente and insisted on normalizing relations between the East and the West. The ideological roots of Willy Brandt's strand of foreign policy lay in the fact that the fears of nuclear apocalypse loomed large. The popular uprisings of East Germany in 1953 and Hungary in 1956 had failed, making it clear to Brandt that the former Soviet Union could not be defeated by using force or encouraging dissent. He advocated the policy of détente or peaceful coexistence, emphasizing the need to promote soft power that could facilitate exchanges between the two blocs. He first began to propose Ostpolitik in 1958 when he was the governing mayor of West Berlin.

He called for improving relations with the former Soviet Union as well as the East European countries aligned with it.

As he believed in the unity of West and East Germany, he rallied for greater cooperation and interactions with East Germany. Initially, Brandt hoped for an open atmosphere between the two German nations; so, he was crestfallen when the Berlin Wall was constructed in 1961. But Brandt did not give up on his goal of peaceful coexistence as he realized that incremental changes were the best way forward given the tense times. He adopted the 'policy of small steps'—mainly aimed at enabling people on either side of the wall to travel to the other side to meet their friends and relatives. His efforts met came to fruition in 1963, with the first accord on travel passes with which thousands of West Berliners could visit their relatives in East Berlin during the 1963 Christmas holidays.[19]

Upon becoming the Chancellor of West Germany in 1969, Brandt was unstoppable. On the one hand, he maintained excellent relations with the US and harshly criticized Soviet repression. On the other hand, he sought rapprochement with the former Soviet Union and other communist countries of Eastern Europe. He implemented his reconciliatory approach almost instantly after coming to power.[20] In 1970, Brandt travelled to Warsaw, despite West Germany not having had diplomatic ties with Poland for over two decades. The famous genuflection of Warsaw, an incident when Willy Brandt walked to the front of the Monument to the Ghetto Heroes and dropped to his knees to beg forgiveness for the crimes of the Nazi era, won him a Nobel Prize for Peace in 1971. What made the gesture particularly remarkable was Brandt's willingness to apologize earnestly on behalf of all Germans, including the Nazis against whom he had fought.[21] By extending such modesty, at his own peril and without caring for the political reaction that he was likely to receive back home, he not only won many a heart, but also managed to push the policy of Ostpolitik ahead.

The second phase of Ostpolitik began after Brandt ceased to be the German Chancellor in 1974. It gathered momentum in the late 1970s and the early 1980s, owing to his campaign to promote dialogue on peaceful coexistence, despite all odds and opposition, as the means of averting a nuclear war. This was in the aftermath of the 1979 invasion of Afghanistan by the former Soviet Union, followed by the crisis in Poland in 1980–81, and the nuclear arms race between the two superpowers reaching a climax in the early 1980s. Brandt was conscious of the volatility of the situation and had discerned the role Europe could play in tempering the conflict. As a result, he pushed for a revitalization of détente and dialogue with the Eastern bloc leaders. Owing substantially to his commitment to peace and reconciliation, and his good relations with Brezhnev and then Gorbachev, the Berlin Wall finally collapsed, leading to the reunification of Germany in November 1989.[22] Whereas Gorbachev's policy of glasnost and the talks with Reagan delivered a decisive outcome for nuclear disarmament and the lowering of tensions between the two blocs, Brandt's contribution to the improvement of relations between the East and West consistently over several years was critical for ending the Cold War without a nuclear apocalypse.

Reagan, Gorbachev and Brandt made fearless efforts to move the world from the risk of total annihilation to partial nuclear disarmament. Critics often wonder how the world did not end in a nuclear Armageddon during the Cold War. What we have just discussed makes it clear that it was not a miracle, nor a chance escape. Responsible leaders took calibrated steps to bridge the divide between the two sides and gradually reduce the motivation to use nuclear weapons.

In modern times, South Korean President Moon Jae-in seems to pursue the détente policy with North Korea, reminiscent of Brandt's Ostpolitik. His officers undertook the groundwork to set up summit meetings between North Korean leader Kim Jong-un and former US President Donald Trump, without claiming any credit for these initiatives. Moon himself has had summit meetings with his North Korean counterpart, taking ahead the work of two of his predecessors, Kim Dae-jung and Roh Moo-hyun; however, the earlier two presidents were mired in controversies. It remains to be seen if Moon Jae-in proves to be the Asian Willy Brandt of the twenty-first century.

The policy shifts introduced by present government leaders for bringing about nuclear disarmament may provide the ground for more initiatives by future leaders to free the world from all weapons of mass destruction. These initiatives were possible because Mahatma Gandhi, Martin Luther King, Jr, and Nelson Mandela over the years popularized the ethics of peace. They proved that peace was a great moral force, much more influential than any weapon of final destruction. Gandhi's non-violent civil disobedience had helped India gain freedom from British colonial rule and, moreover, it had begun a worldwide process of decolonization. Martin Luther King, Jr, aimed at establishing a new, more equitable society in the US. He called for peace and brotherhood, not for revenge by African-Americans over White people for centuries of discrimination. He did not expect the dominance of the Whites to be replaced by the dominance of Blacks, but advocated a society where there would be equality and no dominance. In the famous Washington march in 1963, he said, 'When we allow freedom to ring, when we let it ring from every city and every hamlet, from every state and every city, we will be able to speed up that day when all of God's children, black men and white men, Jews and Gentiles, Protestants and Catholics, will be able to join hands.'[23]

Nelson Mandela followed in King's footsteps in establishing a shared society, rejecting any thought of revenge after apartheid was dismantled in South Africa. He was a legend and much has been and is still being written about him. However, it is relatively unknown that he campaigned for the abolition of nuclear weapons on the floor of the UN and other fora. If Mahatma Gandhi and Martin Luther King, Jr, had been alive in the last quarter of the last century, we can assume that they would have been fasting and demonstrating against nuclear weapons. If they were living among us today, they would be at the forefront of campaigns to ban not only nuclear weapons but also hypersonic missiles, killer robots and neXt weapons and to stop the use of science and technology for the benefit of the forces of mass murder.

Such enlightened leaders do not function in a vacuum. They need public support. In Russia, which emerged as the successor state of the former Soviet Union, Mikhail Gorbachev was criticized and isolated, and was eventually replaced by Vladimir Putin, who enjoys considerable public support for his militant nationalism. Putin's popularity soared after annexing Crimea from Ukraine, and again after invading Ukraine in 2022, and as a result of this, with public opinion in his favour, he is accelerating a new race in nuclear weapons and hypersonic missiles. In the US, Reagan retired from the presidency with one of the highest approval ratings. As a result, his disarmament efforts were taken ahead by his successors George H.W. Bush and Bill Clinton. Clinton's successor, George Bush, Jr, reversed the direction of this journey and strengthened the forces of violence by attacking Iraq and withdrawing from the Anti-Ballistic Missile Treaty. President Donald Trump, who enjoyed high popularity for his aggressive policies, found a partner in Putin to take the arms race for destroying humankind to a new high. What this proved to us is that leaders can mobilize public opinion in favour of peace, as Brandt did, or warfare, as Trump did. Conversely, people can force leaders to move in favour of peace, as the Americans of the 1980s did with Ronald Reagan, or to encourage hostility, as the Russians of the 2010s have done with Putin. The vicious cycle of hostility that fuels the weapons of final destruction can be broken—either by enlightened leaders or by committed people's movements.

Audacity of Peace Seekers

President Reagan's consent to a significant reduction in the stockpile of nuclear weapons jointly with General Secretary Gorbachev was not his original idea. He came to power with a dream of strengthening America's armed forces and of propelling the arms race with the former Soviet Union into space. He had to change his stance in response to the public mood, which was engineered by the Nuclear Freeze Movement led by Randall Forsberg. This shows how ordinary people could force the world's most powerful government to abolish, albeit partially, the world's most destructive weapons.

The Nuclear Freeze Movement of the 1980s stood on the shoulders of giants who had shown the audacity of seeking peace since the 1950s. Joseph Rotblat and Robert Oppenheimer, who were involved in the Manhattan Project,[24] became disillusioned with the US nuclear weapons programme and went on to become the first scientists to advocate nuclear disarmament.

Later, more scientists began to speak up against the US government's testing policies. About 1,000 nuclear tests were conducted in Nevada, the primary site for this purpose from 1951 to 1992. The majority of them were underground tests, resulting in the contamination of aquifers. Since the traces of the toxic chemical element plutonium released in such tests last for 24,000 years, water around the nuclear test sites is permanently at risk. Chemist Linus Pauling, geneticist Ralph Lapp and biologist Barry Commoner, among others, launched public information campaigns to explain the adverse impact of nuclear testing on common people in Nevada and nearby regions where tests were being conducted. Besides Nevada, the US also conducted tests at other sites including Colorado, New Mexico and the Marshall Islands in the Pacific Ocean.

The tests in the Bikini and Enewetak atolls in the Marshall Islands had a damaging impact on the ecology of the marine system. The coral reefs around the area were decimated. The indigenous population of the Bikini atoll had to be shifted to uninhabited islands, where they became fully dependent on external support for survival.[25] The incidence of cancer in the people of the region increased significantly due to the radioactivity generated by the tests. Now it is impossible for the people to return to their original homes in the Bikini atoll due to the contamination of flora, fauna and drinking water.[26]

The populations in the test sites in Russia and China experienced similar tragedies. Testing in Novaya Zemlya in Russia produced radioactive fallout that reached as far as Norway, Alaska and the Arctic region.[27] The Sami, Nenets and Komi people, among other indigenous tribes in Russia's northern coastal region, were exposed to high doses of radiation, leading to death and deformities.[28] The Lop Nor test site in China covers 1,00,000 sq. km, making it the largest in the world. So far, approximately 20,000 sq. km of it has been used for nuclear testing purposes by the country. China has not permitted any independent assessment of the environmental or health impacts of its nuclear testing programme, but anecdotes by local people describing 'dust rain' have been carried by the international media.[29]

In the 1970s, when nuclear tests threatened the environment and health of people living in the vicinity of testing sites, Randall Forsberg emerged as a peace activist in the US. She used to work at the Stockholm International Peace Research Institute, where she came across information on the disastrous consequences of nuclear weapons. This prompted her to move to the US to undertake research on the subject. At the same time, she began giving speeches on nuclear disarmament, networking with peace organizations and mobilizing religious groups to demand the end of nuclear testing, production and deployment. Unlike peace organizations that demanded unilateral action on behalf of the US, she proposed a bilateral freeze jointly by the US and the former Soviet Union.[30] This broadened her support base as many people perceived her to be fair in placing the burden of action on both superpowers alike and not on the US alone. The appeal for a bilateral freeze grew rapidly among various sections of American society. In 1982, 1 million people demonstrated in Central Park, New York, making it one of the largest peace demonstrations in the history of the US.[31] In 1983, protests were held at fifty testing sites in the country.[32] In 1986, hundreds of people walked from Los Angeles to Washington, DC, to demand the freeze.[33]

The Reagan White House initially reacted to the Nuclear Freeze Movement with hostility. The administration launched its own campaign to mobilize public opinion against Nuclear Freeze. But it turned out that people trusted the peace-seekers more than the administration. By 1984, it seemed likely that the electoral mood would swing against Reagan on the nuclear issue and could possibly cost him his second term in office. With this realization, among other factors,

President Reagan changed his mind and began to explore the prospects of nuclear disarmament with the former Soviet leadership.

The anti-nuclear movement had an impact on big media, which in turn had an even larger impact on political leaders such as President Reagan. In 1979, a film on the malfunctioning of a nuclear power plant near Los Angeles received wide appreciation. It motivated a senior executive at ABC to produce *The Day After*, which touched the hearts of millions of people. Thus, the peace movement had a multiplier impact directly through its demonstrations and marches and indirectly through different types of media.

The Nuclear Freeze Movement became an umbrella organization to bring together secular and religious groups, radicals and moderates, apolitical activists as well as elected political representatives. SANE (Committee for a Sane Nuclear Policy), one of the first nuclear weapon abolition advocacy organizations that had been established in 1957, merged with Nuclear Freeze, bolstering the movement further.

However, the policy impact created by the Nuclear Freeze Movement in the US eluded the British peace movement. In Britain, the Campaign for Nuclear Disarmament (CND) was launched in 1958, which subsequently grew to well over 100 local chapters, arranging speeches, fundraising events and staging protests. The CND advocated unilateral disarmament and proposed that Britain should initiate the first step in that regard. With this demand, it began to organize an annual march to Aldermaston, the centre of British nuclear weapons production. But though the CND strengthened its membership numbers, it could not bring about a shift in British nuclear policy.

If we delve deeper to determine why the CND did not succeed whereas the Nuclear Freeze Movement did, we will find a number of reasons. The CND was launched by Bertrand Russell, well-known philosopher, who had co-authored the Russell–Einstein Manifesto in 1955, mobilizing endorsement from several Nobel laureate scientists. On the other hand, the Nuclear Freeze Movement was launched by Randall Forsberg, a young researcher who did not have Russell's charisma. The two organizations differed in their core message. The CND advocated unilateral action by Britain.[34] The Freeze movement emphasized that bilateral action should be jointly undertaken by the two superpowers. As a result, the former was considered radical, while the latter emerged as a mainstream force. Second, the CND appealed to only one segment of the Labour Party, and therefore, a narrow part of the political spectrum. But the Freeze movement was successful in forging a coalition among political, religious, secular and civil society groups. It enjoyed wide support in the Democratic Party, which moved a resolution in the House of Representatives calling for a freeze on the production of nuclear weapons. Third, the Freeze movement was built on the scientific work done by scientists and other professionals, exposing the ill-effects of nuclear tests, such as radioactivity released by the tests causing disease and death as well as contamination of water and nature. There was no such parallel effort in Britain. Overall, the Freeze movement demonstrated that with a pragmatic and clever strategy, a young and unknown catalyst could mobilize public opinion to create potential electoral impact. The movement thereby motivated the key political interlocutor to change his policies to reduce the stockpile of nuclear weapons, going much beyond the demands of the Nuclear Freeze organization. It is a story of how ordinary citizens with determination and the right strategy can force a big change to liberate the world from the weapons of mass destruction.

While the Nuclear Freeze Movement played a key role in influencing US policy, a similar movement in Kazakhstan had an impact on the former Soviet Union. Just as the protests against nuclear testing began in Nevada in the US, a major test site, similar protests were organized in Kazakhstan, which was an important test site for the former Soviet Union. From the first test in 1949 until 1989, Semipalatinsk in Kazakhstan was a host to 456 atomic explosions. The site was 200–300 km from industrial and rural population centres.[35] It was meant to be a secret site, not even shown on the map, but it was not easy to maintain the secrecy.

The nuclear fallout from the tests exposed hundreds of thousands of people to toxic radiation. From 1957 to 1960, a team of Kazakh doctors, with rare permission from the authorities in Moscow, checked the health impact of tests on people in the region. They recorded haemorrhaging of respiratory tracts, mouths, genitals, and changes in the mucous layers and skin of those living in the area surrounding the test site. They also noticed a spike in those suffering from asthenia or extreme fatigue. Many people were exposed to 500–1,000 times the radiation that a normal human being can live with.[36] At this level of radiation exposure, there are significant problems with the blood-forming process in the human body. Antony Butts's film, *After the Apocalypse*, about the people of Semipalatinsk mentions that one in twenty children in the region is born with genetic defects. Besides these problems, it is, of course, a known fact that exposure to radioactive fallout leads to a high incidence of cancer over decades.[37]

Three simultaneous developments awakened the Kazakh nuclear conscience. First, Mikhail Gorbachev emerged as the leader of the former Soviet Union and immediately announced glasnost or openness as his new policy. Second, an industrial accident took place at the Chernobyl nuclear plant in Ukraine in April 1986, with radiation fallout killing many and damaging the health and environment of a large area as far as Belarus. Though far from Kazakhstan, the tragedy stirred the people living in the proximity of the Kazakh test site into action. It was also revealed that radioactive gas had leaked from Semipalatinsk in 1989. Third, Olzhas Suleimenov, a Kazakh poet, in a rare show of courage, articulated opposition to nuclear testing by organizing public rallies against the testing of nuclear weapons. Also, Nursultan Nazarbayev, a favourite of Gorbachev who was sympathetic to the criticism of nuclear testing, was appointed to head the Kazakhstan communist party hierarchy. He would eventually go on to preside over independent Kazakhstan and become the supreme leader of the country.

Olzhas Suleimenov, a man well known in literary circles, played a vital role in mobilizing public opinion at this time. In February 1989, he interrupted a televised recital of his poetry to denounce nuclear testing at Semipalatinsk, appealing to people to form an organization to demand a ban on nuclear testing. Within a week, an anti-nuclear movement called the Nevada–Semipalatinsk Movement was launched. It called for the closure of the Semipalatinsk facility and a clean-up of the area; the end of nuclear weapon production; citizen control over nuclear waste; the creation of a map showing the extent of radiation damage in the Soviet Union; and the elucidation of the plight of radiological victims in the Soviet Union.[38]

The movement announced that its goal was to abolish nuclear weapons worldwide. Their 'High Time' petition received over a million signatures within days. On 1 August 1989, the Supreme Soviet adopted a resolution, authored by Suleimenov, calling for a moratorium on all nuclear testing by the US and the Soviet Union. The movement organized rallies and demonstrations through 1989. In November of that year, the government in Moscow announced its plan to stop testing temporarily at Semipalatinsk, but unfortunately, it wanted to resume doing so at Novaya Zemlya in the Arctic region.

Suleimenov visited the US to turn his movement into an international one. Around this time, the Soviet Union began to cancel tests. Although the Soviet leaders did not have to think of any electoral considerations as they did not have to contest elections like President Reagan of the US, they were forced to be sensitive to public opinion. Gorbachev's policy of glasnost made this further possible. In October 1990, the last nuclear test in the history of the former Soviet Union was conducted at Novaya Zemlya. Weeks later, the Kazakh Parliament introduced a legal ban on testing in the Republic. This was followed by Boris Yeltsin banning nuclear testing in Russia for one year. In fact, the moratorium on Russian testing is still operational in 2022.

In response to the Soviet or Russian initiatives to ban tests, the US moved to introduce a test ban. In September 1992, the US conducted its last test in Nevada. The UK and France have also refrained from testing nuclear weapons since the early 1990s. China conducted its last test in 1996. India and Pakistan did so in 1998.[39] With the sole exception of North Korea, which has conducted six nuclear weapons tests since 2006, there has been a de facto test ban in the rest of the world for the last two decades. This is only a partial success of the nuclear test ban campaign as the Comprehensive Test Ban Treaty remains elusive even now. Until it becomes a legally binding global instrument, the door for testing remains open. In fact, President Trump wanted to resume tests before he was defeated in the US elections in 2020. It will be critical to see if the Biden administration pledges not to test nuclear weapons in the spirit of its commitment to reverse many dangerous policies of its predecessor. In any case, the de facto ban outside North Korea for two decades shows how a determined group of common citizens can change the world.

A few years after the success of American and Russian peace movements in the abolition of intermediate-range nuclear forces and a practical worldwide ban on nuclear testing (with the North Korean exception), another movement involving common citizens succeeded in convincing the world to abolish landmines. It was led by Jody Williams, born in 1950 in Vermont, US. She completed her schooling, undergraduate and graduate studies in her home state. In February 1981, someone handed a pamphlet to her on US war brutalities in El Salvador—where the US was helping a cruel dictator counter communism—while she was waiting to board a train. The similarities between the negative consequences of America's policies in Vietnam and El Salvador aroused her interest and she attended a meeting the very next week in which the situation in El Salvador was discussed in detail. Soon after, she actively began volunteering to educate people about America's operations in El Salvador. Her aim was to shift US policy from interfering in the internal matters of other countries to maintaining a neutral stance.

With a postgraduate degree in teaching Spanish and English, Williams went on to work with different campaigns in Central America, including Medical Aid for El Salvador, in which she was the head of a programme that brought children injured during the war in the country to the US for medical care. She lived in Mexico for two years and spent several months of the year in Nicaragua and the Honduras, maintaining Washington, DC, as her base, since she always wanted to pursue international work and believed that DC would provide her with that opportunity.

In the 1990s, Jody Williams was approached by Bobby Muller of the Vietnam Veterans of America Foundation and Thomas Gebauer of Medico International to coordinate a campaign to ban landmines. She brought together six civil society organizations to form the International Campaign to Ban Landmines (ICBL). The ICBL became involved in advocating a global ban on landmines, holding conferences, arranging meetings with experts, liaising with different NGOs, publishing material on the harmful effects of landmines and other activities. In 1997, Williams was instrumental in drawing up the draft articles for the Ottawa Treaty, sponsored by the Government of Canada, which called for all governments to ban landmines completely. This international agreement prohibits the use, production, stockpiling and transfer of anti-personnel landmines, while additionally outlining mine removal efforts and calling for assistance to the victims of landmines. A decade later, cluster munitions—explosive weapons that eject several bomblets when dropped from the air—were banned, inspired by the landmines ban treaty.

The landmines ban treaty came into force in 1999, with more than 150 countries being parties to it.[40] In the last two decades, almost 50 million stockpiled mines have been destroyed.

Apart from Jody Williams, many other individuals and institutions played a key role in the success of the landmines ban treaty. These included late Canadian Foreign Minister Lloyd Axworthy, Austrian diplomat Werner Ehrlich and representatives of the NGOs that formed the campaign.

The ICBL inspired the birth of the International Campaign to Abolish Nuclear Weapons (ICAN) a decade later. Beatrice Fihn, a Swedish civil society activist, is the executive director of the campaign.[41] She was an intern with a women's peace organization in Geneva where she became familiar with the work of the UN Conference on Disarmament. She steered the growth of the ICAN movement to include more than 500 organizations spread over 100 countries, and under her leadership, the campaign focused on the negative impact of nuclear weapons on humanity.

In 2016, ICAN began efforts to appeal to the UN to adopt a legally binding instrument to prohibit nuclear weapons. In July 2017, a treaty on the prohibition of nuclear weapons was approved by the UN by 122 to 1 votes, but with nuclear power states and their allies choosing not to vote.[42] It is the first time in history that the UN adopted a resolution to abolish nuclear weapons with an objective of eventually eliminating them. It was an arduous diplomatic process, with the treaty coming into force in January 2021. But in this case the glass is only half full: on the one hand, all the nuclear powers and NATO member states have ignored the treaty, without whom it is a vacuous instrument; on the other hand, despite the opposition of nuclear weapons states, the success in convincing the UN General Assembly to create such an instrument demonstrates the power of grassroots movements.

Several organizations launched by common people have awakened the world's conscience about the negative impact of nuclear weapons on humanity. These include the previously mentioned CND in the UK, Green New Deal in the US, Peace Action, Greenpeace and the International Physicians for the Prevention of Nuclear War (IPPNW). The IPPNW was formed by a group of American and Russian doctors in the early 1980s, about the same time that the Nuclear Freeze Movement attracted public attention. The doctors studied the health and medical consequences of a nuclear war and declared that the use of nuclear weapons would unleash a final epidemic that would be incurable. The organization undertook several studies and public information campaigns on the dangerous consequences of nuclear weapons for the world's people and launched the ICAN movement discussed earlier.[43]

The success of the ICBL and the ICAN motivated the launch of the Campaign to Stop Killer Robots in October 2012. It is a coalition of like-minded civil society organizations from around the world that calls for a legally binding instrument to ban lethal autonomous weapons. Since then, several countries have begun to express their views on this issue at various UN meetings. In 2014, the European Parliament adopted its first resolution calling for a ban on the 'development, production and use of fully autonomous weapons which enable strikes to be carried out without human intervention'.[44] A few months later, several faith leaders issued a joint call echoing the same demand.

Experts associated with the campaign and the Nobel Peace Prize laureates supporting its cause have been holding briefing sessions for various legislative and UN bodies since 2014, explaining the dangers associated with the use of lethal autonomous weapons. In July 2015, more than 1,000 AI and robotics researchers, including the late Stephen Hawking, Elon Musk and 15,000 other endorsers, signed an open letter calling for a ban on autonomous weapons. Hundreds of AI workers in countries such as Australia, Belgium and Canada issued national appeals to ban lethal autonomous weapons systems. In July 2018, more than 200 technology companies and organizations from thirty-six countries and 2,600 individuals signed a pledge released by the Future of Life Institute at the International Joint Conference on Artificial Intelligence in Stockholm, committing to 'neither participate in nor support the development, manufacture, trade, or use of lethal autonomous weapons'.[45] By 2021, thirty member states of the UN had called for a legal ban on lethal autonomous weapons as a result of the efforts of the campaign, and almost 175 organizations from more than sixty-five countries had joined it.[46]

However, there is stiff resistance to the campaign's call to ban killer robots. Many governments are not ready to open their minds to this possibility. The farthest they are willing to go is to adopt a voluntary code of conduct but not commit to a legally binding international instrument. But this has not deterred tech workers from practising civil

disobedience. The US Department of Defense had contracted Google
to develop AI for analysing images to help with drone attacks. Over
3,000 Google employees issued a public appeal to the company asking
it to withdraw from the project.[47] Their initiative succeeded as Google
did not renew the contract on its expiry in March 2019.[48] It is quite
plausible that Google and other technology companies might come
under political and financial pressure to continue to cooperate with the
US military without the option of paying heed to the moral appeals of
their employees and consumers. Be that as it may, it is noteworthy that
the collective moral strength of ordinary tech workers had an impact on
a significant corporate decision, and this episode has created a precedent
for similar actions of civil disobedience in future.

Democratic Dividends

The organizations and initiatives discussed in the preceding pages are
mostly grassroots movements. Some have worked with celebrities once
the movements took off, but they did not depend on public figures to
be launched. Common citizens, highly concerned and committed to
peace and disarmament, have steered them. Their impact on national
and global policies is a testament to the power of citizens in a democracy.

All these organizations, except the test ban movement in Kazakhstan,
were started in North America and Western Europe. Invariably, they have
been intellectually and politically opposed by the US administration
and other governments or ignored by them until electoral calculations
forced the political leaders to change their stance. However, the
organizations and individuals leading them have been allowed the
freedom to express their views and organize public opinion. This is
only possible in a mature democracy. It explains why these movements
flourished in North America and Western Europe. The Semipalatinsk
movement in Kazakhstan was founded during Mikhail Gorbachev's
glasnost period, which was the maximum democracy Russia—or the
former Soviet Union—has ever experienced.

If activists from autocratic countries or democracies with autocratic leadership had attempted to mobilize public opinion against lethal weapons, they might have been jailed for life. This would have been construed as an act of treason. In Stalin's and Brezhnev's Russia, they could have been banished to the Siberian gulags. In North Korea, they would have been shot dead. In certain kinds of democracies, they would have been considered anti-national and subjected to harassment, tax raids, brutal investigations, mob violence and media trials. They would have found it difficult to secure permission to organize marches and demonstrations. They might have even found it difficult to secure media coverage to present their views. It is to the credit of genuine, functioning democracies that these movements could grow in the countries in which they were founded and managed, despite opposing nationalist priorities and interests of the military–industrial complex.

The success of these disarmament movements is as much due to the commitment and grit of their leaders as to the democratic dividends they could enjoy in their countries. It is not that people in the former Soviet Union or other countries involved in the pursuit of nuclear weapons, hypersonic missiles, and lethal autonomous weapons approve of the growing lethality of weapons their countries want to deploy. But there is no space to articulate or mobilize against militarist policies, which are blended with nationalistic fervour in these countries.

In the 1950s, the World Peace Council was established in Helsinki, with members primarily from the former Soviet Union and Eastern Europe. It appealed for outlawing of nuclear weapons and organized many public meetings, drawing attention to the consequences of the nuclear bombs dropped in Hiroshima and Nagasaki, highlighting the implications of a potential nuclear war between the US and the former Soviet Union.[49] It may, therefore, appear that there was a peace and disarmament organization in the former communist group of countries. However, the organization did not put the responsibility on the Soviet government, choosing to consider US policies and capitalism as the root of all evils. In effect, it proved to be an instrument of Soviet propaganda.

In contrast, organizations such as the Nuclear Freeze Movement, IPPNW and ICAN held all parties responsible and very much directed their actions towards their own governments. Their experience suggests that the hope for the future disarmament movement would primarily stem from democratic countries in North America and Western Europe. It is not a surprise that all major peace organizations currently operate from North America and Western Europe. Well-known examples include the International Committee of the Red Cross (ICRC), International Peace Bureau, Pugwash, Women's International League for Peace and Freedom, Pax Christi, Global Partnership for the Prevention of Armed Conflict, Mayors for Peace, besides the already mentioned IPPNW, ICLB, Campaign to Stop Killer Robots, ICAN and numerous others. There is no organization or grassroots movement campaigning against nuclear weapons, the arms race or hyper-nationalism that enjoys popularity among the masses and which functions from a country in Asia, Africa, Eastern Europe or Latin America. It is indeed to the credit of the Western democracies that with all their flaws, limitations and abuses, they allow civilians within society to articulate freely against the same military–industrial complex of their countries.

The fact that democracy would enable civic organizations and individuals in North America and Western Europe to organize global disarmament movements does not mean that the burden of eliminating the weapons of final destruction must be entirely on those countries. Any aspiration for the elimination of such weapons must be multilateral.

We have seen how the Nuclear Freeze Movement in the US, the IPPNW and the Semipalatinsk Movement in Kazakhstan in the 1980s and early 1990s succeeded in persuading the two superpowers to stop nuclear testing and eliminate certain categories of nuclear arms because they demanded coordinated bilateral actions. But the peace groups that demanded unilateral actions in the Western democracies failed in changing government policies.

The grassroots movements may initially ask the democratic countries to begin the multilateral disarmament processes since their counterparts in other countries may be restrained due to the restrictions in the free political space. But they must be clear that they urge their countries to negotiate with other countries possessing the weapons of final destruction for a joint or coordinated reduction, not unilateral actions, and eventual abolition of the horrendous weapons from the planet. Such a multilateral approach would not isolate the peace movements from the mainstream in their own societies. An approach that requires action by all countries would convince conservative and nationalist groups that it is not propaganda against their own countries.

It is not realistic to break the chain of proliferation and aspiration for nuclear and post-nuclear weapons with unilateral actions. The grassroots movements working for disarmament realize this. As a result, recent efforts for eliminating all types of lethal weapons have been multilateral. Thus, the conventions to ban landmines, abolish nuclear weapons and ban killer robots are all sought to be negotiated in the UN.

In the 1980s, the US and the former Soviet Union were the only two major powers, and therefore, bilateral disarmament initiatives were adequate. The Nuclear Freeze Movement in the US and the test ban movement in Kazakhstan appealed to their national leaders to negotiate with the other superpower. Now, the US and Russia can further the disarmament agenda in some spheres, but not in all cases. It is necessary to engage their own allies, as well as other nuclear-armed nations, if nuclear weapons are to be abolished. Similarly, aspirations to acquire lethal autonomous weapons, hypersonic missiles and cyberweapons are global and no longer confined to the two superpowers of the Cold War era. We do not even have information about biological weapons and who might be developing them, as they can be produced with a relatively limited amount of resources in secrecy. It is not known what neXt weapons are under research and development and where.

It is essential for any disarmament initiative to engage at least the nine known nuclear powers. If nuclear weapons are not abolished in the next fifteen to twenty years, the number of nuclear powers will at least double to eighteen. In fact, Dr Mohamed ElBaradei, Nobel Peace Prize laureate who was then director general of the International Atomic Energy Agency, said in October 2006 at a symposium in Vienna: 'There is the need to develop a new international or multinational approach to the fuel cycle so as to avoid ending up with not just nine nuclear weapon States, but another 20 or 30 States which have the capacity to develop nuclear weapons in a very short span of time.'[50] With every passing year, the arms race is bound to become increasingly complex with an additional number of players. If Reagan and Gorbachev had agreed on the abolition of nuclear weapons in 1986, as they seemed to, they would have placed heavy political pressure on the other three nuclear powers to follow. India and Pakistan would have never conducted the tests they did in 1998, since India follows the behaviour of major powers and Pakistan pursues what India does. China and Russia would have worked together to curb North Korean nuclear ambitions, as they would not have liked a nuclear-armed country in their backyard when they were willingly giving up their own weapons. The world missed a critical opportunity back then. It is high time now to control the damage before not only nuclear arms but also other weapons of final destruction spread far and wide, exposing the entire world's population to the risk of extinction. A few decades ago, the survival of humankind was threatened by nuclear weapons alone. Now, all weapons of final destruction—including nuclear, chemical, biological, lethal autonomous, hypersonic, cyber and secret neXt weapons—will have to be eliminated in a phased and verifiable manner.

While the specific strategies for ensuring the survival of humankind must change as compared to the last century, the power of common citizens in mature democratic societies remains the same. If these movements can adapt to the new complexity, as they seem to, they can aspire to turn back the Doomsday Clock.

It is necessary for anti-war movements to expand their reach. Such movements seem to attract what are known as liberal political thinkers and activists, but it is necessary for them to engage rural youth, farmers, religious groups and other conservative segments of the population. After all, farmlands in America's Midwestern states and Russia's south-east districts, as well as big cities in Britain, France, India and China, will be the first to be obliterated in a global or regional nuclear war. Relatively weaker countries and unknown groups can damage the nuclear command, control and communication systems of big powers with cyberattacks. It should be reiterated to all that the arsenals of the big countries can wipe out the enemy state but cannot save their own country from the minimum assured damage. Every country is vulnerable: there is no immunity for any nation, however big or small, in a world where nuclear weapons coexist with hypersonic missiles, cyberweapons and robotics. Nationalism can lead to jingoism, resulting in the expansion of arsenals and heightening of rhetoric. But when there is a small nuclear attack on a critical location in a big country, patriotism and nationalism will not help the millions of victims survive the resulting death and destruction.

Sometimes, enlightened leaders such as Brandt, Gorbachev and Mandela change the course of history. But we cannot wait forever in the hope of a great, transformative leader emerging. People's movements can be organized by us, the common citizens. So, instead of merely waiting for Brandt or Gorbachev, our aspiration should be how to convert a Putin, Xi or a future Trump into a peacemaker. Some leaders enter public life for the principles they believe in. Some do it for dominance alone. If those who are in the pursuit of power believe that they can acquire it by proliferating deadly weapons in the name of nationalism, they will do so. If they find that they can gain authority and status by establishing harmony in the world, they will also do so. If they find that jingoism and animosity with enemies within and outside the country improve their electoral prospects, they will spread these vices.

If leaders discover that peace delivers electoral dividends, only then will they choose it. Once a democratically elected leader wants to pursue the path of peace, he or she will have to find partners in authoritarian countries such as China and Russia to negotiate the abolition of the weapons of final destruction.

Although the process of disarmament needs to be initiated by the Western democracies, it would eventually have to include all other existing and aspiring acquisitors of nuclear and other lethal weapons. This is likely to be a much greater challenge than the bilateral agreements between Reagan and Gorbachev. Eventually, the change must embrace the entire world as it would be short-sighted to ignore those countries that have not acquired or declared their intention to acquire the weapons of final destruction. There are always secrets in the world's political closets.

The phased elimination of the weapons of final destruction is only the first step needed to build a secure world. The need of the hour is to go beyond arms control treaties to rethink global norms and institutions. The question is not merely how to avoid the end of human civilization; the questions are how to construct a world where we all live together in peace and harmony and how to progress in the journey of human civilization. The next chapter will discuss the evidence for hope, since the much-neglected truth is that the project of human civilization is a joint venture, and we have already established a platform on which we can construct our future.

5

Before Daylight: Shaping Peace, Preventing Wars

If you step out of Blackwell's bookshop in the medieval centre of Oxford, you will face the Sheldonian Theatre. It is an impressive D-shaped building in yellowish brown. Designed by Christopher Wren, then an Oxford don, it was constructed in the late seventeenth century. Wren was fond of Roman theatres, and this inspired his design of the Sheldonian. Gilbert Sheldon, then Archbishop of Canterbury, provided a princely sum of £15,000 to construct it, and thus was added his name in eternity. It is the university's main venue of congregation. Students matriculate and graduate there. Eminent men and women are conferred honorary degrees in the annual Encaenia ceremony. Behind the theatre is the Bodleian Library, one of the most celebrated libraries in the world. It opened its doors for readers in 1602, decades before the Sheldonian was built, and has 13 million printed items, including books, manuscripts and maps. The third important structure in the complex is the Radcliffe Camera, a circular yellowish building housing a 250-year-old science library. The fence outside the Sheldonian Theatre is decorated with carved figures, known as the Emperor Heads, which gaze at the pedestrians below on Broad Street. Several bicycles are usually parked against the wall beneath the fence.

If you stand outside Blackwell's for some time, you will see students parking their bicycles and then walking past the Sheldonian to the Bodleian Library and the Radcliffe Camera. They are British, American, African, Chinese, Arab, Indian, Indonesian, Fijian, Zambian, Peruvian, Brazilian and Canadian. There are some 5,000 international students from more than 150 countries at Oxford. They carry on the tradition of Emo of Friesland, the first foreign student to arrive at Oxford in 1190, within a century of the university being established. Emo came from Groningen in the northern part of the Netherlands. He returned to his homeland to become a schoolmaster, a priest and an author of numerous works in Latin on virtues and vices.[1] Since then, Oxford has been a home for students and scholars from all over the world to come together, cross-fertilize their ideas and produce knowledge in a collaborative way.

Oxford is only one of several thousand centres of learning where people belonging to different nations, religions and races co-create knowledge. Around 5 to 6 million students are estimated to be studying away from their home countries all over the world at any given time. They live and learn together in dorms and libraries. They work together to produce ideas, concepts and theories. This is not today's story. It has been going on for over 2,500 years since Takshashila University flourished in India, as did the Library of Alexandria in Egypt.

Civilization, a Collaboration

There may be a centuries-old tradition to co-create knowledge, but we rarely hear about a worldwide collaborative endeavour to engender ideas to improve our lives. Instead, we are obsessed with hatred and suspicion of one another. Our tendency to negate each other in the name of religion and nationalism is deliberately cultivated by those commanding politics, media and social media. Our elite are constantly preparing for a war on the pretext of protecting our nations from enemies, while the wise find security in assimilation, mutual trust and harmony.

The human spirit has shown again and again that it can respond to and withstand challenges thrown by those who want to dissipate it. For every mind that conceived of enterprises to avenge long-forgotten historical wrongs, there were others who built houses of wisdom to shelter the works of the finest Christian, Jewish, Persian and Arab minds. If some attacked trains and towers, others joined hands from across continents to eradicate epidemics. If some bombed the houses of unsuspecting mothers and children on the pretext of finding nuclear weapons and promoting human rights, others rushed to save cyclone victims. We must harness the spirit of humanity not only because the alternative is the risk of a catastrophic confrontation. We must harness the spirit of humanity because coexistence is the true human nature.

If indeed we want to discover the true human in us, we must unlearn to believe those who inculcate fear about others, scare us about impending assault and convince us of the need to stockpile lethal arms. These naysayers have brought us close to human extinction, hypnotizing us to glorify war in the name of valour and patriotism. The truth is that bloody battles notwithstanding, our civilization is a collaborative endeavour by people across continents and centuries.

Human civilization as we know it today has its origins in the creation of once avant-garde concepts around 2,500 years ago in China, Egypt, Greece (later Rome), India and Mesopotamia. The seeds of our understanding of physics, chemistry, medicine, philosophy, sociology, mathematics and logic were sown in these regions around the same time in an auspicious coincidence. The Silk Road connecting East Asia to the Middle East and Southern Europe was also established. Other trade routes had opened too. Aden, in today's strife-torn Yemen, was an important port in commerce between India, Arabia and Greece.

As the merchants exchanged goods, they also passed on ideas, religions and advancement in sciences from one part of the world to another. Much of today's scientific innovation depends on the mathematics that was discovered in Mesopotamia, China, Greece, India and Egypt. Today's equations and algorithms owe their existence to the wisdom of the ancient wise men from these lands. The Americans and Russians, followed by others, have produced nuclear bombs using the principles of physics and mathematics developed in a global collaborative endeavour since 500 BCE. Then can we not say that the bombs, missiles, killer robots, killer pathogens and cyberweapons are a betrayal of the spirit of collaboration in knowledge creation nurtured over several centuries?

An honest understanding of the evolution of knowledge is essential because the forces of nationalism and extremism claim their right to possess the instruments of violence merely because of their ability to produce or procure them. In every society, selective interpreters of human experience ignore those parts of world history that do not suit their political needs, while reiterating references that promote their objectives.

We tend to forget that a thousand years ago, the area spanning from today's Iran in the East to Spain in the West and Egypt in the South was the seat of the greatest learning in the world. Here, the Abbasids from their capital in Baghdad, the Ummayads from their base in Cordoba, and the Fatimids from their capital in Cairo created an Age of Enlightenment.

The Abbasid ruler al-Ma'mun, son of Harun al-Rashid, appointed Khalid al-Brmaki, a Persian noble, as his *vazir* or prime minister. Al-Ma'mun ordered the translation of books from other cultures and offered exceptionally high salaries to the translators. He provided patronage and succour to Jewish and Christian scientists who were left beleaguered in the Dark Ages of Europe. He maintained relations with the Byzantine rulers and used diplomacy and rich gifts to acquire books written by Aristotle, Plato, Galen, Hippocrates, Ptolemy, Euclid and Pythagoras, among others. While the Europeans themselves ignored

Greek scholarship, the Arab rulers translated and preserved it. The rulers of Cordoba, like the Abbasids of Baghdad and the Fatimids of Cairo, attracted scholars from across the Middle East to their universities and translation centres. Some of the scholars brought with them the numerical system from India and refined it to produce algebra and algorithms. Some scholars brought the technique of making paper from China and further developed it to make paper from linen instead of tree bark as the Chinese did. Paper mills flourished in the Arab region long before the first one appeared in Europe. The advent of paper led to the production of books and the preservation and spread of knowledge. The emphasis on plurality and coexistence also led to a vibrant trade.

The Arab and Persian scientists improved on experiments done in other parts of the world and produced their own innovations in a wide range of fields, including medicine, irrigation, astronomy and algebra. Thus, we find that the Arab rule around 1,000 years ago served as the main vehicle for the advancement of human civilization: the Arabs absorbed ancient Greek, Indian and Chinese knowledge through translation into Arabic, passing it on to the next generation of Europeans through the translation of their works in Latin.

The Arab rulers also built institutions that made the cross-fertilization of ideas and innovations from different civilizations feasible. Caliph al-Ma'mun, whom we met before, established the House of Wisdom (Bayt al-Hikma) in 832 CE consisting of an observatory, a library and a translation and research bureau. Abd al-Rahman III founded the University of Cordoba in the tenth century. Al-Hakim bi-Amr Allah founded the House of Knowledge, with a public library, in Cairo at the beginning of the eleventh century. He possessed a personal collection of 1,60,000 books. These institutions attracted students from different parts of the world, much like the present-day universities of Oxford, Cambridge, Sciences Po, Tsinghua, Harvard, Stanford, Princeton and Yale.

It is common knowledge that the Arab communities had a penchant for trade. The marketplace (bazaar) was an important aspect of their lives. There was competition to offer the best and the most novel items in the bazaar, motivating traders to look as far as China and India to search for new ideas and goods. Some of the local businessmen improved upon products and technologies imported from abroad. When some traders imported ceramics from China and steel from India, local businessmen developed metallurgy and ceramic glazes to produce superior-quality products locally. It was these traders who came up with the innovative financial instrument called cheques for carrying out financial transactions.[2]

Then there came a time when this flourishing part of the world came under invasion. When the Mongols destroyed Baghdad in 1258, they did not spare anything—hospitals, irrigation networks, centres of learning or libraries. Most significantly, they massacred all scholars. The strides made in the progress of science and culture over 300 years were wiped out in a matter of months. The Arab people never really recovered from a series of assaults beginning with the fall of Baghdad in the thirteenth century.[3] They have so far not managed to rekindle the scientific spirit that enabled the flourishing of the Golden Era. However, the translations of ancient Greek, Indian and Chinese works and the subsequent Arab and Persian improvisation helped launch the European Renaissance from the fourteenth century. The centre of knowledge moved: from Egypt, India, China, Greece–Rome, Mesopotamia during 500 BCE to 500 CE; to Baghdad, Cordoba, Cairo during 800–1200 CE; to Florence during 1300–1400 CE; to the rest of Europe from the 1500s to 1900s.

Continuing a long chain of knowledge generation of over two millennia, Europe saw many discoveries and inventions in the medieval period. By 1500 CE, there were more than eighty universities across Europe—Oxford, Cambridge, Paris, Bologna, Salamanca, Siena, Pisa, Krakow, Vienna, Heidelberg, Barcelona, Glasgow, to name a few. Many of these universities have survived to the present day. Copernicus, Galileo and Newton made path-breaking discoveries on which modern science is founded. Columbus pioneered the search for new lands with the help of advanced equipment such as the astrolabe. In the fifteenth century, Gutenberg established the movable-type printing press. A century later, a couple of hundred printing presses across Europe were producing millions of copies of books. By 1660, there was an adequate critical mass of scientific thinkers to establish the Royal Society in London.

The details of the two industrial revolutions in Europe in the late eighteenth and nineteenth centuries are too well known to be recapitulated here. In the subsequent decades, several scientists migrated from Europe to the US, extending the bridge of knowledge across the Atlantic. They included Joseph Priestley, Alexander Graham Bell, Nikola Tesla, Albert Einstein, Enrico Fermi and Niels Bohr.

The world now, with its functioning underpinned by knowledge and ideas, is an outcome of the merging of millions of streams of learning in the last 2,500 years. Science is not the monopoly of those who dominate it today. They possess it only because of the building blocks of knowledge developed over the last several centuries by different societies. The journey of knowledge and learning that simultaneously began in China, Egypt, Greece, India and Mesopotamia is currently most visible in the US, Russia and Europe, and in recent years also in China and Japan. It remains to be seen where the journey of cooperation will lead our civilization in the future.

Perhaps the greatest discovery of the last century was the Theory of Relativity by Albert Einstein. In 1916, in the middle of the First World War, he published his theory in full mathematical detail. One of the inferences of his work was about the precise deflection of a star's light due to the sun's gravity. Einstein was then in Berlin, and Germany was at war with Britain. Sir Arthur Eddington, a professor at Cambridge, considered Einstein's theory to be highly significant, and he wanted to test it. He received full support in his enterprise from Frank Watson Dyson, Britain's Astronomer Royal, despite the war. Eddington and Dyson concluded that an eclipse due in 1919 would provide an opportunity to measure the deflection of light, as theorized by Einstein. To test this, trips would have to be arranged to Brazil and West Africa.

These two British scientists received the backing from many in the British government to carry out the experiment to test a German scientist's theory. The war ended about six months before the eclipse, and the intended experiment was successfully completed. However, the preparations for it had started in the middle of the war. The results were announced at a Royal Society meeting in London in November 1919, making Einstein eternally famous all over the world.[4]

The endorsement of Einstein's work notwithstanding, other German scientists were boycotted by their American, British and French counterparts for about a decade following the First World War. But no such boycott took place after the Second World War, and several European scientific societies continue to thrive until today. One example is the International Meteorological Organization established in 1879, and now named the World Meteorological Organization (WMO), based in a multistorey building in Geneva.

Besides worldwide scientific cooperation, the world is now integrated through trade, accounting for almost $20 trillion in 2020, and dependent on the use of 17 million shipping containers, almost 30,000 passenger aircraft and over 800 commercial airlines. Alongside, there are thousands of international organizations devoted to benevolent causes. Some of the largest have vast workforces—such as the ICRC and Médecins Sans Frontières, two humanitarian organizations which employ 50,000 personnel. The world is also connected through myriad other ways, one of them being sporting events such as the Olympics. Culture too knits people from all over the globe; the worldwide popularity of events such as the Eurovision Song Contest bearing testimony to that. More recently, the internet has provided new ways to connect all nations, and satellites orbiting the earth enable communication over vast geographical distances.

Yuval Noah Harari explains in his book *21 Lessons for the 21st Century* how ours has truly become one homogenous civilization, and not merely a joint venture of all societies on the planet. Every nation has a flag and a national anthem. The cars, buses, trains, bridges, schools, hospitals, offices, shopping malls, computers and the internet used across countries are no different from one another. The insides of a shopping mall, whether in Ankara or Athens, Beijing or Boston look the same. Every nation is dependent on the use of essentials such as electricity, water and medicines. When flying in an aircraft, regardless of whether one takes off from airports in Beijing, Moscow, New York, Delhi, Islamabad, Paris, London or Tel Aviv, one needs to fasten the seat belt, watch the safety demonstration and follow the same rules.[5]

Despite many such symbols of global cooperation, including that between enemies, and the role played by several cultures and institutions over centuries to create the human civilization that exists today, some people do not fail to emphasize the differences and rivalries between nations. The advocacy of hostility is an easy justification for building lethal arsenals that today threaten our species' existence. Conflict and cooperation are both faces of human reality: preparing for war can one day put an end to the human experiment; preparing for cooperation can enrich our life. There are always some in every society who want to prepare for war, and there are others who work for peace.

The warmongers excel in hypocrisy. The Indian and Pakistani elites who advocate destroying the other's country do not shy away from enjoying the cultural fruits of their rivals. Similarly, Iranians in their denim jeans chat on Apple phones about annihilating the American Satan. The Americans discuss missile attacks on Russia over a glass of vodka, while the Kremlin's favourite billionaires go shopping in London and New York. The People's Bank of China has invested $1 trillion in surplus in reserves in US treasury bills as of 2021. The Arab countries, hated by most US Republicans, finance a small percentage of America's national debt, which makes the Republican agenda of tax reduction possible. An ophthalmologist from the Western Eye Hospital in London leads Syria's military assault against the Western coalition.

If we want humankind to survive, it is essential to see through the games played by the merchants of death. It is important not to be deafened by the daily beats of war drums or to be deceived by theories of deterrence, which as we have discussed earlier, are being turned obsolete by AI. It is necessary to harness what is common between us and construct mechanisms to bind people together from across the planet in the pursuit of a common purpose.

Over the last several centuries, a few courageous scholars and statesmen have withstood the attacks of powerful forces attempting to erase our reality of coexistence and cooperation. They have opposed the efforts to turn the devil of parochialism into the god of patriotism. They have resisted constant endeavours to create discord to provide an alternative vision of concord. They have not stopped at expressing idle wishes for the unity of nations but have proposed salutary institutional architecture to bring nations together, leaving behind their sovereignty and pride. Some of their proposals were for building regional structures, while some had global ambitions. These ideas have progressed over several centuries. Initially, they were limited to securing narrow gains, but eventually, they evolved into proposals for the blueprints of human coexistence. Some of these ideas were of an operational nature, conceived by rulers and their advisers. Some others were treatises by scholars and philosophers. A common aspiration behind all the ideas was the concept of a federation of states to commit countries to our common destiny. It is necessary to examine the trajectory of these ideas before we can envisage an ideal architecture for the future.

Federation of States

Over the past few centuries, a debate on the methods of the world's governance has engaged some of the brightest minds. They belong to two camps.

One school of thought professes that there should be a centralized world government with the monopoly of arms vested with the supreme authority. This will eliminate conflicts between states, and even when there are disputes, the head of the world government can mediate between the nation states that are meant to be equal. If we were to paraphrase George Orwell's words, we could say that all kings will be equal, but one will be more equal than the rest.

The second school of thought advocates a federation of states where all states have equal sovereignty, though not equal strength. In this scheme, no ruler is supreme. All are at the same level. The participating states in the federation would be there on a voluntary basis. In some ways, the UN honours this principle. The President of Kiribati, which has a population of 1,20,000, and the President of China, which has a population of 1.4 billion, follow the same rules of protocol in the UN General Assembly.

Dante, the famous Italian poet, was the first person to advocate a world government. He is celebrated for his poem *Divine Comedy*, which is considered an eternal masterpiece. In the fourteenth century, when Latin was the language of literature, Dante composed this poem in the Tuscan language, creating a revolution in the literary world. Although now Dante Alighieri is renowned as one of the founders of medieval literature, he was also involved in Florentine politics on the side of the White Guelphs, who wanted independence from papal rule. Around 1312, Dante wrote a treatise titled *De Monarchia*, proposing the concept of universal monarchy where one government under one monarch would rule the world. Dante assumed that all religions and all princes on the planet would accept the sovereignty of one monarch, however unrealistic such thought may have been in his time.[6]

Dante's intentions were good, though naive. He believed in the unity of humankind, that humanity had a shared purpose that could be best harnessed by one government led by one monarch to actualize its potential. Dante assumed that the universal monarch would be able to eliminate conflicts between kings, serving as the supreme judge. Whereas kings would be equal chieftains, the monarch would be above them. He suggested that his universal monarch be on par with the Pope and recommended a cooperative relationship between the secular monarch and the Pope. In the conclusion of his treatise, Dante extolled the Holy Roman Emperor as this universal monarch.

So long as Dante tried to create equivalence between the secular and theocratic authority, and therefore between the Holy Roman Emperor and the Pope, it served the purpose of safeguarding the autonomy of Florence, his abode, from religious hierarchy. However, when Dante assumed his universal monarch would govern the whole world, above all the kings whom he considered subsidiary, arose a major problem. Would Dante accept King Edward III of England or Prince Harihara of the Vijayanagara Empire in southern India, Mongol ruler Kublai Khan or Ottoman Emperor Osman I—who were all his contemporaries—as the universal monarch? Would Dante accept the Mamluk Sultan of Egypt, al-Ashraf Khalil, as the universal monarch? Was Sultan Khalil a suitable candidate since he captured Acre, the last Christian estate remaining from the Crusades in 1291, liquidating the Latin kingdom of Jerusalem? If Dante imagined a Christian prince to be the universal monarch when Kublai Khan, Mamluk Sultan Khalil and Prince Harihara were proving their mettle in different regions of the world, of whom Dante might not have been possibly aware, his proposal could be, at best, dismissed as poetic imagination.

Many such proposals for a world government have been floated from time to time; Dante's was the first but certainly not the last. On none of these occasions has the question of who would be accepted as the universal monarch been considered. Therefore, such proposals have not gone beyond theoretical discourse.

Almost 300 years after Dante's death, Émeric Crucé, a French monk, proposed the most ambitious plan for a federation of nations which would act as an alternative to the proposal of universal monarchy. He published it in his treatise *Le Nouveau Cynée ou Discours d'Estat* (The New Cyneas, or a Discourse on the State) in 1623, inspired by Cyneas, a Greek diplomat and statesman from around 300 BCE, who had advocated peace. He was the real founder of the concept of cooperation between states in a binding federation.

Crucé did not attract much attention from historians despite his visionary idea. Only a few researchers have made painstaking efforts to explain his work. One of them, Grace Roosevelt, wrote in *A Brief History of the Quest for Peace* in the Global Policy Forum. She explained that Crucé had proposed a federation of states consisting of a permanent arbitration council of envoys of states and including 'not only the European rulers, but also the Emperor of the Turks, the Jews, the Kings of Persia and China, the Grand Duke of Moscovy (Russia) and monarchs from India and Africa'. She quotes Crucé asserting, 'Hostilities are only political, and cannot take away the connection that is and must be between men. Why should I a Frenchman wish harm to an Englishman, a Spaniard, or a Hindoo? I cannot wish it when I consider that they are men like me, that I am subject like them to error and sin, and that all nations are bound together by a natural and consequently indestructible tie.'[7] Crucé envisioned that the unity of states would be underpinned by prosperity generated by free trade.

Constantine Hadjilambrinos writes in *Iliria International Review*:

Crucé argued that the foundation of a permanent general peace should be the common humanity which overarches the differences of race, humanity and culture. Additionally, he argued that war was the result of pride, posturing and generally, misunderstandings between governments. He argued that the potential for conflict could be reduced and ultimately eliminated through the establishment of free commerce which would increase communication and bring people together. To this end, he proposed a single currency, standardization of weights and measures, and guaranteeing the free movement of people and goods. In order to protect this system of free trade and reduce the prospect of war, Crucé proposed a permanent international body, a council of princes and their representatives, which would be based in Venice (a preeminent global trading power). Crucé's idea for the pursuit of a permanent and universal peace centred on the protection of national sovereignty, while at the same time introducing a system which would make peace increasingly profitable for all states that participated in it.[8]

Émeric Crucé believed that the impetus for war was provided by conflicts between different interest groups *within* a nation, rather than disputes *between* nations. In each country, there are interest groups which have vested interests in war. There are other groups which have an enlightened interest in peace. Crucé described the former as the warring classes dependent on warfare for their own survival, prosperity and ego, while the latter are the mercantile classes which earn from the free flow of goods and capital. His observation holds true for today's realities as well. In his book *To End All Wars: A Story of Loyalty and Rebellion, 1914–1918* Adam Hochschild has provided a detailed account of how in the early part of the last century, Britain had some people supporting war and some opposing it within the same family.[9] A brother who has a bright career in the cavalry sees merit in war, whereas his sister, concerned about London's underprivileged, does not understand the rationale for bloodshed. Similarly, in the US, most presidents find their ego elevated by increasing the lethality of weapons, but civil society activists see benefit in eliminating the weapons of final destruction. There are always some groups in societies which love the culture of war. They often happen to be politicians, government officials, defence contractors, soldiers and media barons. Others view wars as a lose–lose proposition. Then we have Switzerland, Uruguay and over twenty demilitarized countries, where the warmongering groups do not get any popular support to enable their existence. On the other hand are some countries, such as the nine nuclear powers, where the segments of society that benefit by glorifying threats and violence are dominant. This was true in Crucé's time when a thirty-year war wrecked Europe. And this is true in this century, where a devastating war has the potential to wipe out human civilization.

Charles-Irénée Castel, abbé de Saint-Pierre, advanced Crucé's ideas, but limited them to the European arena. He belonged to a noble family and had obtained entry into Parisian high society through salons hosted by elite women authors. He also had connections to French royalty as he was appointed as a chaplain to the king's sister-in-law. In 1712, he proposed a peace plan introducing the idea of a confederation of the Christian states of Europe with a uniform economic policy and a common defence policy. He improvised the plan a few times in the following decade. Originally, he had proposed a global confederation much like Émeric Cruce, but he amended the plan to confine it to Europe for pragmatic reasons. His federation would allow member states to retain their political systems, while eschewing war to settle differences between them and defending each other in the case of external aggression. Therefore, some scholars consider his proposal to be a precursor of the present European Union. He was influenced by Hobbes's *Leviathan* to maintain domestic order and believed that there should be a supranational authority to maintain international stability. Such an authority could be governed by an assembly of the representatives of the participating states to resolve disputes and craft common policies. If any one state disobeyed the decisions of the federation, all other states would collectively use force against such a miscreant to establish order.

Saint-Pierre proposed that perpetual peace could be achieved if the states surrendered their right to make war and peace to a federation formed by a common will, which would ensure the protection of their basic interests such as internal stability, territorial integrity and growth of commerce. He also proposed that the union of Christian sovereigns should make peace with the Muslim rulers and that the European Union should encourage the Asian princes to form a similar union of their own.[10]

Some of the elements in this plan may be criticized for maintaining the status quo. But it cannot be denied that other elements are visionary and radical. They emphasize renunciation of war, promotion of diplomacy, expansion of trade, democratic voting to determine key policies of the union, rotating presidency of the senate, freedom of religion, common standards for weights and measures, and, most importantly, the provision that the commander-in-chief of the new federation would not belong to any sovereign family and that there would be a limit of 6,000 soldiers for the army of each kingdom. While Émeric Crucé had proposed Venice as the headquarters of the federal body, Saint-Pierre proposed Utrecht.

Kant and Perpetual Peace

Saint-Pierre inspired Immanuel Kant to advocate the idea of 'perpetual peace'. Kant was born in Kaliningrad, a part of Prussia that is today in Russia. He read theology and physics at the University of Königsberg and then taught logic and metaphysics at the same university. He shot to fame in 1781 with the publication of *Critique of Pure Reason*. Kant believed that nations, like individuals, must enter into a legal system through a union of states. He proposed a permanent congress of nations to deliberate differences and resolve them in a civil way, eschewing warfare.

Immanuel Kant was inspired by Saint-Pierre's peace plan. Initially, he echoed Saint-Pierre's proposal of a federation with supranational coercive powers. However, Kant slowly changed his mind as he was inspired by the birth of a republican state in France and in later years, he abandoned the idea of the use of force by the federation of states. He relied more on his interpretation of human destiny with the formation of a world republican state as the ultimate goal. He did not use the term 'end of history', but to Kant, the history of the human species would culminate in such a world republican state. We should be careful here to not confuse Kant's long-term objective of the world republican state with Dante's idea of universal monarchy. The latter would lead a global dictatorship, whereas Kant wanted a system where people would be the supreme power. In the interim period, he preferred a federation of sovereign states that were republican for such a body to succeed. He was so impressed by the republican state in France that he believed it to be potentially at the centre of an international republican union.

In 1795, he published his essay 'Perpetual Peace: A Philosophical Sketch' with the following articles:[11]

1. No Treaty of Peace Shall Be Held Valid in Which There Is Tacitly Reserved Matter for a Future War.
2. No Independent States, Large or Small, Shall Come under the Dominion of Another State by Inheritance, Exchange, Purchase, or Donation.
3. Standing Armies (*miles perpetuus*) Shall in Time Be Totally Abolished.
4. National Debts Shall Not Be Contracted with a View to the External Friction of States.
5. No State Shall by Force Interfere with the Constitution or Government of Another State.
6. No State Shall, *during* War, Permit Such Acts of Hostility Which Would Make Mutual Confidence in the Subsequent Peace Impossible: Such as the Employment of Assassins (*percussores*), Poisoners (*venefici*), Breach of Capitulation, and Incitement to Treason (*perduellio*) in the Opposing State.

Kant appealed, 'It follows that a war of extermination, in which the destruction of both parties and of all justice can result, would permit perpetual peace only in the vast burial ground of the human race. Therefore, such a war and the use of all means leading to it must be absolutely forbidden.'

This was more than 250 years before the development of atomic weapons and more than 300 years before the deployment of killer robots and hypersonic weapons in the armies of powerful nations. Kant had clearly foreseen the dangers of the arms race.

Kant proposed that the states should have republican constitutions for perpetual peace to become a reality.

If the consent of the citizens is required in order to decide that war should be declared (and in this constitution it cannot but be the case), nothing is more natural than that they would be very cautious in commencing such a poor game, decreeing for themselves all the calamities of war . . . But, on the other hand, in a constitution which is not republican, and under which the subjects are not citizens, a declaration of war is the easiest thing in the world to decide upon, because war does not require of the ruler, who is the proprietor and not a member of the state, the least sacrifice of the pleasures of his table, the chase, his country houses, his court functions, and the like.[12]

Kant believed that the rulers wanted wars and the people wanted peace. He did not foresee the menace of jingoism in future democracies. Since the publication of Kant's essay, wars have resulted in millions of deaths and some of these wars have had massive public support in the republican states. The US, Great Britain, India, Israel and France, which have the greatest tradition of democracies, have been waging wars with significant popular support during the last several decades. These republican countries also possess the weapons of final destruction, along with some of the authoritarian or military-dominated countries like China, Russia, Pakistan and North Korea.

Since Kant's publication of 'Perpetual Peace', nobody else has proposed an international federation of nations for over a hundred years. The Congress of Vienna in 1815 could have been used to establish an international federation had there been visionaries at the negotiating table. Instead, the four big powers—Russia, Austria, Prussia and Britain—mainly concentrated on expanding their respective territories and establishing a balance of power between themselves, ignoring the undercurrent of destructive nationalism in many countries. Subsequently, much of the world outside Europe was colonized and had no power to influence the shaping of the new order. The nineteenth century did not see any proposals for bringing the nations of the world together, either from statesmen or scholars. In 1899 and 1907, the Hague Peace Conferences proposed an arbitration mechanism to settle international disputes that did not materialize. In any case, the two conferences did not go as far as proposing a permanent federation. But they sowed the seeds of the future League of Nations.

Gandhi and Einstein

In the twentieth century, Mahatma Gandhi and Albert Einstein, both dedicated apostles of peace, made significant contributions to the debate on a world government versus a federation of nations. Einstein, like Dante, proposed a world government. Gandhi, like Émeric Crucé, Saint-Pierre and Kant, advocated a federation of states. The former changed our understanding of the universe, while the latter was the torchbearer of India's freedom movement. Although these stalwarts knew of each other, they lived on different continents and never met.

Gandhi was influenced by Leo Tolstoy's ideas, which in turn were inspired by Adin Ballou's non-violent resistance or non-resistance.[13] Tolstoy believed in non-violence and renunciation of enmity with everyone. Gandhi practised non-violence while leading India's freedom movement and adopted it as a strategy for societal transformation. On one occasion, when the freedom fighters set a police station of the British rulers on fire, thereby breaking the code of non-violence, Gandhi suspended the agitation for independence. Thousands of tomes have been written on his experiments with non-violence and civil disobedience, which can together be described as non-violent resistance. He went on to inspire many leaders around the world, particularly Dr Martin Luther King, Jr, of the US. The thinkers Gandhi was inspired by, and the leaders who followed him refrained from indulging in violence in their struggle against repression and injustice. Moreover, Gandhi also articulated profound views on how the world order should be structured on the principles of non-violence through a world federation of nations. But this aspect of his work has received relatively less attention.

Speaking at a public meeting in Rangoon on 9 March 1929, and
then writing in *Young India* on 4 April 1929, Gandhi proclaimed:

> My mission is not merely freedom of India, though today it
> undoubtedly engrosses practically the whole of my life and the
> whole of my time. But through realization of freedom of India,
> I hope to realize and carry on the mission of the brotherhood of
> man. My patriotism is not an exclusive thing. It is all-embracing
> and I should reject that patriotism which sought to mount upon
> the distress or the exploitation of other nationalities.[14]

In *All Men Are Brothers*, a UNESCO publication on Gandhi's thoughts
in his own words, we find the following:

> I do suggest that the doctrine [of non-violence] holds good
> also as between States and States. I know that I am treading on
> delicate ground if I refer to the late war. But I fear I must in
> order to make the position clear. It was a war of aggrandizement,
> as I have understood, on either part. It was a war for dividing
> the spoils of the exploitation of weaker races—otherwise
> euphemistically called the world commerce . . . It would be
> found that before general disarmament in Europe commences,
> as it must someday, unless Europe is to commit suicide, some
> nation will have to dare to disarm herself and take large risks.
> The level of non-violence in that nation, if that event happily
> comes to pass, will naturally have risen so high as to command
> universal respect. Her judgments will be unerring, her decisions
> firm, her capacity for heroic self-sacrifice will be great, and she
> will want to live as much for other nations as for herself.[15]

Gandhi's concept of non-violence envisaged encompassing the whole
world. He was a nationalist and internationalist at the same time and
imagined a world federation that would combine national interests

with global good. In 1942, he introduced a resolution at a meeting of the Indian National Congress, which was the principal liberation movement in India under colonial rule, that said:

> While the Indian National Congress must primarily be concerned with independence and defence of India in this hour of danger, the Committee is of the opinion that the future peace, security, and ordered progress of the world demand a world federation of free nations, and on no other basis can the problems of the modern world be solved. Such a world federation would ensure the freedom of its constituent nations, the prevention of aggression and exploitation by one nation over another, the protection of national ministries, the advancement of all backward areas and peoples, and the pooling of the world's resources for the common good of all.[16]

Gandhi's idea was in many ways close to Kant's concept of perpetual peace, but Gandhi believed that all nations, and not only the republican states, should belong to the federation of states. In his writings and speeches, he clarified that the world federation he had in mind would involve renunciation of arms by all member states. He did not see value in the collective use of force by the federation as advocated by some of the earlier exponents of the international federation of states, including Saint-Pierre. Gandhi went beyond the earlier exponents in extending the use of the federation's resources for the common good of humanity, particularly backward communities.

The Bombay Sarvodaya Mandal has compiled a sampling of Gandhi's views on world federalism published in *Young India* and *Harijan*, the two periodicals he edited. Some of his remarks published in these two journals provide clues to his inner thoughts. Writing in *Young India* on 17 July 1924, and again on 26 December of the same year, he strongly supported the interdependence of nations in a federal structure. He said that he was opposed to any notion of absolute independence and held that though an international federation was a long-term vision which could take years to become a reality, the countries should prepare themselves for such a future. Moreover, he thought that the nations of the world should consider interdependence on their own to create voluntary partnerships.[17]

Explaining his logic for renouncing violence in international affairs, he wrote in *Young India* on 21 October 1916 that the unity of nations had to be founded on superior moral fibre and this would involve giving up the use of gunpowder.[18] Gandhi was persistent about his proposal about the federation of nations and advocated it several times from the 1910s to the 1940s. About the same time that he moved the resolution in the Congress Party, he also made a strong plea in *Harijan* on 9 August 1942:

> Federation is undoubtedly a greater and nobler end for free nations. It is a greater and nobler end for them to strive to promote Federation than be self-centred, seeking only to preserve their own freedom . . . The very first step to a world Federation is to recognize the freedom of conquered and exploited nations.[19]

Gandhi's proposal of an international federation of states did not have any collective authority at its core. A few years later, Albert Einstein began advocating the idea of a global federation of states, but this would be headed by a world government with a monopoly on the use of arms.

Initially, Einstein wanted the US to produce a nuclear bomb to counter Hitler. He was aghast when the bomb was used against the Japanese population and a nuclear arms race between the US and the former Soviet Union threatened human extinction.

In 1946, Einstein suggested that the only hope for the survival of humanity was a world government. He proposed: 'A world government must be created which is able to solve conflicts between nations by judicial decision. This government must be based on a clear-cut constitution which is approved by the governments and nations and which gives it the sole disposition of offensive weapons.' In order to realize Einstein's vision, it was necessary for every state to surrender its armed forces and weapons to the international authority. By the time he wrote his essay, the UN had already been established, but Einstein did not consider the UN to be the world government of his dreams because it did not control the world's military. The only other way forward was an agreement between the US and the former Soviet Union to disarm themselves and persuade other countries to follow them. But this would require mutual trust.[20]

Einstein believed that the world government would be ineffective if it merely depended on moral authority, as any powerful state could bypass it. Therefore, he proposed that there be an international arbitration mechanism to resolve conflicts between countries, and the power to wage war monopolized by the collective leadership of the federation. With these two conditions, Einstein very much reflected Saint-Pierre's proposals with global application. He believed that in the absence of a supranational authority, the world would slide into a major war.

In order to move towards global disarmament, Einstein proposed a concrete plan, the first step of which would be the mutual inspection of military facilities by major powers. This should be concomitant with an exchange of scientific and technical knowledge between them in spheres that would have implications for the arms race. The next step would be an exchange of military personnel between the major powers and gradual recruitment of soldiers and technicians for a supranational military force. Simultaneously, the major powers would begin drafting the constitution of the supranational military command and the international arbitration institution. Once there was an agreement between the big powers, all other nations would be invited to join the supranational organization. In the end, national armies would be disbanded.[21]

Even though Einstein lamented the weakness of the UN he preferred to create the world government through the UN, since it had already come into existence, and he saw no value in reinventing the wheel. Writing in the *Atlantic* in November 1947, he suggested that the world government should solely deal with hard security and military matters and not try to be too expansive in its mandate by including economic and other agendas.[22] As we shall see, he was almost prophetic in this approach as the UN has now become so overburdened with the economic and social agenda that it has proved to be substantially ineffective in maintaining peace and security and preventing wars.

Einstein extensively advocated his proposition from 1945 until his death in 1955, emphasizing that the world government had to be created through negotiations between countries, irrespective of their political systems, and not by the victors of a future war.

League of Nations

In the debate between the world government and the federation of states, the federation approach found acceptance in the realm of international politics in the last century. About 300 years after Émeric Crucé outlined his framework of a global and inclusive federation, the first serious effort to create such an organization was made in the aftermath of the First World War in 1920. In the last hundred years, the League of Nations and the UN have existed as live experiments in operating an international federation of states, albeit much weaker than imagined by Crucé, Saint-Pierre, Kant and Mahatma Gandhi.

The League of Nations was the first intergovernmental organization established for the maintenance of peace. It resulted from the Paris peace conference of 1919 to 1920, though its genesis can be traced to various private initiatives in the UK, France and the US from 1915 to 1919. For example, international women's peace groups were very active in demanding a new intergovernmental organization to resolve conflicts between countries through negotiation and arbitration. In the midst of the First World War, British and American think tanks floated proposals for institutional structures. In 1919, a drafting committee for the covenant of the future League of Nations was established under US President Woodrow Wilson's chairmanship, with members from the

US, several European nations, China and Japan.[23] At the time of the foundation of the organization, forty-four states signed the covenant, with more members gradually joining it, taking the maximum number of members to fifty-eight in 1935.[24]

The Swiss government provided a palatial building to the League to set up its office on the shores of Lake Geneva. Presently, it is the head office of the UN High Commissioner for Human Rights and is named Palais Wilson after US President Wilson. The street where it is located is Quai Wilson, and a hotel in the adjoining building is President Wilson.

The core structure of the League was not too different from today's UN. It had three layers, including the general assembly, the council made up of permanent and non-permanent members, and the secretariat. In addition, it had some specialized organs associated with it.

The main business of the League was to resolve conflicts between countries. Accordingly, it was involved in the Åland crisis between Finland and Sweden; the Corfu dispute between Greece and Italy; the Hatay region dispute between Turkey and Syria; the Mosul dispute between Iraq and Turkey; and the Leticia dispute between Peru and Colombia, among others. However, three of the five permanent members of the League's council were involved in invading other countries, and the League could not prevent their breach of international peace and security: Japan invaded Manchuria in 1931–32; Italy annexed Ethiopia in 1936; and Germany attacked Austria in 1938.

The League had the lofty objective of achieving worldwide disarmament. Several proposals for arms control had been in circulation for twenty to thirty years, particularly debated at the Hague Peace Conferences, and the League convened an international disarmament conference in the 1930s. Although it seemed that there was agreement on disarmament principles in the beginning, as mentioned earlier, it collapsed after Hitler's election in Germany, leading to Germany's withdrawal from the conference as well as the League of Nations. Japan, too, withdrew around the same time.

Therefore, the League failed in its two primary objectives: collective security and disarmament. As a result, it could not prevent the outbreak of the Second World War, and the failure of the organization in achieving its noble goals has become the subject of study by many scholars.

The League was formed in haste in 1920 without a strong foundation. At the time of its creation, the US, Germany and the former Soviet Union were not its members. Germany joined in 1926 and the former Soviet Union in 1934. The US never joined. In some quarters, the League was seen as a personal tribute to President Wilson and not as an American project. President Wilson failed to get the US Senate on board, particularly on the matter of collective security, as the Senate did not want the US to provide military aid to resolve conflicts and maintain peace. Thus, they did not support the League's core objective. Also, the American defence industry was opposed to disarmament plans. President Wilson, however, insisted on including the covenant of the League in the Treaty of Versailles, forcing other countries to accept it. He established an ambitious organization without the US taking any responsibility for it; in the absence of some of the most influential countries from the League of Nations, it became a hollow organization. The membership was constantly changing, not expanding, with some members joining and some leaving the organization from time to time.

During the lifetime of the League of Nations, forces of hyper-nationalism and fascism gathered strength in Germany, Italy, Japan and the former Soviet Union, among other countries. Obviously, extreme nationalism was intrinsically opposed to international cooperation. Many countries in Asia and Africa were under colonial rule and hardly had any voice in international affairs. The League was, therefore, reduced to a club of its original permanent members: Britain, France, Italy and Japan.

The League of Nations succeeded in promoting international cooperation in socio-economic areas, including labour, health, education, transport and refugees. It brought about significant technical cooperation in these fields by convening meetings for exchanges and cooperation between experts from different countries, resulting in many conventions and agreements. But the most significant contribution of the League was that an idea of an intergovernmental organization was now accepted in the minds of statesmen and diplomats. Until the League was founded, for over 600 years, an international federation of nations was a theoretical proposition in scholars' pamphlets and books. The League made it a functioning reality, however feeble and vacuous. That finally made the founding of the UN feasible.

The United Nations

The UN was founded in 1945 with fifty-one member states. Currently, it has 193 states as members and two associate members (Vatican City and Palestine). It is a truly global federation of nations, including almost all countries on the planet. In the universality of its membership, it has far surpassed the League of Nations. It has its headquarters in New York with other offices in Geneva, Vienna, the Hague and Nairobi.

The concept of the UN was developed in Washington, DC, and London, much like the League of Nations. Committees were set up in the US State Department and the British Foreign Office to develop proposals for an institutional architecture after the end of the Second World War, and President Roosevelt took a personal interest in the groundwork being done by the State Department on the future UN. His Secretary of State Cordell Hull put Leo Pasvolsky in charge of the secretive 'advisory committee on the post-war foreign relations'. Pasvolsky brought with him an inclusive approach that gave a special role to the big powers but not an absolute veto in matters of decision-making. He wanted a democratic world where the big powers would not have excessive control, but in this he was opposed by other groups in the US State Department and the former Soviet Union, with Moscow insisting on an absolute veto. Finally, a compromise was reached whereby the big powers were given a veto on substantive matters, but not on the procedural ones. Pasvolsky was also the lead author of the

Charter of the UN and the main negotiator in finalizing its provision in consultation with the key players.[25]

The Charter of the UN says:

We the peoples of the United Nations determined

- to save succeeding generations from the scourge of war, which twice in our lifetime has brought untold sorrow to mankind, and
- to regain faith in fundamental human rights, in the dignity and worth of the human person, in the equal rights of men and women and of nations large and small, and
- to establish conditions under which justice and respect for the obligations arising from treaties and other sources of international law can be maintained, and
- to promote social progress and better standards of life in larger freedom,

And for these ends

- to practice tolerance and live together in peace with one another as good neighbours, and
- to unite our strength to maintain international peace and security, and
- to ensure, by the acceptance of principles and the institution of methods, that armed force shall not be used, save in the common interest, and
- to employ international machinery for the promotion of the economic and social advancement of all peoples,

Have resolved to combine our efforts to accomplish these aims.[26]

The structure of the UN is in some ways similar to the League of Nations. It has a Security Council with permanent and non-permanent members, a General Assembly of all member states, a permanent secretariat headed by the secretary general and a plethora of adjunct organizations. Following the League of Nations, and in a hugely greater proportion, the UN has facilitated social and economic cooperation. There are nineteen independent bodies under the auspices of the UN that deal with food and agriculture, development, environment, climate change, finance, atomic energy, civil aviation, labour, education, health, industry, telecommunication, tourism, drugs and refugees. There are also ad hoc committees. For instance, UN Water brings together more than twenty-five stakeholder organizations. There are many regional social and economic commissions and thousands of quasi-governmental initiatives on global cooperation. Currently, the UN is promoting Sustainable Development Goals to be achieved by 2030 in seventeen dimensions of human development.

The question is whether in the pursuit of its development agenda, the UN has ignored its peace and security objectives, the primary reason for which it was set up. The Preamble of the UN Charter opens with 'to save succeeding generations from the scourge of war', an objective in which it has mostly failed.

First, the UN has not been able to prevent wars. Second, the UN has not managed to restrain the arms race. The League of Nations, too, had failed in realizing these two objectives, which resulted in the Second World War. Will the failure of the UN with respect to these objectives lead to the Third World War and the end of human civilization? The successes of the organization in social and economic spheres do not make up for its failure to achieve peace and disarmament.

Some of the limitations of the UN are latent in its structure. Although it is called the United Nations Organization, it really functions as a 'United Governments Organization'. Daisaku Ikeda, the Japanese philosopher, points out that the Preamble of the UN Charter is in the name of 'we the people', but the UN has always acted as an organization of governments. He says: 'All its decisions have been made by those governments and the people have been relegated to the backstage.'[27] At its heart, it is a federation of states, although it cannot be denied that it does create opportunities to listen to the voices of civil society on the margins. Those who conduct UN affairs are ambassadors and plenipotentiaries of the member states. In such a federation, national sovereignty and territorial integrity are cardinal principles.

The UNSC is the highest organ of the organization. In order to attract major powers, the founding fathers provided for five states to be permanent members with a veto—against the advice of Leo Pasvolsky, as we have seen. This has created internal contradictions. Without such a monopoly of power, the big powers may not want to be in the UN; with such powers, the UN has created a discriminatory hierarchy rooted in the 1940s. The world has changed since then and will continue to change in the future. In a dynamic world, five states having permanent veto powers open up fault lines in the international system rather than resolving conflicts. As a result, the UNSC is often paralysed due to the deadlock between its permanent members.

The genocide of Srebrenica in Bosnia and Herzegovina in July 1995, in the aftermath of the breaking up of Yugoslavia, is one of the moments of shame in the UN's history. More than 8,000 Bosnian men and boys were killed under the UN's watch in about a week in that fateful month. The UNSC had declared Srebrenica a 'safe area' in the spring of 1993 at the initiative of the US, France and Britain, but not enough troops were deployed for the protection of these safe areas. In the UN Secretary General's assessment, some 35,000 troops were required to protect the local Bosnian population from the Serb troops trying to massacre them. But only 7,000 troops were provided due to inefficient decision-making in the UNSC. The Serb troops led by General Ratko Mladic, who was later found guilty of war crimes, crimes against humanity and genocide, overran the UN zone.[28] The UNSC was paralysed because the US, Britain and France were ready to support the beleaguered people of Bosnia, but Russia was firmly on the side of Serbia. Article 2(4) of the UN Charter prohibits member states from breaching the territorial integrity and political independence of any country. This essentially means that if any country uses force against another country, it violates the provisions set out in

Article 2(4) and makes such a country liable to be termed an aggressor by the UNSC. However, this very body failed to term Serbia as an aggressor as it would then have ipso facto triggered the provisions of Chapter VII of the UN Charter.[29] Chapter VII allows the UNSC to authorize the use of military force if, in its opinion, there is a threat to international peace. By failing to apply Chapter VII, the UN avoided military action to contain Serbia. On the twentieth anniversary of the Srebrenica, massacre in 2015, the UNSC acknowledged its failure in protecting the people of Srebrenica, which led to the genocide of many Bosnian Muslims. Even on this occasion, Russia vetoed a UNSC Resolution, which would have used the term 'genocide' to describe the mass killing of 8,000 Bosnian Muslims.[30]

Another genocide that the UNSC failed to prevent took place in Rwanda in the early 1990s. In 1994, the then Hutu–dominated regime killed ten UN peacekeeping officers to prevent international intervention, and the UN wanted to flee from the scene. In only three months, the Hutus brutally murdered about 8,00,000 Tutsis and raped nearly 2,50,000 women in Rwanda, while UN troops abandoned the victims or just stood by as spectators while the horrific and brutal violence raged on.[31] Observers familiar with the UNSC deliberations during the period say that the council's time was primarily consumed by the question of withdrawing the peacekeepers, ignoring the need to strengthen the mission to save the local population.[32]

The next major clash that has turned into a disaster is the Syrian conflict, which has resulted in half a million deaths in ten years from 2011 to 2021, and seemed to be unending at least until the autumn of 2022. The UNSC has been plagued by the constant use of vetoes by its permanent members blocking any serious effort to resolve the conflict and stop the violence. The first series of vetoes, cast in October 2011 and February 2012, blocked resolutions that contained condemnatory statements and threatened sanctions against the Assad regime. In July 2012, a resolution, if it had not been vetoed, would have imposed sanctions on the Assad regime if it did not cease troop movements and the use of heavy weaponry in and around population centres. In May 2014, another veto was cast that blocked a resolution on the referral of the situation in Syria to the International Criminal Court.[33] Other vetoes have precluded access to humanitarian agencies in Aleppo and the prevention of the use of chemical weapons. As late as September 2019, Russia and China blocked a resolution that would have demanded an end to fighting in the Syrian province of Idlib, the final stronghold of the opposition.[34]

If the permanent members of the UNSC can stubbornly refuse the resolution of conflicts in Bosnia and Syria, it is easy to imagine how they would behave if there is a situation of a conflict directly involving them. If the present structure continues, it will prove to be increasingly ineffective. If it is changed to deprive the established powers of their privileges, they may leave the organization, making it hollow. It is worth recalling how Germany and Japan left the League of Nations in the 1930s.

There is no way to establish justice if one or more permanent members decide to attack another country, either with or without the sanction of the UNSC. Such attacks have taken place since the birth of the UN and been justified on ideological grounds. There is no mechanism in the UN to challenge the permanent members when they violate peace and security, and to force them to modify their behaviour. Therefore, collective security provisions mostly apply to conflicts between relatively smaller nations.

The UN has no enforcement powers. It does not have an army or a court empowered to deliver legally binding judicial decisions. The UNSC can introduce economic sanctions, but this is never possible against permanent members since they can use their veto to block the resolution aimed at them or their close allies.

Ikeda recommends that the UN General Assembly be brought to the centre of UN decision-making, as the UNSC wields too much power yet delivers little result when it comes to bringing about lasting peace. 'The current state of the United Nations—with the UNSC in a position of pre-eminence and the General Assembly playing a subordinate role—is undesirable. If we are to enhance the qualities of what should become a parliament of humanity, I believe we should do all we can to strengthen and further empower the General Assembly.'[35] It might be possible to find creative ways to enhance the role of the General Assembly to balance partially the powers of the UNSC. The question is, if there exists political will to bring about such a reform. Many countries would prefer to find a place for themselves in the UNSC than increase the institutional powers of the General Assembly.

Several authors have analysed the strengths and weaknesses of the UN. It is the only federation of states that includes almost all countries in the world. This itself is a great advantage to the world community as it provides a platform for every nation on an equal basis. The UN has contributed tremendously to the development and security of several generations of people. It has given birth to many new concepts. But it has a limited capacity to maintain peace and promote disarmament, particularly where the national interests of the big powers or their allies are involved. It has passed a resolution adopting a treaty to prohibit nuclear weapons, but it has not succeeded in convincing the nations possessing such weapons to give up their arsenal. The reduction of nuclear weapon arsenals by Reagan and Gorbachev took place outside of the UN framework.

At this time, hypersonic weapons, lethal autonomous weapons and cyberweapons are being developed by most of the nine nuclear weapon–owning states. It is still early days, but the nuclear weapons powers will deploy them in battle-ready condition before long, and indeed the US, China and Russia have already inducted them into their defence forces. There is nothing to indicate that the UN has the capacity to prevent the use of such weapons of final destruction and save people from the scourge of war.

Beyond a Federation

As we have seen, in the last 700 years, several proposals for establishing a federation of states were floated by scholars, kings and governments. We have discussed the main contours of the debate between the idea of the world government and the proposal for the federation of states. Let us make a quick summary review of the main features of these proposals before we look at the future.

Dante and Einstein wanted a world government supported by a monopoly on military power. Both had pious intentions, but they did not foresee the dangers of concentrating political prowess and military forces into a centralized authority.

The federation envisaged by Émeric Crucé, abbé de Saint-Pierre, Kant and Gandhi emphasized a number of points: the reduction or abolition of armed forces by individual member states; arbitration mechanisms to resolve conflicts between federation members; use of collective security for the defence of members from external aggression or against a miscreant member trying to destabilize the union; non-interference in the internal affairs of member states; and economic incentives and free trade to bolster the union.

The essence of these proposals was that the individual states would surrender their sovereign right to make war and peace to the federation, which would design a mechanism for collective decisions and create a way to arbitrate and resolve disputes between the members. Most of the proposals were aimed at reducing armaments to the minimum, or possibly eliminating them altogether. In these two respects, the League of Nations and the UN were fundamentally different. Neither organization had the mandate for the elimination of weapons, surrendering the right of making war and peace to the federation or for carrying out binding international arbitration of disputes. In fact, both the League and the UN emphasized the principle of national sovereignty.

The League of Nations did not include the most influential states in the world for much of its lifetime and could not convince the US to join at any stage. Moreover, the countries under colonization could not participate in its functions in a free and effective way. It did not have a strong conflict resolution machinery, with the questions on war and peace being determined from a nationalist perspective and not from a universal human angle. The League tried to reduce arsenals, but a disarmament conference convened to discuss these arrangements failed without any conclusion.

The UN is the first federation of states with universal membership. It provides collective security in specific conflicts, mostly in countries where the veto-bearing permanent members have marginal interest. The members have not surrendered their right to make war and peace to the federation, and the diplomacy on the arms race and arms control mostly takes place outside the UN framework. There is no arbitrary mechanism in place to make binding decisions that would apply to other states. Further, the UN has no army or any other enforcement capability to implement decisions in the maintenance of peace and security.

The UN does not reflect the visions enunciated by Émeric Crucé, abbé de Saint-Pierre, Kant and Gandhi. It has not prevented wars and it cannot be trusted to prevent any major global conflict, particularly if it involves the permanent members or their allies.

The theoretical and functional propositions for the proposed international federations have always considered the state as the basic unit. Rousseau has explained that states and not men are primarily responsible for wars. He writes in *The Social Contract*:

> Men are not naturally enemies, if only because in their original independence they do not have sufficiently stable relationships to constitute either the state of peace or of war. War is not a relation between man and man, but between State and State. There, private individuals are enemies only by accident, not as men or even as citizens, but as soldiers—not as members of the homeland, but only as its defenders. And they can be killed only while armed and acting as defenders; once they lay down their arms and cease to be soldiers, they become simply men again, and no one has any longer a right to their lives.[36]

Rousseau asks in *A Lasting Peace*:

> Each one of us being in the civil state as regards our fellow citizens, but in the state of nature as regards the rest of the world, we have taken all kinds of precautions against private wars only

to kindle national wars a thousand times more terrible, and that in joining a particular group of men, we have really declared ourselves the enemies of the whole race?[37]

The centrality of the state in warfare is the reason why all thinkers from Dante to Gandhi have concentrated on the relations between states, and not people. This is also the reason why the UN is a 'United Governments Organization'. But the modern state, singularly or collectively, is not competent to manage many kinds of global dynamics. These include fast-spreading infectious diseases, as we saw in the case of COVID-19, or environmental catastrophes such as hazardous smoke from forest fires and radiation. We live in a dual world where the states are units for organizing societies as well as for conducting competition between countries, but forces outside their purview enable intercourse between countries and societies. States have no control over natural phenomena: rivers flow without caring for national borders; diseases do not need passports to spread; and atmospheric gases are not limited in their ability to travel the world.

A federation of states cannot provide an adequate remedy to the fault lines experienced by humankind, often resulting in wars, because states are only relevant to some aspects of human affairs. If the relations between people and societies around the world must be recalibrated, we need to develop a dual approach. We need one track involving relations between states and another one involving relations between the individual and the world. In 1762, Rousseau showed how a social contract could create a civil state within a society. Since then, the world has been intensely integrated, making total reliance on the societal social contract within national boundaries redundant to address our challenges. The time is upon us now to forge a global contract.

6

Morning at Last: A World without War

Hope Valley is a small town in the coal-mining region of Alberta, Canada. In this town, ordinary people go out of their way to nurture the community. Children gift their favourite toys to the young ones in newcomer families. Little girls competing to play Mary in the Christmas pageant abandon their moment of glory to protect friendships. Adults open their homes for miners injured in a mudslide. A bride offers her banquet to famished neighbours who have lost their belongings in a flood. The compassion of the Hope Valley residents is seen not only in calamities. It can be observed in many small things during daily life. A restaurateur always finds free hands willing to repair her kitchen. A nurse cancels her wedding to a banker in another city in order to serve the ailing. A bandit becomes a pastor. An heiress becomes a schoolteacher. An orphan becomes a son. It is a town where jealousies, corruption and suspicions prevail like any other small town.

But the wise folks of Hope Valley believe that a habit of happily living together and understanding one another is better than squabbling for profit or ego.

There is only one person in Hope Valley who enjoys fostering confrontation. He is rich, greedy and cunning. He is the mayor; and he knows how to capture power, even though his ethos is not the same as that of the people. The town folk build their community of care despite the mayor's antics. They go on constructing the fabric of society and finally change his mind.

This fictional town in the Hallmark series *When Calls the Heart* has become popular in many parts of the world because, deep inside our hearts, we want to live in Hope Valley. We cherish kindness. We appreciate empathy. We long for togetherness.

In many regions of the world, north as well as south, towns and villages like Hope Valley exist. In thousands of such milieus, civility and kindness triumph over hatred and vanity. With the advent of technology, we have even created international hope communities.

Our spirit of humanity is especially kindled when a disaster takes place due to nature's fury or human folly. Visuals of the elderly and children in distress pull at our heartstrings. The human capacity for compassion for victims of disasters in faraway places is truly remarkable. It is natural that people primarily rush to the aid of victims in their vicinity. In an earthquake or a flood, many Samaritans risk their own lives to rescue stranded people. Communities donate food, clothes and money to help the needy. Emergency mass kitchens pop up. Volunteers appear in the hundreds from nowhere. We see this happening in different parts of the world almost every day. Whether it is a train accident or a burst dam, there is always a reservoir of empathy. When such a sentiment is extended to victims of calamities in other countries, where there is no personal investment, it is only because of the subconscious association we feel with humankind.

Much like Hope Valley, people around the world do not confine their human spirit to adversities. We like to love, respect and help despite our ego, jealousies and other frailties. We cry when death assaults our lives. We laugh when life wins.

It is human nature to be considerate. But then, why do we glorify violence and accept the weapons of final destruction? It is because we humans have created states that tend to be malevolent. These states have convinced us to swallow the poison of nationalism and made us forget our humanity.

States brawl with each other for any and every reason they can invent. The *Onion*, an American satirical magazine, published a headline about the eve of the First World War: 'Austria declares war on Serbia declares war on Germany declares war on France declares war on Turkey declares war on Russia declares war on Bulgaria declares war on Britain. Ottoman empire declares war on itself.'[1]

If the *Onion* were to tell the story of the 2020s, it would publish the same headline with a different cast of players: 'Russia declares war on the US declares war on North Korea declares war on Japan declares war on China declares war on India declares war on Pakistan declares war on Israel declares war on Iran declares war on Saudi Arabia declares war on Turkey declares war on Greece. Brazil, feeling left out, declares war on itself. Nations struggle to distinguish between allies and enemies. Switzerland leads fifty countries to proclaim neutrality. Rival alliances come together to confer on whether they should bomb neutral states, whose peaceful actions insult the glory of war, before they annihilate each other.'

When left to themselves, states articulate general will from Rousseau's social contract: this represents the legitimate political community. Common interest must underpin general will. Those who control states look to expand their authority. If they try to coerce in the pursuit of power, it does not reflect general will. Neither does coercion serve common interest. Rousseau suggests that people can overthrow such rulers.

Beyond the boundaries of nation states, there is no legitimate political community. As there is no general will between countries, there is no common interest. States do not hesitate to encroach on others when it is opportune for them. If each state tries to expand its sphere of influence or its territory, sooner or later, it is bound to confront and come in conflict with others. Some states in some periods may observe restraint, but the possibility of war does not disappear.

Immanuel Kant and others believed that the formation of a federation would create a social contract between states reflecting 'common general will' underpinned by mutual interest. It was a pious hope. States have treated federations more as markets to bargain for their national interest than as political communities to find a common purpose. When they indeed discovered unity of purpose, they created a political community and eschewed wars, as in the European Union since the 1950s. Otherwise, they have pursued national interests without any bounds. The so-called national interest is often a euphemism for the ruler's ambition or ego and the so-called national glory is the manipulation of patriotism for the worship of violence. States ignore federations by pretending to honour a holy book or a rectangular standard, hiding their ulterior motive of profiteering and greed. The examples of this over the years are aplenty: Japan quit the League of Nations when it wanted to attack Manchuria; the US snubbed the UN when it wished to bomb Iraq, and so on.

Since a federation of states does not seem to be capable of ending wars, it is necessary to conceive of a global social contract for humankind where people can find a general will beyond national frontiers and voluntarily harness the common interest of our planet, the only known world in the universe inhabited by humans.

Boundaries of States

The goal of the human race should be to establish a global social contract that eliminates war and violence and creates scope for actualizing the greatest good of our species. If we do not aim for such an objective, there is a risk of increasingly lethal armaments devouring our species. There is no middle way. On the one hand, the survival of human civilization is at stake and on the other is the prospect of its advancement. The main obstacle in this journey is the propensity of states to aggrandize their interests by using violence on a massive scale.

A small beginning has been made in the journey towards the right direction, with over twenty nations having renounced arms. Some have abdicated wars for decades and a few of them for centuries. These states are beacons of hope, but they are relatively few in number. It is not realistic to expect an instant transformation of the world from one where most states do not hesitate to wage wars to one where all choose to abolish war forever. Thus, it is necessary to progress in phases.

The next phase should be to confine wars only to the institutional boundaries of the rival states. A war is an act involving two or more states where the objective is to threaten, pre-empt, undermine, humiliate or even destroy the opponent. However, many a time, states do not confine their assault to the institutional boundary of the rival state. They wilfully ravage societies beyond the state structure, for example, by bombing schools, monuments, hospitals, civilian infrastructure and population centres. This is not a war; it is criminal aggression against a part of humankind. In order to distinguish between hostile actions between states and those aimed at the greater society beyond the state structure of another country, it is necessary that we understand the conceptual boundaries of a state.

A state is more than a government but less than a society. It is an organized political community in the society. It is a plethora of institutions underpinning the government. Such institutions include the political leadership, civil service, legislature, judiciary, security forces, political institutions, defence production capacity and all other organizations that are engaged in the accumulation and exercise of power vis-à-vis constituents of the country or other countries. The society includes population centres, educational institutions, health facilities, agriculture, industry, civil infrastructure and civil society, in addition to the institutions of the state. Some organizations, such as scientific research centres and defence production facilities, can overlap between the conceptual horizon of the state and the society outside it. The hospitals and schools owned by the government can be part of the state by ownership, but outside it by their use or by the absence of relevance to the accumulation and exercise of power.

The sovereignty of a nation rests in the state, which exercises general will. The state is responsible for the formulation and implementation of laws. Outside of the state, society is fabricated by formal and informal social relations, which are conducted through customs and voluntary actions.

It is the state that conducts a war and not society, though the latter may be persuaded or manipulated to support an armed conflict. Some ingredients required to sustain a war, such as food for soldiers, scientific and technological input, heavy metals and equipment, may be obtained from the society; in fact, such input may also be obtained from a foreign society. It is common knowledge that often offensive equipment used in warfare by countries is imported from abroad and manufactured by commercial enterprises in some third country. Notwithstanding the fact that the society arranges supply lines for several of the essential requirements of the state, it is not the same as the state.

International Humanitarian Law (IHL) prohibits attacks against parts of society which are not engaged in combat. It establishes, as per Article 22 of Geneva Convention IV that 'the right of belligerents to adopt means of injuring the enemy is not unlimited'. Certain fundamental principles of IHL as codified in the Geneva Conventions are pivotal in limiting the effects of armed conflicts. These principles relate to humanity, proportionality and military necessity. Most significantly, the principle of distinction is fundamental and provides that the parties to an armed conflict must 'at all times distinguish between the civilian population and combatants and similarly between civilian objects and military objects and accordingly shall direct their operations only against military combatants and objects'.[2] This implies that random attacks and the use of indiscriminate means and methods of warfare are prohibited. But we only have to take a look at the rubble of schools and hospitals in current war-ravaged zones of the world for ample evidence of how this principle is violated regularly.

In astronomy, there is an event horizon denoting the boundary that clearly indicates the outer limit of a black hole. Similarly, there is an 'event horizon' around the state, and IHL makes a distinction between combating and non-combating dimensions of the state. The fact that the state controls population and territory and cannot exist without them does not mean that the state itself is the population and the territory. No state can legitimately engage in indiscriminate destruction of the parts of society which do not constitute the rival state.

The weapons of final destruction are, by their very nature, indiscriminate. They do not recognize boundaries of states and annihilate whole societies. They may even damage neighbouring countries that are not involved in the hostilities. Thus, we have to accept that they have been developed in violation of IHL. In 1996, the International Court of Justice concluded that the use of nuclear weapons would be generally contrary to the principles and rules of IHL. However, it used confusing language, allowing the use of nuclear weapons in an extreme situation where the survival of the state would be in jeopardy. The Court said: 'In view of the current state of international law and of the elements of fact at its disposal, [it] cannot conclude definitively whether the threat or use of nuclear weapons would be lawful or unlawful in an extreme circumstance of self-defence, in which the very survival of a State would be at stake.' This opinion of the court has been criticized for its ethical ambiguity. It is not firmly either here or there. This is despite the fact that about 4 million 'declarations of public conscience' in forty languages against nuclear weapons were delivered to the Court as an expression of public opinion.[3] The Court seems to have forgotten that there might be many realities in diplomacy, but only one truth in morality.

In 2012, Switzerland, on behalf of several countries, told the First Committee of the UN that all rules of IHL apply fully to nuclear weapons, notably the rules of distinction, proportionality and precaution, as well as the rules of prohibition on causing superfluous injury or unnecessary suffering and prohibition on causing widespread, severe and long-term damage to the environment.[4] Prior to that, in 2011, the Council of Delegates of the International Red Cross and the Red Crescent Movement had adopted a resolution emphasizing not only the incalculable human suffering resulting from any use of nuclear weapons, but also stressing the incompatibility of such deadly weapons with the rules of IHL.[5]

The proponents of nuclear weapons, lethal autonomous weapons, hypersonic missiles, killer pathogens, neXt weapons and other weapons of final destruction in their arguments take refuge behind the fact that these weapons are not specifically mentioned in any of the Articles of the Geneva Conventions. However, such a specific reference is not necessary. Articles 51 and 54 of the Additional Protocol of the Geneva Conventions are comprehensive enough to cover the implications for all weapons of mass destruction. These Articles confirm general protection for the civilian population and individual civilians, as well as civilian objects, from all military operations. The experience of the bombing of Hiroshima and Nagasaki shows that it is impossible for nuclear weapons to observe the principle of distinction between civilian and military targets. Some lethal autonomous weapons and neXt weapons may be designed for precision attacks on military targets. But if they are combined with nuclear warheads, the social, economic and environmental consequences would be in violation of Articles 51 and 54 of the Additional Protocols. The consequences of future biological weapons for the civilian population would be catastrophic and unpredictable and, therefore, in direct violation of IHL. Nevertheless, the ICRC and other international organizations should explore how all weapons of final destruction, including those existing now and those that might be created in future, can be specifically brought under the ambit of IHL.

Following Rousseau, we can say that the state is the sovereign that expresses general will. A society cannot articulate general will. General will directs the state to the object for which it is constituted—

common good. What makes the will general is the common interest uniting people. Without general will, or common interest, the state has no purpose. Thus, the state cannot perform functions that may consciously destroy general will. The destruction of humankind with the weapons of final destruction in no way fulfils general will, since it is not logical for people in any society to have a common interest in the extermination of the population and prevention of the birth of future generations. The political elite in nuclear-armed countries may argue that their intent is not to destroy the population of their own countries but rather to protect them by threatening the destruction of an adversary state. Such thinking ignores the possibility that the enemy state can think in the same way and inflict minimum assured destruction. To flirt with the possibility of such minimum assured destruction, even to a marginal degree, is to expose segments of the population in nuclear-armed countries to the risk of extermination.

There are now two immediate tasks before the human race. The first is to force the world's leaders to agree to a phased elimination of all weapons of final destruction and to commit not to use science and technology in future to develop such weapons. As we have seen, such weapons should not be employed in wars between states since their consequences are bound to extend much beyond their boundaries. The second is to force the world's leaders to agree to the rules of war using conventional weapons and to observe the boundaries of states in warfare. The good news is that IHL already incorporates both demands, and there is no need for a novel legal instrument. However, the challenge that faces it is political. The real task is to persuade or force states to implement these provisions of the Geneva Conventions.

Beyond the 'Event Horizon'

At this stage, it is useful to assess the ability of individual states and the federations of states to address problems faced by humankind beyond the question of human extinction by the weapons of final destruction. Take the case of air pollution. Pure Earth, a think tank, says that air and water pollution moves all over the world and is not restricted to any one nation. Air particulates, heavy metals and some pesticides can move in the air and water and transmit globally through the food and product chains. Even if some states invest in pollution control technology, they are helpless if pollutants enter from another country. The Pure Earth report *Pollution Knows No Borders*, for example, suggests that a quarter of the air particulates in the San Francisco Bay Area come from China; Korea, Japan and other Asian countries transfer pollutants to one another via air currents;[6] and France is impacted by coal pollution from neighbouring countries in Europe. Other reports suggest that ozone travels from Southern Asia to Colorado. Emissions from industry and transport in the Asian countries react to form ozone in the presence of sunlight. This ozone from Asia then drifts across the Pacific Ocean to the US and impacts high-altitude sites such as the Yellowstone and Yosemite national parks.

As air currents carry emissions from one part of the world to another, many glaciers have begun to retreat in the last 150 years. No continent has escaped this phenomenon within their middle latitudes—from the Tropic of Cancer to the Arctic and from the Tropic of Capricorn to the Antarctic. Mountain glaciers in North America, South America, Africa, Europe and Asia are retreating. Glaciologists have published detailed reports on how much specific glaciers have retreated in every region of the world. Writing in *National Geographic*, Daniel Glick narrates the story of the Glacier National Park in Montana, US.[7] It was created a hundred years ago, encompassing 150 glaciers. Now, only thirty of them remain in a diminished form, and they are expected to disappear by 2050. The water from melting glaciers flows into the sea where it warms, expands in volume, and contributes to rising sea levels.

There are many other examples to show how environmental disasters do not care for the authority of any state or the UN or any other federation of states. In late 2019, hundreds of wildfires spread in southeast Australia, burning millions of acres of forest land and killing animals by droves. By the beginning of 2020, media reported that the smoke from these forest fires had moved approximately 11,000 km across the South Pacific Ocean to Chile and Argentina.[8] There was nothing that the states in South America could do to stop the smoke from travelling to their territories. On this particular occasion, the smoke disappeared in a few days and there was no noticeable long-term impact in the South American countries. However, it is difficult to predict future dangers due to the flow of air currents and gases from one continent to another.

These stories are enough to show us that global warming cannot be addressed within the boundaries of individual states. Without immediate collective action, the damaging impact of climate change on the world will become irreversible. In this respect, international organizations have to lead the coordination efforts between states. But as we have seen, states tend to be guilty of protecting their parochial interests when they participate in any global dialogue rather than considering mankind's common future.

Another danger, recently made clear to us, is that of pandemics that can ravage human civilization if there is no proper cooperation between states. The Spanish Influenza that raged from 1918 to 1920 infected more than 100 million people out of the then world population of 2 billion, with some estimates putting the number of the infected at as high as 500 million.[9] It killed between 30 and 50 million people. In other words, that epidemic likely killed more people than the First World War, though accurate and verifiable estimates of death are not available. Although there are different hypotheses about the origin of the flu, it is largely held that the infection started in a military camp in Europe after it was transmitted from birds or animals, and it followed troop movements across the continent. It reached the US in the spring of 1918. Eventually, it killed millions of people in India, China, Japan, New Zealand, Brazil, Russia and Africa. Since this pandemic occurred immediately after the First World War, suitable infrastructure to contain the spread of the disease was not in place, nor were health facilities and nutrition adequately available for the victims. The capacity of institutions to respond to the crisis was particularly weak and, most significantly, there was no coordination between the various countries in the aftermath of the First World War. The aggregate impact was much worse than it should have been.

In the 1950s, the Asian flu spread from China to Singapore, then to the rest of East Asia and later to the US, from where it reached Great Britain. This pandemic lasted for around two years and claimed 1 to 2 million lives.[10] A decade later, it emerged again as the Hong Kong flu. Within a few months, it had proliferated to Southeast Asia, India, Northern Australia, Europe and California, claiming another 1 million victims.

In the first two decades of the twenty-first century, three pandemics threatened the world population. The first was the Severe Acute Respiratory Syndrome (SARS) virus identified in 2003. It was thought to be an animal virus from an as-yet-uncertain animal reservoir, perhaps bats, that spread to other animals (possibly civet cats) and first infected humans in the Guangdong province of southern China in 2002. The SARS epidemic affected twenty-six countries in North America, South America, Europe and Asia and resulted in more than 8,000 infections in 2003 and a death toll that was just under 1,000. This time, the World Health Organization (WHO) managed to encourage member states to cooperate to take preventive measures and develop a vaccine. As a result of this coordinated effort, the damage from this pandemic was limited as compared to others.[11]

A swine flu pandemic involving the H1N1 virus lasted for almost two years from January 2009. The official death toll confirmed by the WHO was 18,000.[12] But some research centres place it at a much higher number of around a quarter million[13]—about the same as people dying from seasonal flu every year. Originating from a pig farm in Mexico, the virus managed to travel all over the world within a matter of months, mostly spread by people travelling by air.

Although a number of coronaviruses have been circulating in the world for a while, a novel coronavirus, later named COVID-19, originated in 2019 and attacked the world at the beginning of 2020. It was set to infect 200 million people and cause more than 5 million deaths by the end of 2021. Originating in Wuhan, China, the pandemic spread to almost all the 200 countries and territories in the world, including to small islands in the Pacific Ocean. The impact of the exceptionally fast pace of the virus' spread was made worse by the absence of international cooperation in containing it. In September 2019, the Global Preparedness Monitoring Board, jointly established by the World Bank and the WHO, had publicly warned that a fast-moving pandemic causing respiratory infection could cause millions of deaths. In October 2019, an initiative of the Gates Foundation involving health leaders from public and private sectors in the US indicated that a fast-spreading pandemic could bring the world economy to a standstill. However, such prophetic warnings issued by eminent institutions were largely ignored, and by the end of January 2020, the WHO had declared a 'global health emergency' resulting from the novel coronavirus. Nevertheless, no urgent plans were announced by the governments of important countries to cooperate; this delayed an international response in terms of a coordinated ban on travel, mobilization of medical equipment such as masks and ventilators, or a joint search for a vaccine and remedial medicine.

Around the middle of February 2020, two weeks after WHO's declaration of a global health emergency, senior government ministers of several countries spent a few days together in a hotel in Munich at an international conference. Even at this stage, there was no indication of the government leaders having utilized their time together to discuss or plan an emergency response to a developing health crisis. Within a month following the meeting, country after country all over the world announced economic lockdowns and a ban on travel. Although initially these measures were expected to be in place for a short time, they had to be extended for almost two years. It was soon clear that the virus had not only created a health emergency, but it had also caused economic and humanitarian disasters. Even after the global economy was brought to a standstill and millions of people were suffering from disease as well as unemployment by the autumn of 2021, there was no evidence of the major powers engaging in international cooperation. On the contrary, as vaccines were gradually being developed in different countries in 2021, they indulged in competitive 'vaccine nationalism'.

We are familiar with environmental and health disasters. With the fast growth of modern technologies such as AI, synthetic biology and nanotechnology, we may be exposed to unpredictable risks in the future. Perhaps that future is not too far away when a new risk will emerge of AI evolving into Artificial General Intelligence, where algorithms will learn to operate on their own, write their own codes without human intervention and proliferate based on their own initiative. We have discussed in an earlier chapter how Stephen Hawking, Elon Musk and other experts have expressed concern about the AI overreach, including malicious algorithms spreading to critical infrastructure facilities such as electricity, water storage, nuclear plants, military high commands, financial markets and banks. They may interfere with the workings of such infrastructure facilities and damage them or impact their supplies and transactions, therefore, leading to a global catastrophe. In the next phase of development, AI will evolve into superintelligence, which is a technical term to denote machines that have acquired a thinking ability similar to humans and that can act on their own without human intervention. Even if it sounds fantastic, the time is perhaps not too far when such machines will develop the ability to create situations where they begin to control humans!

So far, Artificial General Intelligence and superintelligence are merely at the level of concepts in science fiction. Several scientists believe that such advanced, autonomous AI capacity beyond human control may become a reality within decades, though not within years. Max Tegmark, a leading AI researcher, has warned: 'We could one day lose control of AI systems via the rise of superintelligences that do not act in accordance with human wishes—and that such powerful systems would threaten humanity.'[14] Stephen Hawking told the BBC in 2014, 'The development of full Artificial Intelligence could spell the end of the human race.'[15] He continued to issue warnings on existential threats to humankind until his death in March 2018. Max Tegmark, Nick Bostrom, Martin Rees and other authors continue to caution the world on this subject.

The advancements in genomics and synthetic biology might also have worrisome consequences. Just as researchers may find cures to disease, in particular cancer and Alzheimer's, they may inadvertently create new pathogens or biological entities. Once self-replicating pathogens are born in laboratories and begin mutating on their own, biological agents that are not even imaginable to us today can devastate large parts of the population. Accidents have been known to occur in matters such as this. For example, Australian scientists accidentally created a fatal variant of the mousepox virus by adding the IL-4 gene at the beginning of the twenty-first century. In this case, the concerned scientists published their findings in a reputed journal. However, we cannot expect such high ethical standards in all cases; there might be instances that we may never know of, if information regarding them is treated in secrecy.[16]

There are risks that, in future, CRISPR, the technology to make genetic alterations in organisms, will be manipulated to produce chimaera by blending genes of two different species.[17] There are already some indications of Chinese scientists producing a hybrid of humans and monkeys. Such experiments, too, can accidentally produce biological entities that can threaten humans.

Based on world events till now, we can boast of no evidence which proves that any organization—the UN or another interstate entity or any individual state—possesses the required competence to prevent or control the consequences of technological and biological accidents, particularly if the resulting harmful organisms or viruses spread from one country to another within hours. Thus, it is questionable how the states or the UN will be able to prevent the spread of nuclear radiation, fissile material particles, debris and other forms of fallout, which will occur within a few hours of a nuclear attack. When states have time and again proven to be ineffective in managing issues with civilizational dimensions, it is extremely doubtful if they will be able to exert any control over newer technological advancements that may easily turn out to be detrimental to life on this planet.

Besides the efficacy issues discussed earlier, there are also ethical questions raised by Professor Martha Nussbaum. She says, 'We cannot solve the problem of global justice by envisaging international cooperation as a contract for mutual advantage among parties similarly placed in a state of nature.' In her view, the application of the social contract at the international level results in bargaining for national interest with other states. Moreover, states are represented by governments in the process of international bargaining, but in some cases, governments may not necessarily represent the people's interest. Nussbaum criticizes the accordance of 'moral person' status to a state: 'Let us now consider the analogy between states and "moral persons". One of its problems is that many nations of the world do not have governments that represent the interests of the people taken as a whole. Even when a nation has a government that is not a mere tyranny, large segments of the population may be completely excluded from governance.'[18]

Nussbaum rejects the Kantian social contract theory between states to advocate entitlements for the individual from the world at large. She is driven by a sense of justice, equality and human dignity. The mechanism she proposes is characterized by modified behaviour by states, multinational corporations and governments of rich countries to transfer resources, capabilities and human rights. Such an approach is reflected in human development indicators, sustainable development goals and universal basic income. It essentially treats the human development agenda as the global social contract. If fully realized at the global level, it will ensure that the human development needs of all people are satisfied. However, it does not explain how to manage the global catastrophic risks that are currently threatening human survival. Thus, as our previous efforts have proved to be ineffective in controlling mankind from hurtling down the path of self-destruction, it is now of utmost importance to conceive of an all-new global social contract premised on common interest among the world's people on civilizational issues.

Third Dimension

In this endeavour to find a more just path towards achieving the common good, it is necessary to extend the scope of the social contract to include one between the individual and the world. Although the social contract between individuals has existed for some time now, and institutional arrangements between states have been structured, the main function of such a third dimension will be to represent universal general will and produce common good of humankind in the aspects affecting our species' survival. The global social contract so created should go beyond the facets of human affairs that are already adequately addressed by states and interstate federations. This new contract should in fact be limited to civilizational issues such as the threat of the extinction of human civilization from the weapons of final destruction that exist today and new weapons that may be developed in future; threat of the fragmentation of human civilization from global warming and climate change; threat of the suspension of human civilization from pandemics; threat of extinction, fragmentation or suspension of human civilization from mishaps in the evolution, functioning and fusion of high technologies in AI and different branches of biology, physics and chemistry.

Generally, we find that political principles and laws stem from past experiences and present conditions and that they respond to specific requirements. For instance, separate arms control treaties are negotiated for different kinds of weapons, and as new weapons are developed, new treaties are required to prevent their proliferation. This approach precludes the anticipation and prevention of arms of the future that might be unimaginable today. To avoid such a pitfall the arrangements to be made under the global social contract must be forward-looking.

It has to be made clear that the global social contract is not a proposal to draft a treaty or a declaration. It is not another arms control agreement or a disarmament convention or a UN resolution. Instead, it is envisaged to be a living doctrine to realize universal common interest in securing human civilization from extinction, fragmentation or suspension on a continuous basis. Just as the social contract has worked for the last several centuries, the global contract is expected to underpin relationships in the centuries and millennia to come if humankind is not to annihilate itself in a cataclysmic global war. Such a global social contract will require a supranational institutional architecture to express the general will of humankind.

The supranational architecture should not be a representation of the system of states in any form. Presently, the UN member states nominate candidates to lead international organizations such as the main UN secretariat, WHO, World Trade Organization, Food and Agriculture Organization by lobbying for them. It is the same with regional organizations such as the Commonwealth, Organization for Security and Co-operation in Europe (OSCE) and regional development banks. The UN sometimes appoints independent panels to address a specific issue for which it asks member states to nominate candidates. Once in the panel, the members are expected to function independently, but they subconsciously represent the interests of their home country. A panel on new threats to global security may focus on terrorism if there are members from the Western states, or on the expansion of the UNSC if they are from India or Brazil, but not on the threats posed by lethal autonomous weapons or killer pathogens. Thus, even though a UN panel may function independently, if its members are appointed by the sovereign states, its recommendations are likely to reflect the concerns of the nominating states. It is, therefore, necessary that the states have no nominating authority or representation in the supranational architecture embodying the global social contract.

The supranational civilizational architecture thus created should engage with people around the world through various means of digital and direct communication. It should have powers to take decisions that are binding on the states, but these should only be confined to civilizational matters; it should not interfere in issues within the ambit of national governance. This new organization should also provide binding direction to the various associations of states, including the UN, on issues that may threaten the existence of human civilization. One of its major tasks should be to propose solutions based on compromise for conflicts between states so that there is no incentive to take recourse to arms.

Such an architecture can be the initial step for the transition to a global social contract. However, this should be conceived of in a creative way as it should not be mired in the current problems that plague our existing organizations, such as an excessive adherence to hierarchy; in any case today there are too many international organizations that do precious little to make any real difference in civilizational matters and adding to that tally will not make a difference. The new architecture can be a form of network that brings civilizational issues to surface in a dynamic process and pulls together the weight of the world's public opinion on government leaders to implement solutions. It may be possible to use technology to achieve this aim, though there are dangers of the technology being misused by vested interests. It must be underpinned by the moral unity of the world's people transcending national borders. The weight of such moral unity must be so significant that it can persuade powerful nation states to act for global good.

Eventually, the people of the world need to unite and legislate through a world parliament. It would be a long and arduous process to conceptualize such a parliament independent of states. It should be more effective and different from the current Inter-Parliamentary Union (IPU), which is a federation of current parliaments operating with the principle of state representation. Its activities are governed by the Speakers of member parliaments, who are intrinsically linked with their national governments. It is common to see parliamentary representatives of many countries representing the views of their respective states in the IPU assemblies.[19] The future world parliament must be based on a novel formula. If it is formed with nomination from the states, it would in effect become a platform for representing and negotiating states' interests, and if it is formed as per population, it would be dominated by the most populous countries. The European Parliament (EP), which is the only major multinational legislature, may inspire some ideas for the model of a world parliament. The EP membership composition is set out by the European Union treaties. The allocation of seats in the EP is not proportional to each state's population, nor does it reflect any particular mathematical formula; however, it is stated in the treaties that the distribution of seats should be 'degressively proportional' to the population of the member states. This means that the smaller states receive more places on a pro rata basis than the more populous states.[20] Other important questions will surface. For example, countries that have never experienced democracy and do not hold elections for their national legislature might not be willing to hold elections for a global one.

Several civil society organizations have launched a campaign to create the UN Parliamentary Assembly.[21] Many different formats of the proposed organization are under discussion. The easiest path would be the evolution of the IPU into a robust parliamentary body. Another option under discussion is the establishment of a subsidiary body under the UN General Assembly. But this option creates a hierarchy, giving primacy to the organization representing the states over the one representing people. The League of Nations had considered and rejected the proposal to create a People's Assembly in the 1920s. It is possible that the UN might reject a similar proposal in this century to avoid a turf competition. Those committed to having people's representation in global governance may have to contemplate other ways and means to pursue this objective.

The supranational organization to manage civilizational issues will also need an independent judicial organ. It is the perceived absence of justice that is at the root of violence. Justice ensures peace. And this is true at local, national and global levels. When we consider justice in the context of civilizational survival, we must be certain of the protection of the world's population from the scourge of a devastating war, or slow death from environmental, biological and technological mishaps, without any discrimination. This requires an effective mechanism for arbitration, conflict resolution and dispensation of justice.

The only mechanisms for international justice presently available are the International Court of Justice (ICJ) and the Permanent Court of Arbitration. However, both organizations have many limitations. In the case of the ICJ, the judges are nominated by the member states of the UN and are elected by members of the General Assembly and the UNSC. As is to be expected, the nominating countries lobby for their candidates. There is also a provision for re-election of a judge after nine years in office, and so the judge depends on his home country for re-nomination or for a respected life after retirement. This ensures that there is an invisible bond between the judge and the sponsoring state. Moreover, the ICJ is a courthouse of states, where only states can be parties to contentious cases. And even when it comes to the states, the ICJ only has jurisdiction based on consent, not compulsory jurisdiction. Thus, if there is a dispute between two states, and one of the states refuses to grant consent by treaty, by specific agreement once the dispute has arisen or by some other declaration, the ICJ cannot hear the case.[22]

The ICJ has not proved to be competent in resolving conflicts between big powers, especially when national honour is at stake. As we have seen earlier, it has also proved to be inadequate in resolving global problems by pronouncing a vague advisory opinion on nuclear weapons. Whether the ICJ evolves into an effective role or another structure is found to be more suitable in the new proposed architecture is a question for further consideration.

The other international judicial body operating now is the Permanent Court of Arbitration, which was created by the first Hague conference in 1899. It is not a UN body, and as the name suggests, it provides arbitration services. As with the ICJ, the consent of the parties to the conflict is required for the Permanent Court to consider a dispute,[23] diluting its original purpose of finding solutions to disputes that would lead to big wars. The nuclear-armed countries do not want to take critical conflicts to the Permanent Court of Arbitration. If the original purpose of the Permanent Court can be revived when setting up an international judicial body within the framework of the global social contract, the new organization may provide a reliable foundation for resolving disputes to prevent wars and litigation in the future. The key to success would be to address the main issue of defining how to use such a mechanism more fruitfully.

The concepts of a supranational institution with powers to take decisions binding on states and people on civilizations issues, a world parliament, and an international judicial authority, need to evolve through deliberations. It is not appropriate to capture these concepts in narrow operational frameworks.

The Third Hague Conference

The discussion on a new supranational institutional architecture must involve the states. They will resist as their absolute powers will be reduced, but that is precisely why an engagement with them will be essential. The processes of global consultations can be initiated at the third Hague Peace Conference, drawing lessons from the previous two conferences.

Tsar Nicholas II of Russia took the initiative in August 1898 to convene the first Hague conference.[24] It was a period of growing international disputes and increasing militarization. The China–Japan war and the US–Spain wars were fresh in the public's mind. The underlying rivalry between France and Germany led to brewing tensions. Moreover, it was the beginning of the modernization of the armament industry thanks to the Industrial Revolution. Military budgets were increasing in most countries. Germany and Britain were engaged in a competition to control the seas, and the US and Japan had newly entered the international power game, challenging the old and established powers. Ironically, it was also the time when an international peace movement was emerging with the involvement of civil society and parliaments in the Western countries. However, Russia did not have either a parliament or a peace movement. It was, therefore, an unlikely party to convene an international peace conference, and Tsar Nicholas's invitation to the ambassadors at the weekly foreign office reception in August 1898 surprised everyone. The Tsar had chosen the Hague as a neutral location.

When Tsar Nicholas II issued his invitation, he did not attract a favourable response from the major powers. But the peace movements in various countries of the West were enthusiastic and pushed the governments to participate in the conference. The programme as outlined in a circular issued by the Russian government at the end of December 1898, and compiled for historical record by the Carnegie Endowment of International Peace, included the following agenda:

> An understanding stipulating the non-augmentation, for a term to be agreed upon, of the present effective armed land and sea forces, as well as the war budgets pertaining to them; preliminary study of the ways in which even a reduction of the aforesaid effectives and budgets could be realised in the future.
>
> Acceptance, in principle, of the use of good offices, mediation, and voluntary arbitration, in cases where they are available, with the purpose of preventing armed conflicts between nations; understanding in relation to their mode of application and establishment of a uniform practice in employing them.[25]

All the remaining proposals on the agenda were about prohibiting the use of new weapons, with significant focus on firearms and the navies.

The first Hague conference finally took place in 1899. The meetings were hosted in the Orange Hall of the Huis ten Bosch palace and the high representatives stayed at Hotel Des Indes. While the walls of the palace witnessed formal negotiations, the hotel saw back-channel talks and informal discussions. The formal as well as informal persuasion by the Tsar's diplomats did not have any impact on the disarmament agenda as it was rejected by most delegates, who stated that they were willing to bear the cost of war and its preparation. There was also strong opposition to stopping the modernization of armaments. The proposals for creating arbitration mechanisms were more positively received. Initially, they were resisted, especially by Germany. But the pressure of peace movements in the Western countries and the growing popularity of socialist politics forced the delegates to accept arbitration, albeit with some limitations. An agreement was reached on the rules of war with regards to the treatment of prisoners, sparing public buildings and undefended towns from bombarding, prohibition of the use of projectiles and certain types of bullets. However, the US did not accept this last point on the prohibition of projectiles and bullets.

The second Hague conference was convened by US President Theodore Roosevelt in 1907 and attended by almost fifty countries, as compared to twenty-six in the first conference.[26] It strengthened the arbitration mechanism created in the first conference and also clarified several issues pertaining to naval war.

The third Hague conference was proposed for 1915. It didn't take place as the First World War had broken out.[27] The conference has not been revived yet, though 10,000 peace activists and civil society representatives from around the world gathered for the Hague Appeal for Peace in May 1999.[28] If the institutional architecture of the global social contract is to be promoted, it will be essential to convene the third Hague conference at some stage.

More than a hundred years after the second conference and in the backdrop of rapid strides in military technology, the third Hague conference will need to consider an ambitious agenda:

- Phased elimination of all weapons of final destruction, including nuclear, chemical, biological, lethal autonomous weapons and hypersonic missiles, beginning with worldwide ratification of the treaty prohibiting nuclear weapons;
- Prohibition on applying advances in all technologies, including AI, genomics and synthetic biology, to produce weapons of final destruction;

- Gradual reduction in military expenditure in a coordinated fashion;
- Establishment of supranational institutional machinery to address global catastrophic risks;
- Establishment of a binding arbitration mechanism to resolve conflicts between countries arising out of all issues, including those concerning boundaries and the perceived honour of nations.

The third Hague conference should aim to produce global solutions to break the chains of militarization. The current trend during international meets is to resolve specific conflicts with local or regional solutions. There are also arms control initiatives to reduce specific kinds of lethal weapons. But there is no integrated and comprehensive plan for general and complete disarmament, including prohibition on the production of future lethal weapons. Neither is there any mechanism to resolve conflicts involving the great powers. If a third Hague conference is convened, it should present a grand scheme to end all international conflicts in the world and introduce a plan for general and complete disarmament. The conference should aim at rewriting the rules of conduct of international affairs and establish principles of the rule of law.

The first two Hague conferences were in session for a few months each. The third conference will require a much longer timespan. It may be assumed that it will not be easy for states to compromise on the status quo and that the talks may take place over years and not months.

An example of a productive multilateral security conference on which the third Hague conference may be modelled is the Conference on Security and Cooperation in Europe (CSCE) that took place in Helsinki and Geneva from July 1973 to July 1975.

The CSCE process took place in a context determined by two main variables that, at first glance, appeared contradictory: a novel policy of détente on the one hand and the unchanged policy of confrontation between the two main power blocs on the other.[29] In this sense, it was similar to the contradictions existing at the time of the first Hague conference. While the détente was based on an increasing level of cooperation between NATO and the Soviet blocs, there was also mutual anxiety and distrust, resulting in a relative instability of the relationship between them. But, with the realization that hostile policies were unsustainable in the long run, especially after the experience of the near-catastrophic Cuban missile crisis in 1962, both sides aimed at a policy of détente through Strategic Arms Limitation Talks (SALT) and other measures.[30] Efforts such as these culminated in 1973 in the USSR proposal for the CSCE, which aimed at maintaining the status quo between the power blocs, so that no boundaries could be shifted by the use of force.

After several rounds, the Helsinki Final Act was signed in 1975. It emphasized improving relations between the signatory nations, with the focus being on the principles of conduct of international relations.[31] They had to do with the concept of the inviolability of frontiers, state sovereignty and non-intervention in internal affairs. While most of these principles were already enshrined and agreed upon when the participating states had signed the Charter of the UN, they fulfilled the major goal of containing the anxiety of the former Soviet Union about losing spheres of influence. It was agreed that all boundaries that separated the Warsaw Pact countries from the West were now, in principle, not to be changed by force. In return, the USSR made certain concessions regarding the protection of human rights and liberties.

The CSCE process took place over two years and was not rushed to be completed in two to three months. It also enjoyed popular support in member countries.

There is a lesson to be drawn from the relative failure of the two Hague conferences and the relative success of the CSCE process. The geopolitical context often has mutually contradictory patterns. So long as there is one trend in favour of peace and reconciliation, and countries want to protect their status quo without aspiring for more influence, it is possible to craft rules of the game to provide political stability.

It is also obvious from these examples that it is essential for major players to take the initiative. In the case of the first Hague conference and the CSCE process, Russia or the former Soviet Union took the initiative. Only if a great power takes the initiative for the third Hague conference, if the parties are willing to invest a few years in negotiations and if they genuinely want to reduce the risk to human survival will such an idea translate into reality. Small countries and NGOs can contribute to building a conducive atmosphere for such an initiative, but they do not have the political capital to convene the third Hague conference. The large powers are not likely to be enthusiastic about a global social contract in which the influence of the system of states is bound to weaken. Therefore, stakeholders in the international community will have to play different roles depending on their respective strengths to make such an endeavour possible. The final success will depend on the negotiators structuring a formula where everyone gains something—each of the major powers at the table receives concrete public goods, and the new institutional arrangement is invested with the potential to mitigate global catastrophic risks. Before such a conference is convened, considerable effort will be required to think about incentives for the lethally armed countries to give up their weapons of final destruction and commit not to use technological advancements for military purposes. It is a tall order, but one that is essential for the survival of humankind.

New Global Ethic

The third Hague conference will have to aim to resolve transactional and institutional aspects of the global contract. There is a danger of such solutions not lasting for a long time. It will, therefore, be necessary to think of a new moral and psychological framework for the world. A long-term and sustained global change will only take place when our mindset is transformed.

The global social contract should also not be confused with its institutional expressions. It is a much deeper doctrine. It is about the will of every individual on the planet to commit voluntarily to the global architecture on civilizational issues, even when such a commitment may not coincide with the national objectives of the state to which the person belongs. It is about creating a mindset of dual loyalty—with one loyalty to the state, and another loyalty, limited to the civilizational survival framework, to the human race. So far, the proposals for federations of states have assumed undivided loyalty to the state and its competence to bargain with other states. The global social contract will divide loyalty between the nation and human civilization and require a new kind of thinking. But the alternative, if such a global social contract is not developed, is the end of humankind. The choice before all of us is to live with such divided loyalty or be willing to perish.

Einstein once said:

> A new type of thinking is essential if mankind is to survive and move toward higher levels. Often in evolutionary processes, a species must adapt to new conditions in order to survive. Today the atomic bomb has altered profoundly the nature of the world as we knew it, and the human race consequently finds itself in a new habitat to which it must adapt its thinking . . . In previous ages, a nation's life and culture could be protected to some extent by the growth of armies in national competition. Today, we must abandon competition and secure cooperation. This must be the central fact in all our considerations of international affairs; otherwise we face certain disaster. Past thinking and methods did not prevent World Wars. Future thinking must prevent wars.[32]

He also said:

> The destiny of civilized humanity depends more than ever on the moral forces it is capable of generating. Without 'ethical culture', there is no salvation for humanity.[33]

Responding to the civilizational crisis by going beyond national frontiers is also about redefining the concept of power. Nations want the most lethal weapons because they want to expand their power. Those who control the levers of state want to deepen their personal power. So long as there is an obsession with and greed for power, the lethality of weapons will go on increasing and humankind will move closer and closer to the precipice. The risk is not limited to countries that control global politics at any specific moment in the world history, as the players keep on changing. The real issue is formulating the rules of the game. In 2020, there were nine nuclear-armed states. This number will quite possibly double before 2050 if power continues to be the cardinal principle for determining the destiny of nations, assuming the incumbent nine have not blown up the earth in the meantime.

There are different concepts of power. In 1922, Max Weber defined power as the ability to assert one's own will against the resistance of others, thus making it about unilateral domination. He defines domination as 'the probability that certain specific commands (or all commands) will be obeyed by a given group of persons'. The features associated with domination are obedience, interest, belief and regularity. Weber notes that 'every genuine form of domination implies a minimum of voluntary compliance, that is, an interest (based on ulterior motives or genuine acceptance) in obedience'.[34] It is power over something or someone, not only in a personal relationship but also in the management of human affairs at the broader level.

According to Bertrand Russell, power relates to the ability to achieve intended outcomes.[35] We can describe this as the power of our inner resources. It is the power of the child when she or he first masters the ability to stand erect, walk and speak the first magic words. It is the power of the architect, the artist, the poet, the singer, the gardener to create something out of nothing. If the power-holders treat power with this perspective, it will become a vehicle for positive change.

Hannah Arendt, distinguishing power from force, says that positive power depends on the consent of numbers, while force depends on implements. Joy Ann James elaborates: 'Hannah Arendt argues that power is communication, not coercion and control: power radically differs from control, domination or violence in that it cannot be exercised over someone; it can only be exercised with others through communication and cooperation. Political power is shared power, collective action by members of a political community with an understanding of power as communication not as coercion. Arendt argues that traditional political philosophy misrepresents power as ruling and confuses it with domination.'[36]

Thus, we can see that there is a clear difference between domination and power. Domination instigates fear and violence and needs implements. The greater the ambition for domination, the deadlier the instruments that are required.[37] It is true of individuals as well as nations. The nations that desire the most sophisticated weapons are the ones aspiring for global domination. On the other hand, power can be destructive or constructive. If it is treated as a constructive concept, it would be capable of bringing about pleasant change such as art, innovation and development. The difference between domination and power leads to the difference between fear and hope.

A critical question for the world's people to consider is if they want to live in fear or hope. If people desire fear, they should accept domination, its implements and its violent consequences to the extent of the possible termination of human civilization. If they want hope, they should demand constructive discharge of power leading to the advancement of human civilization—the same way that people demanded and obtained the end of colonization, the end of apartheid, the ban on nuclear testing and the rejection of racism. If they want domination, they should be prepared for authority being exercised from above to decide their fate along with that of millions of people. If they want constructive power, they should enjoy the possibility of their participation in the processes that determine their own future, giving up the inertia that characterizes our dominant reaction towards the weapons of final destruction. Whether the world is ruined in a series of mushroom clouds or allows the last person to enjoy happiness will depend on whether we consciously choose fear or hope.

People would obviously prefer hope to fear if their eyes are open. But they cannot see the options before them because they are blinded by the smoke of national pride. Once obsessed with nationalism and the desire to aggrandize the interests of their nation states, people forget that the interest and glory of their nation is a convenient cover for the ambition and greed of their leaders. They are led to believe that there is a choice between pride and humiliation. But the real choice is between fear and hope.

Several philosophies around the world provide a framework for global coexistence. Jōsei Toda, a Japanese spiritual leader, and his follower Daisaku Ikeda, about whom we have read earlier in this book, have introduced the concept of *chikyu minzokushugi*. Toda first mentioned this term in the 1950s, when he was the second president of Soka Gakkai International. Ikeda is the third president of the organization. He says that this phrase is directly translated as 'global nationalism' or the 'underlying unity of the world's peoples', corresponding to what today we would call 'global citizenship'. Toda was convinced that wars among states and peoples would end and a peaceful world society would be constructed when people realized this ideal and took full responsibility as members of a single human community. Ikeda has described it as placing humanity before the state or one's own country. In order to translate the concept into a practical reality, it is necessary to promote the culture of peace. The Soka Gakkai approach calls for a psychological change to transcend loyalty to a nation and instead embrace loyalty to humankind.[38] Ikeda says: 'We cannot think in terms of the future of humanity with our minds bound to the narrow confines of the sovereign state. We are living in an era where such a narrow mindset can undermine the very basis of our survival.'[39]

The Japanese concept of chikyu minzokushugi is akin to the Indian concept of vasudhaiva kutumbakam, originating from ancient Indian scriptures. It means the world is one family and is an important precept in Hindu philosophy. The term is engraved in the entrance hall of the Indian Parliament, as well as on the walls of several other public buildings. It is mentioned often by Indian leaders and scholars in their speeches. Mahatma Gandhi's philosophy of non-violence and his proposal for an international federation of states can be considered an extension of his belief in this philosophy.

Even though the Japanese and Indian philosophies emphasize the 'one world' concept, the two states have often deviated from it in the treatment of their neighbours as well as groups within the respective countries. The two countries have also experienced the rise of popular nationalism in the twenty-first century. However, the fact that the Indian and Japanese states and the elite do not implement this philosophical concept does not invalidate the philosophy itself.

Southern Africa has a similar philosophy known as *ubuntu*, meaning 'I am, because we are'. It is a part of the Xhosa phrase '*Umuntu ngumuntu ngabantu*', which literally means that a person is a person through other people. Ubuntu has its roots in humanist African philosophy, where the idea of community is one of the building blocks of society. It is a creative notion of common humanity and oneness.

According to Michael Onyebuchi Eze, South African philosopher, the core of ubuntu can best be summarized as follows: 'A person is a person through other people strikes an affirmation of one's humanity through recognition of an "other" in his or her uniqueness and difference. We are because you are, and since you are, definitely I am.' Eze says on his website: 'Humanity is a gift, a quality we owe to one another!'[40]

Just like the problems with the Japanese and Hindu edicts, ubuntu has not been practised by the African states, and yet again the failure of the elite to learn from their wisdom cannot negate the wisdom itself.

These concepts have one belief in common: humankind's good is more desired than the interests of the nation state, for the progress of the world will automatically lead to the progress of each nation. The rivalry between nations will bring all of them down, though some may seem to gain in the short term. The model based on the domination, exercise of constructive power, pursuit of national ego and militarism has not created permanent victors. Every superpower is diminished, and every empire has collapsed.

The doctrine of a global social contract intends to embody the spirit of chikyu minzokushugi, vasudhaiva kutumbakam and ubuntu. It aims to transform the concept of power from dominance to construction. It aims to convert the context of fear into that of hope.

It is only natural that such a fundamental revision of our world view will be opposed by those who gain from the status quo. Popular nationalism is the reality of the day and has been so for over a century. Several hundred million have lost their lives in the name of national interest since the rise of nationalism. Those who control the levers of power have succeeded in creating a smokescreen of the choice between national glory and national humiliation for several decades. They will not like tectonic shifts in the belief systems that will shake their palaces and close their war factories. They would rather risk human extinction than their own irrelevance.

It is for us to determine whether to continue to be blinded by the smoke of national pride, dominance and arrogance or to wake up and build up a common home of humankind and explore the huge potential of our civilization. I am because we are. Each one of us is because we all are.

Politics of Delegitimizing War

A global social contract to actualize the common interest of all people on earth must be rooted in the global ethic of coexistence, constructive power and dual loyalty to the nation and humankind.

Such a transformation can happen through a change in our mindset. It is a social and psychological process. As we have seen, a global social contract needs a supranational institutional architecture comprising mechanisms for responding to civilizational crises, world parliament and an impartial machinery for conflict resolution. The institutional issues require structured discussion through a political process.

It is clear that our political leaders do not care about the cost of war. They only understand the cost of losing power. They know that war is a matter of choice. Their preponderant belief is that supporting war preparedness ensures their place in the saddle of the nation's capital. But if they suspect that militarism can throw them out of power, they will rather give up war than their power and honour.

Only when politicians lose elections for surrendering humanism to nationalism, development to destruction, wisdom to vanity will there be hope. Otherwise, our march to the precipice will continue unabated. If we want to turn back, people's movements will have to convince the world's population that there will be no victors in the next war involving the weapons of final destruction. The cost of the next war is beyond calculation. It is ultimate.

The grassroots movement will have to prove to the politicians in democracies that their support for deadly weapons, and the underlying psychology of hyper-nationalism, will cost them elections. Some political leaders may become worried about being devoured by a Frankenstein's monster and give up militarism on their own. But most will not care for the risk of human extinction if jingoism helps them win elections. Only if they see masses demonstrating on the streets and in cyberspace, demanding a world without war, will they change their ways. If people demand peace, the rulers will have to give in.

Since the only language politicians understand is that of power, a new kind of politics needs to emerge around the global social contract, and it must aim to defeat traditional political groups in a democratic competition.

The experience of world history over the past many centuries has shown that democratic politics is a constantly evolving process.

In Great Britain, the US, Sweden and other countries, various groups evolved from factions into parties starting from the seventeenth to the nineteenth century. For example, the initial electoral politics in Great Britain was about the palace and place of the British royalty. The Tories wanted the monarchy to rule the country; the Whigs, and later the Liberals, wanted a constitutional monarchy with real power vested in an elected government. In other parts of the world, towards the end of the nineteenth century, many socialist parties sprang up.

In the last century, the political spectrum the world over was essentially divided on a socio-economic basis. The conservative parties supported the perpetuation of strong economic interests, including landlords and businessmen. The communist and socialist parties advocated workers' rule and varying degrees of state control over the economy. The political right represented the conservatives, whereas the left represented the communists and socialists.

More recently, in the last fifty years, green parties advocating environmental protection and nationalist parties aiming at fostering national pride have become popular. Earlier, the political right meant parties with a conservative economic agenda of free enterprise, and the political left included parties in support of the state regulation of the economy. Increasingly, the political right has now come to mean parties nurturing identity based on nationalism, anti-immigration policies, cultural heritage, old glory and religion. The new left advocates a caring and compassionate society with open doors for immigration and religious tolerance. In the meantime, conventional conservative and socialist parties are moving towards the centre of political and economic policies.

In order for the efforts to enable a global social contract, underpinned by peaceful coexistence and disarmament, to yield political results, it will be necessary to shape them in tune with the new political dynamics. The movement to abolish the weapons of final destruction can find a common cause with green parties, to which are closely related the concerns for health, climate and peace. At the same time, it is equally important to reach out to people who join hyper-nationalist politics out of ignorance. Many of them tend to be supporters of tradition and religion. They must be made aware that all religions are opposed to the politics of human extinction. It is necessary to explain to deeply religious people that god has not given anyone the exclusive power to destroy his creation. It is necessary to explain to the rank and file of the political right that there is a difference between patriotism and hyper-nationalism. Patriotism can be good for society by developing brotherhood and a sense of common purpose, whereas hyper-nationalism can divide the country and ruin the world.

The growing support for nationalist and communal politics stems from a sense of rootlessness when social and economic problems mount and the state fails to deliver. Nationalist politicians find scapegoats and ascribe such woes to an enemy, either within or without. Hitler discovered the Jews. Milošević found the Bosnians. Trump found China. Putin found the US. The Kims have found Japan and the US. India and Pakistan have found each other. In an atmosphere of fear of the enemy, a nationalist leader emerges to protect his people. He needs to demonstrate that he is a strongman and the head of a strong state. It is then necessary to acquire and flaunt weapons. The more lethal the weapons are, the more popular the leader is. But the moment the leader feels that he could lose power by peddling hawkish rhetoric, he changes his tune. Serbian President Aleksandar Vučić was once a trusted lieutenant of ultra-nationalist Slobodan Milošević in the 1990s. He was known for aggressive views towards minorities and others who would disagree with the regime. Soon after Milošević died as a war criminal in a prison cell in the Netherlands in 2006, amidst large-scale condemnation of his policies around the world, Aleksandar Vučić changed his political party, renounced pugnacious politics and became the leader of a new party. Once his goal of controlling the power apparatus in Serbia was achieved with election to the presidency of Serbia, he was again found to be walking on the authoritarian path.

On the surface, global transformation may appear to be a utopian dream. But currents beneath the surface often indicate different realities.

People have more power than they realize. We have already encountered some powerful examples of civil movements dictating the moves of politicians. When the Tsar issued invitations for a peace conference at the end of the nineteenth century, the leaders of Great Britain, France and the US did not want to accept it. Peace organizations in those countries forced their governments to go to the Hague. President Reagan wanted to build the strongest American army ever. The Freeze movement forced him to reduce nuclear arsenals in partnership with his Russian counterpart. Russia, or the former Soviet Union, wanted to go on testing nuclear weapons till the end of mankind. But a poet's followers forced the mighty nation to halt the testing forever.

'So what?' the cynics might ask. The Hague conference did not stop the World Wars. The decrease in the number of nuclear warheads was made up for by the increase in their lethality. The moratorium on nuclear testing did not prevent nations from going beyond nuclear arms to lethal autonomous weapons and hypersonic missiles. The savage has not been tamed. There is no need to celebrate piecemeal success.

We have to realize that there will always be tactical successes and failures. Warmongers must be defeated in elections again and again until they realize that belligerence does not pay. What matters even more is the legitimacy of ideas. From cannibalism to colonization to communism, many cruel ideas have collapsed. Liberty and love are ideas that have succeeded.

Containing combat at the edges of institutional boundaries of states is a question of tactics. The global social contract is the need of the hour for an integrated civilization facing the risk of extinction. We may not be able to eliminate the weapons of final destruction any time soon. But we can deprive them of popular legitimacy. We may not be able to end violence. But we can deprive it of its glory. We may not be able to vanquish hyper-nationalism instantly. But we can expose its hollowness.

Political leaders must realize that they cannot gain popularity by worshipping weapons and wars. They must be shown that they cannot earn respect by stoking nationalism. They must not win at the hustings by promoting hatred. When political leaders accept that the idea of war, the idea of national pride and the idea of animosity have lost popular legitimacy, they will change their ways.

The question of paramount importance before us is not limited to defeating war and nationalism in the political game but how to do so in the contest of ideas. Once ideas win, actions will follow.

Switzerland has proven that it is possible to renounce wars. Costa Rica has shown that it is possible to forego weapons. South Africa has demonstrated that it is possible to eliminate nuclear warheads. However, the courage that Switzerland, Costa Rica and South Africa have shown is missing in the big powers. It is because the powers that are militarily grand and economically huge are often strategically frightened and morally small. They know that no emperor or despot lasts forever: after all, Kaiser Wilhelm II had to hide in exile and Hitler had to kill himself. If we abandon our fear of the petty leaders of these superpowers, we will be able to build hope.

Sometimes, though rarely, great men walk the earth and show light to the rest of humanity. Mahatma Gandhi, Martin Luther King, Jr, and Nelson Mandela proved that the idea of non-violence could defeat the idea of dominance. Willy Brandt made the idea of reconciliation win over the idea of hostility. Gorbachev shamed the idea of colossal brutality, helping the idea of peace win.

Similarly, US President John F. Kennedy and Russian leader Nikita Khrushchev produced something valuable that could have transformed the world more than half a century ago. Although their initiative has not received the attention it deserves in international discourse—it is almost treated as a secret—it is encouraging that the details of their endeavour can be found in news media and on the internet. It is this open secret about Kennedy and Khrushchev that can provide the foundation stone of the Global Hope Valley we have proposed here and gradually help us to withdraw from the precipice of ultimate destruction.

Global Hope Valley

It may appear unrealistic, utopian and naive to propose a global social contract with dual loyalty to the state and the human race, to create a supranational organization to determine issues of civilizational consequence, to usher in politics of delegitimizing violence, to confine the scope of war to the combating elements in the state structures, and to bring about general and complete disarmament. It may appear that anyone proposing such a transformation of the world must be an Ivory Tower scholar unaware of the tortuous ways of the real world or a hermit living in a mountain cave in isolation or a peace-loving but hallucinating hippie.

But can these appellations apply to a man who worked as the assistant secretary of war during the Second World War with responsibility for arms procurement, the founder of the predecessor organization of the CIA and the creator of the US National Security Council? Can we describe the man who became president of the World Bank and the chairman of one of the largest private American banks as a hermit living in isolation in a mountain cave? Can we describe a high-flying Wall Street lawyer trusted by large energy companies as a hippie? John McCloy was a highly pragmatic war planner, banker and lawyer.

McCloy worked with Valerian Zorin of the former Soviet Union on an important mission. Zorin was an apparatchik of the Community Party of the Soviet Union from its early days. As a hardcore communist party official, he worked in its foreign relations department. Like McCloy, he was by no measure a monk or a hippie.

John Kennedy and Nikita Khrushchev, who had reached the highest positions in their respective countries with great political skill and acumen, had commissioned McCloy and Zorin respectively to negotiate a new agreement between the US and the Soviet Union. McCloy and Zorin met in Belgrade, in the former Yugoslavia, on 20 September 1961 with instructions from their leaders. They agreed on an accord to propose the following principles for disarmament negotiations: that disarmament is general and complete, and war is no longer an instrument for settling international problems. To this end, the programme for general and complete disarmament would contain the necessary provisions, with respect to the military establishment of every nation for:

- The disbanding of armed forces, the dismantling of military establishments including bases, the cessation of the production of armaments as well as their liquidation or conversion to peaceful uses;
- The elimination of all stockpiles of nuclear, chemical, bacteriological and other weapons of mass destruction, and the cessation of the production of such weapons;
- The elimination of all means of delivery of weapons of mass destruction;
- The abolition of organizations and institutions designed to organize the military efforts of states, the cessation of military training, and the closing of all military training institutions; and
- The discontinuance of military expenditures.[41]

Were Kennedy and Khrushchev unrealistic, utopian and naive to authorize their special envoys to agree on such an ambitious plan for disarming nation states and abolishing war? They were involved in a tussle over Berlin at the same time as they had deputed McCloy and Zorin to negotiate peace. In fact, the meeting of the special envoys in Belgrade took place when Berlin was being divided with a new wall. This was one of the most difficult phases in the relations between the US and the former Soviet Union.[42]

Such all-encompassing disarmament was not a mere fancy of two leaders. Within three months of the McCloy–Zorin accord, 104 member states of the UN unanimously passed the UN General Assembly resolution 1722 (XVI) on 20 December 1961, which officially welcomed the accord and recommended that 'negotiations on general and complete disarmament under effective international control be resumed at the earliest possible time'.[43]

The McCloy–Zorin accord, the UN General Assembly resolution and its follow-up were being negotiated while the tension between the two superpowers was building up and nuclear testing was going on. The Cuban missile crisis exposed the world to the vulnerabilities of a third world war. As a result, the momentum for peace began to grow. However, with the signing of the Partial Test Ban Treaty in August 1963, which banned atmospheric and underwater (but not underground) tests of nuclear weapons, the peace movement became complacent. Finally, President Kennedy's tragic assassination in November 1963 ended the momentum for disarmament.

The Kennedy–Khrushchev initiative has given the world a resolution of the UN General Assembly, which unanimously endorses the concept of general and complete disarmament to the extent that nation states have to abolish armies, except for domestic purposes and UN peace-keeping missions, and renounce war as an instrument of settling international disputes. Thus, General Assembly Resolution 1722 is a de facto declaration of the intent to create a world without war.

The initiative has also given us the experience of what a successful process in this regard could be like. The demand for general and complete disarmament began with peace movements in the US and Europe. At the same time, the non-aligned nations—countries that then did not identify with either of the two superpowers—played a major role in mobilizing worldwide public opinion. In fact, two weeks before the McCloy–Zorin accord, the non-alignment movement met at the summit level in Belgrade and appealed for general and complete disarmament.

Once demand for peace was created by grassroots movements within the Western democracies and the non-aligned movement internationally, Kennedy and Khrushchev acted like statesmen and appointed special envoys to discuss a disarmament negotiation plan with far-reaching consequences. They took the envoys' accord to its logical conclusion by seeking the endorsement of the UN General Assembly. But the hope for global transformation withered away with President Kennedy's death in 1963.

We have seen in an earlier chapter how history was repeated twenty-five years later when the Nuclear Freeze Movement and international public opinion enabled disarmament negotiations between President Reagan and General Secretary Gorbachev.

These two historical experiences at the height of the Cold War prove that world leaders can be amenable to the pressures brought to bear on them by peace movements within their countries and by the community of nations globally. Kennedy was convinced of the need for disarmament. Reagan acted in consideration of the electoral outcome and, to some extent, the influence of movies on nuclear disasters.

These lessons suggest a pathway for the future. Common people must wake up from their slumber and demand disarmament, especially the phased elimination of all weapons of final destruction and a prohibition on future investments in dangerous weapons and technologies. In the context of the technological realities of the twenty-first century, it is also necessary to campaign for restricting the use of AI in military matters, and particularly nuclear weapons and their delivery systems. Neutral countries have to raise their voices in their conclaves and on the floor of the UN. The demand from sane voices for disarming the world should go on building until the day the presidents of the US, Russia and China decide to negotiate collectively a plan for disarmament and peaceful resolution of all conflicts between themselves and all nation states in the world.

Such a realization may dawn on world leaders and the general population after a nuclear accident ravages a city, killing a few million people. It may come from a 'close call' where a nuclear Armageddon nearly takes place but is averted by a few seconds and someone in the military command structure goes public with details. Or it may come with enlightened leaders and catalysts mobilizing the world's conscience.

We must be aware of the dangers that a peace plan can encounter, as happened in the case of President Kennedy's assassination. It is, therefore, necessary to look beyond disarmament and conflict resolution. We must create a global social contract, dual loyalty to the state and the human race, and an institutional machinery that represents our species and not our nations. It is time we embraced the spirit of chikyu minzokushugi, vasudhaiva kutumbakam and ubuntu.

If we don't use the legal foundation laid down by UN General Assembly Resolution 1722 and inspire our leaders to launch a new initiative echoing the Kennedy–Khrushchev enterprise, we must remember that we are choosing to stare at universal death full in the face. We may postpone such a moment of human extinction by years or a few decades, but we will never avert it completely. With technologies taking over military decisions from humans, it may happen sooner than we would imagine. We may ridicule the pursuits of peace and the global social contract as impractical, utopian and naive, and the advocates of such a path as idealistic dreamers. But let's remember that Gandhi and Mandela, Kennedy and Khrushchev, McCloy and Zorin, Reagan and Gorbachev and Willy Brandt had more experience of the real world than millions of peddlers of personal interests, arrogance and ambition who pretend to promote national interests.

We, the people of the planet earth, must consciously decide whether we want to ignore the risks of the most dangerous epoch in our species' history and commit collective suicide or whether we want to create a Global Hope Valley where partnerships replace partisanship, communities replace countries, solidarity replaces soldiers, collaboration replaces competition, responsibility replaces recklessness, and humanity replaces horrors.

Appendix 1

Table A1: Nine Nuclear Power Countries—Estimates of Weapons, 2020

No.	Country	Estimate of nuclear weapons
	Russia	6,370
	US	5,800
	France	300
	China	290
	UK	215
	Pakistan	150
	India	130
	Israel	80
	North Korea	20
TOTAL		13,335

Source: *Bulletin of the Atomic Scientists*, Hans M. Kristensen and Matt Korda, 'Nuclear Notebook'

Table A2: Global Military Expenditure, 1949–99

Year	USD billion (2016 constant values)
1949	251
1950	302
1951	579
1952	813
1953	865
1954	865
1955	761
1956	726
1957	747
1958	780
1959	765
1960	777
1961	765
1962	798
1963	869
1964	874
1965	859
1966	861
1967	988
1968	1,117
1969	1,144
1970	1,116
1971	1,096
1972	1,029
1973	1,055
1974	1,033
1975	1,045
1976	1,026

Year	USD billion (2016 constant values)
1977	1,032
1978	1,089
1979	1,106
1980	1,115
1981	1,081
1982	1,170
1983	1,316
1984	1,287
1985	1,326
1986	1,401
1987	1,419
1988	1,462
1989	1,394
1990	1,344
1991	1,079
1992	1,124
1993	1,085
1994	1,049
1995	1,003
1996	983
1997	1,001
1998	993
1999	1,016

Source: Data from SIPRI (including USSR expenditure as the median between 37.5 per cent of US military expenditure and CIA estimates for USSR from 1949–88)

Note: Figures for 2019–25 calculated as per growth rate of expenditure at the rate of 1.85 per cent, mean growth rate for 2016–18.

Table A3: Global Military Expenditure, 1998–2025

Year	USD billion (2016 constant values)
1998	993
1999	1,016
2000	1,051
2001	1,074
2002	1,146
2003	1,227
2004	1,305
2005	1,360
2006	1,401
2007	1,457
2008	1,540
2009	1,646
2010	1,672
2011	1,674
2012	1,669
2013	1,645
2014	1,642
2015	1,638
2016	1,638
2017	1,739
2018	1,788
2019	1,821
2020	1,854
2021	1,854
2022	1,923
2023	1,958
2024	1,994
2025	2,031

Source: Data from SIPRI

Table A4: Military Expenditures of Big Powers in Europe, 1870–1914

Military Estimates of Great Powers (GBP million)						
Year	Germany	Austro–Hungary	France	Great Britain	Italy	Russia
1870	10.8	8.2	22	23.4	7.8	22
1880	20.4	13.2	31.4	25.2	10	29.6
1890	28.8	12.8	37.4	31.4	14.8	29
1900	41	13.6	42.4	116	14.6	30.8
1910	64	17.4	52.4	68	24.4	63.4
1914	110.8	36.4	57.4	76.8	28.2	88.2

Source: A.J.P. Taylor, *Struggle for Mastery in Europe: 1848–1918* (Oxford University Press, 1954).

Table A5: Global Military Expenditure

Arms expenditure in USD (billion), 2017 Constant				
Year	Total	US	Countries possessing or aspiring for nuclear and post-nuclear weapons besides the US: Russia, China, UK, France, India, Pakistan, South Korea, Saudi Arabia, Iran and Israel	Rest of the World
2010	1,708	784	476	447
2011	1,711	775	488	448
2012	1,706	731	515	459
2013	1,683	673	539	471
2014	1,681	631	576	473
2015	1,677	616	604	456
2016	1,678	612	604	461
2017	1,696	605	616	474
2018	1,741	633	624	483

Source: SIPRI database (1949–2018)

Note: North Korea has not been included as data is unavailable for that country.

Appendix 2
The Normandy Manifesto for World Peace
Issued in Normandy, 4 June 2019

'Shall we put an end to the human race; or shall mankind renounce war?'

Russell–Einstein Manifesto, 1955

The existential question posed by the Russell–Einstein Manifesto in the midst of the Cold War is even more pressing today than it was then. Nuclear weapons are several thousand times more deadly. Over 2,500 warheads are on hair-trigger alert. Deadly pathogens threaten life as we know it. And with major powers preparing to deploy killer robots, we are on the edge of a black hole; the possibility of machines determining our fate is morally repugnant. Global military expenditure has doubled since the end of the Cold War. It is set to increase further with plans to modernize existing weapons and develop new systems of destruction and decimation. The risk of a war by accident, incident or intent remains a distinct possibility against the backdrop of the climate crisis, growing inequality, ultra-nationalism and the erosion of ethical values.

An international treaty to ban and eventually eliminate nuclear weapons was recently concluded, though it awaits universal acceptance. Efforts are underway to prohibit lethal autonomous weapons and bring the weaponization of genes and biotechnology within the purview of the Biological Weapons Convention. Despite these positive signs, we still face the risk of human extinction. The major powers oppose the new arms control initiatives; they are abandoning existing treaties. They are dragging their feet to reverse global warming and gross socio-economic inequality. Historical evidence shows that no empire lasts forever. The collapse of each and every strong nation in history is a testament to the naiveté of the arrogant. Technology was much less advanced when earlier empires collapsed, killing millions but sparing the earth.

War is not innate to human nature. It is a function of choice. Cooperation, much more than conflict, underpins evolution. Life became possible two billion years ago when cells learnt to thrive together. Civilization came into existence 12,000 years ago when human beings learnt to live together in communities. We can draw strength from the fact that the human spirit has shown resilience for millennia. It has bounced back after every crisis to create a better world. The world possesses a vast pool of wisdom. Time and again, we have proved ourselves capable of reason. We have banned mustard gas, blinding laser weapons, landmines and cluster munitions. We must now make war implausible and gradually renounce it so that we can go ahead and solve real problems such as poverty, climate change and disease.

We have come together in Normandy to appeal to all the people of the planet that we are one. We all breathe, think, love, hate, fear and hope. What we have in common is greater than our differences.

We recall here what Russell and Einstein told us: *Remember your humanity; forget the rest.*

———·———

In order to render war implausible, establish sustainable peace, reconstruct ethical values and harness our common humanity, we need a New Global Contract underpinned by a fresh approach to international security. We must build an inclusive international security system rooted in the rule of law, respecting universal human rights. We need to design a reliable collective security architecture that everyone can have confidence in. Unless there is such a security alternative, states will continue to acquire weapons of war. We need to develop a time-bound integrated action plan for the elimination of all weapons of mass destruction, including nuclear, biological, chemical and lethal autonomous weapons systems.

We believe that the phased elimination of weapons of mass destruction will not compromise security, quite to the contrary; twenty-two countries without standing armies have not been attacked from the moment they disavowed the idea of military. The evidence shows that security arrangements that do not depend on weapons are more effective than the ones that depend on the potential use of force. We must re-engineer our collective security system guided by evidence of success rather than fear of failure.

Peace is not the absence of war; the implausibility of war is. We need to transform the United Nations, particularly the Security Council, into a robust instrument of conflict prevention and conflict resolution. We must harness the power of dialogue in order to pre-empt the use of force.

Sustainable peace thrives only when there is sustainable development. The Sustainable Development Goals, the Kyoto Protocol on greenhouse gas emissions, and the Paris Agreement on combating climate change provide elements of the New Global Contract. We require a global budget to underpin these agreements, with resources raised from a future decrease in military expenditure, increase of development partnership commitments, and the consideration of new and creative sources of revenue.

We must ensure every day, every minute and in every corner of the world that all human beings are treated with dignity and are equal and empowered participants, without distinction of any kind such as race, gender, colour or faith.

Our call for a universal, inclusive, rule-based collective security system, global budget for sustainable development, and the commitment to human dignity and human rights of all is enshrined in the core values of tolerance, trust and cooperation. It is an appeal to ignite the spirit of ubuntu, which means 'I am because we are'. In the seventeenth century, John Donne reminded us, 'Any man's death diminishes me, because I am involved in mankind.'

We have a tendency to establish peace only after a prolonged devastating war. The Treaty of Westphalia, the Final Act of Vienna, the League of Nations, the United Nations were all conceived after millions of young men and women lost their lives, families were ruined, and humanity was shamed. There will be no opportunity to negotiate a new Peace Agreement after the next world war, because there will be no negotiators, no people, no flowers and no trees.

Let us conceive and establish sustainable peace before someone initiates the next war. If we do not, we will be sleepwalking into collective suicide. If we do, we will have the possibility of achieving the apex of humanity and entering an era of summum bonum.

Signed by
Mohamed ElBaradei (Nobel Peace Prize laureate),
Leymah Gbowee (Nobel Peace Prize laureate),
Anthony Grayling (Master of New College of the Humanities),
Denis Mukwege (Nobel Peace Prize laureate),
Jody Williams (Nobel Peace Prize laureate),
Sundeep Waslekar (President of Strategic Foresight Group)

Notes

1. Approaching Midnight: The Threat of Human Extinction

1 'Ukraine: 'We need peace now' declares Guterres, warning of global hunger meltdown'. *UN News*, 14 March 2022. Retrieved from https://news.un.org/en/story/2022/03/1113882.

2 Mecklin, J. 'Closer Than Ever: It Is 100 Seconds to Midnight'. *Bulletin of the Atomic Scientists*, 23 January 2020. Retrieved from https://thebulletin.org/doomsday-clock/current-time/#full-statement.

3 Grayling, Anthony, Denise Mukwege, Jody Williams, Leymah Gbowee, Mohamed El Baradei and Sundeep Waslekar. *The Normandy Manifesto for World Peace* (Normandie Pour La Paix), 4 June 2019. Retrieved from https://normandiepourlapaix.fr/en/read-online-manifesto.

4 Soka Gakkai Youth Division, ed. *Hiroshima and Nagasaki: That We Never Forget: Hibakusha Share Their Testimonies of Survival*, 2017. Daisanbunmei-sha.

5 International Campaign to Abolish Nuclear Weapons. *Catastrophic Humanitarian Harm*, August 2015. Retrieved from https://d3n8a8pro7vhmx.cloudfront.net/ican/pages/749/attachments/original/1575657291/CHH-Booklet-WEB-2015.pdf?1575657291.

6 'Cap on Trident nuclear warhead stockpile to rise by more than 40%'. Guardian, 15 March 2021. Retrieved from https://www.theguardian.com/

uk-news/2021/mar/15/cap-on-trident-nuclear-warhead-stockpile-to-rise-by-more-than-40.

7   Center for Strategic and International Studies. *Avangard*, 3 January 2019. Retrieved from https://missilethreat.csis.org/missile/avangard/.

8   Segarra, L.M. 'Read President Trump's Speech Threatening to "Totally Destroy" North Korea'. *Time*, 19 September 2017. Retrieved from https://time.com/4947942/trump-totally-destroy-threatens-north-korea-un-speech-transcript/.

9   Arbatov, A. *Nuclear Deterrence: A Guarantee or Threat to Strategic Stability?* Carnegie Moscow Center, 22 March 2019.

10 Bristow, D.L. *Flight to the Top of the World: The Adventures of Walter Wellman.* Lincoln, US: University of Nebraska Press, 2018, p. 211.

11 Faulkner, W. 'William Faulkner Banquet Speech', 10 December 1950. Retrieved from https://www.nobelprize.org/prizes/literature/1949/faulkner/speech/.

12 Marder, A.J. *From the Dreadnought to Scapa Flow. Vol. 1: The Road to War 1904–1914.* Great Britain: Seaforth Publishing, 2013, p. 272.

13 Tian, Nan, Alexandra Kuimova, Diego Lopes Da Silva, Pieter D. Wezeman and Siemon T. Wezeman. *Trends in World Military Expenditure, 2019.* Sweden: Stockholm International Peace Research Institute, 2020. Retrieved from https://www.sipri.org/sites/default/files/2020-04/fs_2020_04_milex_0.pdf.

14 Dusek, M. '4 ways leaders can strengthen Europe's economic resilience'. World Economic Forum, 21 May 2022. Retrieved from https://www.weforum.org/agenda/2022/05/4-ways-leaders-can-strengthen-europe-economic-resilience/.

15 Dupuy, T.N. *The Evolution of Weapons and Warfare.* California: Hero Books, 1984.

16 Megadeth (n.d.). *Albums.* Retrieved from https://megadeth.com/releases/.

17 Union of Concerned Scientists. 'Frequently Asked Questions about Hair-Trigger Alert'. January 2015. Retrieved from https://www.ucsusa.org/resources/frequently-asked-questions-about-hair-trigger-alert.

18 Woolf, A.F. *U.S. Strategic Nuclear Forces: Background, Developments, and Issues.* Washington, DC: Congressional Research Service, 2020.

19 Nuclear Threat Initiative. *Russia: Nuclear.* August 2018. Retrieved from https://www.nti.org/learn/countries/russia/nuclear/.

20 Stone, R. '"National Pride Is at Stake". Russia, China, USA Race to Build Hypersonic Weapons'. *Science*, January 2020. Retrieved from https://www.sciencemag.org/news/2020/01/national-pride-stake-russia-china-united-states-race-build-hypersonic-weapons.

21 Sayler, K.M. *Defense Primer: U.S. Policy on Lethal Autonomous Weapons Systems.* Washington, DC: Congressional Research Service, 2019. Retrieved from https://fas.org/sgp/crs/natsec/IF11150.pdf.

22 Nieroda, C. 'Killer Robots & Autonomous Machines . . . 3 New Technologies You Need to Know About'. NATO Association of Canada, 13 December 2016. Retrieved from http://natoassociation.ca/killer-robots-autonomous-machines-3-new-technologies-you-need-to-know-about/.

23 Campaign to Stop Killer Robots. 'Artificial Intelligence Experts Call for Ban'. 28 July 2015. Retrieved from https://www.stopkillerrobots.org/2015/07/aicall/.

24 Schummer, J. 'Ethics of Chemical Weapons Research: Poison Gas in World War One'. *HYLE: International Journal for Philosophy of Chemistry*, 2018, pp. 5–28.

25 Sun, Y. *Field Detection Technologies for Explosives*. Hertfordshire, UK: ILM Publications, 2009.

26 Austin, B. 'Wireless in the Boer War'. *IEEE Electromagnetic Compatibility Magazine*, 6(1), 2017, pp. 30–35. Retrieved from https://ieeexplore.ieee.org/stamp/stamp.jsp?arnumber=7931979.

27 Smithsonian National Air and Space Museum. (n.d.) 'The Wright Brothers: The Invention of the Aerial Age'. Retrieved from https://airandspace.si.edu/exhibitions/wright-brothers/online/age/1908/index.cfm.

28 Atomic Heritage Foundation. (n.d.) 'Otto Hahn: Nuclear Chemist, Germany'. Retrieved from https://www.atomicheritage.org/profile/otto-hahn.

29 Ministry of External Affairs, Government of India. 'Frequently Asked Questions on Mission Shakti, India's Anti-Satellite Missile Test Conducted on 27 March, 2019'. 27 March 2019. Retrieved from https://www.mea.gov.in/press-releases.htm?dtl/31179/Frequently_Asked_Questions_on_Mission_Shakti_Indias_AntiSatellite_Missile_test_conducted_on_27_March_2019.

30 Nuclear Threat Initiative. 'Lop Nor Nuclear Weapons Test Base'. 26 July 2012. Retrieved fromhttps://www.nti.org/learn/facilities/710/.

31 Hern, A. '"Industroyer" Virus Could Bring Down Power Networks, Researchers Warn'. *Guardian*, 13 June 2017. Retrieved from https://www.theguardian.com/technology/2017/jun/13/industroyer-malware-virus-bring-down-power-networks-infrastructure-wannacry-ransomware-nhs.

32 Klare, M.T. 'Cyber Battles, Nuclear Outcomes? Dangerous New Pathways to Escalation'. *Arms Control Association*, 2019. Retrieved from https://www.armscontrol.org/act/2019-11/features/cyber-battles-nuclear-outcomes-dangerous-new-pathways-escalation.

33 Devanesan, J. 'Japan's Fugaku Is the World's Fastest Supercomputer'. *Techwire Asia*, 26 June 2020. Retrieved from https://techwireasia.com/2020/06/japans-fugaku-is-the-worlds-fastest-supercomputer/.

34 Anderson, M. 'Will China Attain Exascale Supercomputing in 2020?' *IEEE Spectrum*, 7 January 2020. Retrieved from https://spectrum.ieee.org/computing/hardware/will-china-attain-exascale-supercomputing-in-2020.

35 Peckham, O. 'LLNL Highlights Magma's Role in NNSA's Computing Arsenal'. *HPC Wire*, 11 March 2020. Retrieved from https://www.hpcwire. com/2020/03/11/llnl-highlights-magmas-role-in-the-nnsas-computing-arsenal/.

36 Turney, J. 'Our Final Century by Martin Rees: How a Bored Teenager Could Destroy the Planet'. *Independent*, 29 April 2003. Retrieved from https://www. independent.co.uk/arts-entertainment/books/reviews/our-final-century-by-martin-rees-117154.html.

37 Callaway, E. '*E. Coli* Bacteria Engineered to Eat Carbon Dioxide'. *Nature*, 27 November 2019. Retrieved from https://www.nature.com/articles/ d41586-019-03679-x#:~:text=Ewen%20Callaway&text=Steve%20 Gschmeissner%2FSPL-,E.,sugars%20or%20other%20organic%20molecules.

38 Cohen, J. 'The Untold Story of the "Circle of Trust" behind the World's First Gene-Edited Babies'. *Science*, 2019. Retrieved from https://www.sciencemag. org/news/2019/08/untold-story-circle-trust-behind-world-s-first-gene-edited-babies.

39 Kania, Elsa and Wilson VornDick. 'China's Military Biotech Frontier: CRISPR, Military–Civil Fusion, and the New Revolution in Military Affairs'. *China Brief*, 19(18), 8 October 2019. Retrieved from https://jamestown.org/ program/chinas-military-biotech-frontier-crispr-military-civil-fusion-and-the-new-revolution-in-military-affairs/.

40 Kania, Elsa and Wilson VornDick. 'Weaponizing Biotech: How China's Military Is Preparing for a "New Domain of Warfare"'. *Defense One*, 14 August 2019. Retrieved from https://www.defenseone.com/ideas/2019/08/ chinas-military-pursuing-biotech/159167/.

41 Tegmark, M. *Life 3.0: Being Human in the Age of Artificial Intelligence*. UK: Penguin, 2017.

42 Kimball, D.G. 'Nuclear False Warnings and the Risk of Catastrophe'. *Arms Control Association*, December 2019. Retrieved from https://www. armscontrol.org/act/2019-12/focus/nuclear-false-warnings-risk-catastrophe.

43 Future of Life Institute. (n.d.) 'Accidental Nuclear War: A Timeline of Close Calls'. Retrieved from https://futureoflife.org/background/nuclear-close-calls-a-timeline/.

44 Shephard, Alex and Melville House. 'Here's a List of Every Time Someone Lost Control of Their Nukes'. *Business Insider*, 23 May 2013. Retrieved from https://www.businessinsider.com/list-of-broken-arrow-nuclear-accidents-2013-5?IR=T#:~:text=Since%201950%2C%20there%20have%20 been,been%20lost%20and%20never%20recovered.

45 Walsh, B. *End Times: A Brief Guide to the End of the World, Asteroids, Supervolcanoes, Rogue Robots, and More*. UK: Hachette, 2019.

46 Lau, M. 'Chinese President Xi Jinping Gives Army Its First Order of 2019: Be Ready for Battle'. *South China Morning Post*, 5 January 2019. Retrieved from

https://www.scmp.com/news/china/politics/article/2180772/chinese-president-xi-jinping-gives-army-its-first-order-2019.

47   Chirikov, S. 'Russia Allows Nuclear Response to Conventional Attacks'. *Moscow Times*, 3 June 2020. Retrieved from https://www.themoscowtimes.com/2020/06/03/russia-allows-nuclear-response-to-conventional-attacks-a70471.

48   *Economic Times*. 'Musharraf Planned to Use Nukes against India after 2001 Attack, Claims Report'. 14 July 2018. Retrieved from https://economictimes.indiatimes.com/news/defence/musharraf-planned-to-use-nukes-against-india-after-2001-attack-claims-report/articleshow/59789364.cms.

49   *UN News*. 'Pakistan's Khan Warns of All-out Conflict Amid Rising Tensions over Kashmir; Demands India Lift "Inhuman" Curfew'. 27 September 2019. Retrieved from https://news.un.org/en/story/2019/09/1047952.

50   *Week*. 'Imran Khan Warns of Nuclear War If Pakistan Loses in Conventional Warfare'. 15 September 2019. Retrieved from https://www.theweek.in/news/world/2019/09/15/imran-khan-warns-of-nuclear-war-if-pakistan-loses-in-conventional-warfare.html.

51   *ABC News*. 'North Korea's Kim Jong-un Threatens "Shocking Action" against US with "New Weapon"'. 1 January 2020. Retrieved from: https://www.abc.net.au/news/2020-01-01/north-korea-threat-new-strategic-weapon-us/11836450; Shinkman, P.D. 'North Korea Threatens US: Nuclear Attack "The Only Option Left"'. *U.S. News*, 26 June 2020. Retrieved from: https://www.usnews.com/news/world-report/articles/2020-06-26/north-korea-threatens-us-with-nuclear-attack.

52   Kimball, D. 'START I at a Glance'. *Arms Control Association*, February 2019. Retrieved from https://www.armscontrol.org/factsheets/start1.

53   Reif, K. 'New START at a Glance'. *Arms Control Association*, January 2020. Retrieved from https://www.armscontrol.org/factsheets/NewSTART.

54   Boese, W. 'U.S. Withdraws from ABM Treaty; Global Response Muted'. *Arms Control Association*, 2002. Retrieved from https://www.armscontrol.org/act/2002-07/news/us-withdraws-abm-treaty-global-response-muted.

55   Reif, K. 'Russia Completes CFE Treaty Suspension'. *Arms Control Association*, 2015. Retrieved from https://www.armscontrol.org/act/2015-04/news-briefs/russia-completes-cfe-treaty-suspension.

56   Bugos, S. 'U.S. Completes INF Treaty Withdrawal'. *Arms Control Association*, September 2019. Retrieved from https://www.armscontrol.org/act/2019-09/news/us-completes-inf-treaty-withdrawal.

57   Davenport, K. 'Timeline of Nuclear Diplomacy with Iran'. *Arms Control Association*, April 2020. Retrieved from https://www.armscontrol.org/factsheets/Timeline-of-Nuclear-Diplomacy-With-Iran.

58   Nuclear Threat Initiative. 'Treaty between the United States of America and the Russian Federation on Measures for the Further Reduction and Limitation

of Strategic Offensive Arms (New START)'. 11 February 2020. Retrieved from https://www.nti.org/learn/treaties-and-regimes/treaty-between-the-united-states-of-america-and-the-russian-federation-on-measures-for-the-further-reduction-and-limitation-of-strategic-offensive-arms/.

59   US Department of Defense, Office of the Secretary of Defense. *Nuclear Posture Review*. Washington, DC, 2018. Retrieved from https://media.defense. gov/2018/Feb/02/2001872877/-1/-1/1/EXECUTIVE-SUMMARY.PDF.

60   Arbatov, A. 'Nuclear Deterrence: A Guarantee or Threat to Strategic Stability?' Carnegie Moscow Center, 22 March 2019.

61   Pinker, S. *The Better Angels of Our Nature: Why Violence Has Declined*. UK: Penguin, 2011.

62   Ibid., pp. 235–36.

63   The Institute for Economics and Peace. 'Global Peace Index'. 2012. Retrieved from https://www.economicsandpeace.org/wp-content/ uploads/2015/06/2012-Global-Peace-Index-Report.pdf.

64   Teller, E. *The Pursuit of Simplicity*. Pepperdine University Press, 1980, p. 151.

65   Haworth, Alida, R. Scott, D. Sagan and Benjamin A. Valentino. 'What Do Americans Really Think about Conflict with Nuclear North Korea? The Answer Is Both Reassuring and Disturbing'. *Bulletin of the Atomic Scientists*, 75(4), 2 July 2019. Retrieved from https://thebulletin.org/2019/07/what-do-americans-really-think-about-conflict-with-nuclear-north-korea-the-answer-is-both-reassuring-and-disturbing/.

66   Valentino, S.D. 'Revisiting Hiroshima in Iran: What Americans Really Think about Using Nuclear Weapons and Killing Noncombatants'. *International Security*, 42(1), 2017. Retrieved from https://www.mitpressjournals.org/doi/ full/10.1162/ISEC_a_00284.

67   Brown, C. 'Public Opinion about Using Nuclear Weapons'. Roper Center for Public Opinion Research, 18 February 2015. Retrieved from https:// ropercenter.cornell.edu/blog/public-opinion-about-using-nuclear-weapons.

2. Dark Times: Menace of Nationalism

1   Office of the United Nations High Commissioner for Human Rights. 'Report on the Human Rights Situation in Ukraine, 16 November 2019 to 15 February 2020'. 2020. Retrieved from https://www.ohchr.org/Documents/ Countries/UA/29thReportUkraine_EN.pdf.

2   Harash, R. 'Muslim Holds Ancient Key To Jesus Tomb Site in Jerusalem'. *Reuters*, 30 November 2017. Retrieved from https://in.reuters.com/article/ religion-jerusalem-church/muslim-holds-ancient-key-to-jesus-tomb-site-in-jerusalem-idINKBN1DU180.

3   Tilly, C. *Coercion, Capital and European States: AD 990–1992*. Vol. 1, *Studies in Social Discontinuity*. Wiley, 1993.

4   Arendt, H. *The Origins of Totalitarianism*. UK: Penguin, 2017.

5   Brooks, D. 'Do Democrats Know What Unites Us?' *New York Times*, 5
    November 2018. Retrieved from https://www.nytimes.com/2018/11/05/
    opinion/democrats-midterms-immigration-nation.html.

6   Prabook. (n.d.) 'Vasil Uladzamiravich Bykau'. Retrieved from https://
    prabook.com/web/vasil.bykau/720907.

7   Chesney, G. *The Battle of Dorking: Reminiscences of a Volunteer*. Dodo Press,
    2008.

8   Brooke, R. *1914 and Other Poems*. UK: Sidgwick & Jackson, 1911, p.15.

9   International Peace Bureau. (n.d.) 'History: Over a Century of Peace Making'.
    Retrieved from http://www.ipb.org/history/over-a-century-of-peace-
    making/.

10 Marx, K. *The Civil War in France*. 1871. Retrieved from https://www.marxists.
    org/archive/marx/works/download/pdf/civil_war_france.pdf.

11 Tharoor, I. 'The Nanjing Massacre: Scenes from a Hideous Slaughter 75
    Years Ago'. *Time*, 13 December 2012. Retrieved from https://world.time.
    com/2012/12/13/the-nanjing-massacre-scenes-from-a-hideous-slaughter-
    75-years-ago/photo/sino-japanese-war/.

12 Tillman, B. *D-Day Encyclopedia: Everything You Want to Know about the Normandy
    Invasion*. US: Regnery Publishing, 2014.

13 *BBC*. 'French Casualties on D-Day: "What I Saw . . . Was So Horrible"'.
    3 June 2019. Retrieved from https://www.bbc.com/news/av/world-
    europe-48489460/french-casualties-on-d-day-what-i-saw-was-so-horrible.

14 Reif, K . and Bugos, S. 'UK to Increase Cap on Nuclear Warhead Stockpile'.
    Arms Control Association, 2021. Retrieved from https://www.armscontrol.
    org/act/2021-04/news/uk-increase-cap-nuclear-warhead-stockpile.

15 Linton, R. *The Study of Man*. US: D. Appleton-Century, 1936, pp. 326–27.

16 Huntington, S.P. *The Clash of Civilizations and the Remaking of World Order*.
    New York: Simon and Schuster, 2007.

17 Isachenkov, V. *Putin Says Russia Is Leading World in Hypersonic Weapons. ABC News*,
    25 December 2019. Retrieved from https://abcnews.go.com/International/
    wireStory/putin-russia-leading-world-hypersonic-weapons-67911604.

18 Soon, S. 'Amid Economic Challenges, China Displays "A Military Show of
    Strength" at Its 70th Birthday Bash'. *CNBC News*, 1 October 2019. Retrieved
    from https://www.cnbc.com/2019/10/01/china-displays-a-military-show-
    of-strength-at-70th-anniversary-parade.html.

19 Central Intelligence Agency. (n.d.) 'Russia'. The World Factbook. Retrieved
    from https://www.cia.gov/library/publications/the-world-factbook/geos/
    rs.html.

20 Conant, E. 'Ethnic Russians: Pretext for Putin's Ukraine Invasion?' *National
    Geographic*, 2 May 2014. Retrieved from https://www.nationalgeographic.

com/news/2014/5/140502-russia-putin-ukraine-geography-crimea-language/.

21   Akhmatova, A. 'The Poet and the Motherland: On the 119th Anniversary of Anna Akhmatova's Birth'. Russkiy Mir Foundation, 25 June 2008. Retrieved from https://russkiymir.ru/en/publications/139547/.

22   Atomic Heritage Foundation. 'Tsar Bomba'. 8 August 2014. Retrieved from https://www.atomicheritage.org/history/tsar-bomba.

23   Beebe, G.S. *The Russia Trap: How Our Shadow War with Russia Could Spiral into Nuclear Catastrophe.* US: St Martin's Publishing Group, 2019.

24   Allison, G. 'The Thucydides Trap: Are the U.S. and China Headed for War?' *Atlantic,* 24 September 2015. Retrieved from https://www.theatlantic.com/international/archive/2015/09/united-states-china-war-thucydides-trap/406756/.

25   Xinhua. 'The Largest Military Orchestra Appeared on the National Day Parade'. 1 October 2019. Retrieved from http://www.xinhuanet.com/politics/2019-10/01/c_1125063670.htm.

26   Joe, R. 'Reviewing China's National Day Parade'. *Diplomat,* 21 October 2019. Retrieved from https://thediplomat.com/2019/10/reviewing-chinas-national-day-parade/.

27   Huang, E. 'As Dissent Is Silenced, Xi Jinping Lauds a Massive Student Rebellion 100 Years Ago'. *Quartz,* 3 May 2019. Retrieved from https://qz.com/1609382/china-lauds-100-years-since-the-1919-may-4th-protests/.

28   Curtis, K. and Hansen V., eds. *Voyages in World History,* Vol. 1. US: Wadsworth Cengage Learning, 2008, pp. 411–14.

29   Piven, B. 'North Korea Celebrates "Juche 101"'. *Al Jazeera,* 10 April 2012. Retrieved from https://www.aljazeera.com/indepth/features/2012/04/2012410111258757121.html.

30   Ronkin, N. 'On the Centennial of the March First Independence Movement of Korea'. Stanford University, Freeman Spogli Insititute for International Studies, 13 May 2019. Retrieved from https://fsi.stanford.edu/news/centennial-march-first-independence-movement-korea.

31   Blake, S. '10 Myths North Koreans Are Told about Kim Jong-un'. *Northern Star,* 15 April 2017. Retrieved from https://www.northernstar.com.au/news/10-myths-north-koreans-believe-about-kim-jong-un/3166963/.

32   Branigan, T. 'Kim Jong-un's Uncle Jang Song-thaek Executed, Say North Korean State Media'. *Guardian,* 13 December 2013. Retrieved from https://www.theguardian.com/world/2013/dec/12/north-korea-jang-song-thaek-executed.

33   Ellis-Petersen, Hannah and Benjamin Haas. 'How North Korea Got Away with the Assassination of Kim Jong-nam'. *Guardian,* 1 April 2019. Retrieved from https://www.theguardian.com/world/2019/apr/01/how-north-korea-got-away-with-the-assassination-of-kim-jong-nam.

34 Beauchamp, Z. 'Juche, the State Ideology That Makes North Koreans Revere Kim Jong-Un, Explained'. *Vox News*, 18 June 2018. Retrieved from https://www.vox.com/world/2018/6/18/17441296/north-korea-propaganda-ideology-juche.

35 Albert, E. 'North Korea's Military Capabilities'. Council on Foreign Relations, 20 December 2019. Retrieved from https://www.cfr.org/backgrounder/north-koreas-military-capabilities.

36 Malice, M. 'Going Nuclear: What Is the Ideological Justification of North Korean Militarism?' *Observer*, 14 January 2016. Retrieved from https://observer.com/2016/01/going-nuclear-what-is-the-ideological-justification-of-north-korean-militarism/.

37 Klug, F. 'Juche Rules North Korean Propaganda, but What Does It Mean?' *Associated Press*, 30 September 2019. Retrieved from https://apnews.com/d63d00ce9de042dc88b9df2c40be53ee.

38 Popham, P. '"The World's Most Dangerous Place" Is Already at War'. *Independent*, 18 March 2000. Retrieved from https://www.independent.co.uk/news/world/asia/the-worlds-most-dangerous-place-is-already-at-war-282458.html.

39 Kazimi, D.M. 'Special Report: The Legendary Liaquat, 1895–1951'. *Dawn News*, 19 October 2017. Retrieved from https://www.dawn.com/news/1362909.

40 *UN News*. 'Pakistan's Khan Warns of All-out Conflict Amid Rising Tensions over Kashmir; Demands India Lift "Inhuman" Curfew'. 27 September 2019. Retrieved from https://news.un.org/en/story/2019/09/1047952.

41 Baker, L. 'With Trump Sitting Nearby, Macron Calls Nationalism a Betrayal'. *Reuters*, 11 November 2018. Retrieved from https://www.reuters.com/article/us-ww1-centenary-macron-nationalism/with-trump-sitting-nearby-macron-calls-nationalism-a-betrayal-idUSKCN1NG0IH.

42 Singh, B. 'Patriots and Nationalists'. *Statesman*, 27 November 2018. Retrieved from https://www.thestatesman.com/opinion/patriots-and-nationalists-1502711594.html.

43 Fromm, E. *The Sane Society*. New York: Open Road Integrated Media, 2013.

44 Viereck, G.S. 'What Life Means to Einstein'. *Saturday Evening Post*, 26 October 1929. Retrieved from http://www.saturdayeveningpost.com/wp-content/uploads/satevepost/einstein.pdf.

45 Tagore, R. *Nationalism*. New Delhi: General Press, 2019, pp. 38–102.

3. In Twilight Hours: War, a Choice

1 Horgan, J. *The End of War*. US: McSweeney's, 2012, p. 5.

2 Asbridge, T.S. *The Crusades: The Authoritative History of the War for the Holy Land*. US: Harper Collins, 2010, pp. 15–33, 519–50.

3   Goldschmidt Jr., Arthur and Ibrahim Al-Marashi. *The High Caliphate. A Concise History of the Middle East.* UK: Hachette, 2015.

4   Grousset, R. *The Empire of the Steppes: A History of Central Asia* (translated by N. Walford). US: Rutgers University Press, 1970, p. 434.

5   Powell, C. 'Remarks at the World Economic Forum'. US Department of State, 2003. Retrieved from https://2001-2009.state.gov/secretary/former/powell/remarks/2003/21810.htm.

6   Waslekar, Sundeep. *Cost of Conflict in the Middle East.* Mumbai, India: Strategic Foresight Group, 2009. Retrieved from https://www.strategicforesight.com/publication_pdf/39166Cost%20of%20Conflict%20in%20the%20Middle%20East.pdf.

7   Berreby, D. *Us and Them: The Science of Identity.* US: University of Chicago Press, 2008, pp. 157–223.

8   Nah, L.T. 'What's behind North Korea's Missile Testing?' *Diplomat*, 4 December 2019. Retrieved from https://thediplomat.com/2019/12/whats-behind-north-koreas-missile-testing/.

9   *Limitation of Naval Armament.* 43 Stat. 1655. 6 February 1922. Retrieved from https://www.loc.gov/law/help/us-treaties/bevans/m-ust000002-0351.pdf.

10 The Office of 'Disarmament'. *Disarmament in 1932: The Yearbook of the Disarmament Information Committee.* Geneva: League of Nations Union, 1932, pp. 11–15. Retrieved from https://www.peacepalacelibrary.nl/pmfiles/D10-13-006.pdf.

11 Van Berchem, Mathieu. 'Swiss Divided over Legacy of 1515 Battle'. Swissinfo. ch, 2 January 2015. Retrieved from https://www.swissinfo.ch/eng/500-year-controversy_swiss-divided-over-legacy-of-1515-battle/41189286.

12 Aeschimann, S., et al. (n.d.) *Swiss Neutrality.* Swiss Federal Department of Defence Civil Protection and Sports and Federal Department of Foreign Affairs. Retrieved from https://www.files.ethz.ch/isn/14841/broch_neutrality_e22.pdf.

13 Republic of Austria, Parliament. (n.d.) *1955—State Treaty and Neutrality.* Retrieved from https://www.parlament.gv.at/ENGL/PERK/HIS/REP2/1955/index.shtml.

14 Macias, A. *From Aruba to Iceland, These 36 Nations Have No Standing Military. CNBC News*, 3 April 2018. Retrieved from https://www.cnbc.com/2018/04/03/countries-that-do-not-have-a-standing-army-according-to-cia-world-factbook.html.

15 Barquero, J.C. 'Does International Humanitarian Law Play Any Role in Demilitarized Countries? A Policy Analysis of Costa Rica and Panama'. *Revista Relaciones Internacionales*, 84, 2012, p. 111. Retrieved from https://www.corteidh.or.cr/tablas/r32018.pdf.

16 The Nobel Prize. (n.d.) 'Oscar Arias Sánchez'. Retrieved from https://www.nobelprize.org/prizes/peace/1987/arias/facts/.

17 Derbyshire, J. Denis and Ian Derbyshire. *Encyclopedia of World Political Systems*, Vol. 1. US: Routledge, 2016, p. 736.

18 Thucydides. *The History of the Peloponnesian War* (translated by R. Crawley). London: Longmans, Green, and Co., 1874, pp. 41–74, 396–421.

19 Tzu, S. *The Art of War* (translated by T. Huynh). India: Jaico Publishing House, 2010.

20 Kamal, K. 'Kautilya's Arthashastra: Indian Strategic Culture and Grand Strategic Preferences'. *Journal of Defense Studies*, 12(3), July–September 2018, pp. 27–54. Retrieved from https://idsa.in/jds/jds-12-3-2018-kautilya-arthashastra-kajari-kamal.

21 Teller, E. 'Fallout and Disarmament: A Debate Between Linus Pauling and Edward Teller'. KQED television, 20 February 1958. San Francisco.

22 Harrer, G. 'Cicero on Peace and War'. *Classical Journal*, 14(1), 1918, pp. 26–38. Retrieved from http://www.jstor.org/stable/3288190.

23 Tornau, C. 'Saint Augustine' (edited by E. Zalta). *Stanford Encyclopedia of Philosophy*, 2020. Retrieved from https://plato.stanford.edu/archives/sum2020/entries/augustine/.

24 Kaufman, R.G. 'Just Prudence: Defending Aquinas on Preemption, Prevention, & Decisiveness in War'. *Providence*, 27 September 2017. Retrieved from https://providencemag.com/2017/09/just-prudence-defending-aquinas-on-preemption-prevention-decisiveness-in-war/.

25 Khaldun, I. *The Muqaddimah: An Introduction to History* (translated by F. Rosenthal). US: Princeton University Press, 2005.

26 Hobbes, T. *Leviathan*, Vol. 1, Part 1. Andrew Crooke, 1651, pp. 61–62.

27 Bertram, C. 'Jean Jacques Rousseau' (edited by E. Zalta). *Stanford Encyclopedia of Philosophy*, May 2017. Retrieved from https://plato.stanford.edu/archives/sum2020/entries/rousseau/.

28 Grayling, A. *War: An Enquiry*. US: Yale University Press, 2017, pp. 9–10.

29 International Committee of the Red Cross. 'Convention (IV) Relative to the Protection of Civilian Persons in Time of War. Geneva, 12 August 1949'. 1958. Retrieved from https://ihl-databases.icrc.org/applic/ihl/ihl.nsf/COM/380-600005?OpenDocument.

30 Einstein, A. *Einstein on Peace* (edited by O. Nathan). Pickle Partners Publishing, 2017s.

31 Please see https://en.unesco.org/courier/marzo-1993/why-war-letter-freud-einstein.

32 Korab-Karpowicz, J. 'Political Realism in International Relations' (edited by E. Zalta). *Stanford Encyclopedia of Philosophy*, 2018. Retrieved from https://plato.stanford.edu/archives/sum2018/entries/realism-intl-relations/.

33 John F. Kennedy Presidential Library and Museum. 'Archives: Address before the United Nations General Assembly, 25 September 1961'. 1961. Retrieved

from   https://www.jfklibrary.org/asset-viewer/archives/JFKWHA/1961/
JFKWHA-050/JFKWHA-050.

34 Marinoff, L. *On Human Conflict: The Philosophical Foundations of War and Peace.*
US: Hamilton Books, 2019, pp. 1, 183, 427, 429.

4. Dawn on the Horizon: Where Peace Dares

1   Buddemeir, Brooke, et al. 'National Capital Region: Key Response Planning
Factors for the Aftermath of Nuclear Terrorism'. Lawrence Livermore
National Laboratory, U.S. Department of Homeland Security, 2011. Retrieved
from https://fas.org/irp/agency/dhs/fema/ncr.pdf.

2   Robock, A. and O.B. Toon. 'Self-Assured Destruction: The Climate Impacts
of Nuclear War'. *Bulletin of the Atomic Scientists*, 12 September 2012. Retrieved
from https://thebulletin.org/2012/09/self-assured-destruction-the-climate-
impacts-of-nuclear-war/.

3   Klingaman, W and N. Klingaman. 'Tambora Erupts in 1815 and Changes
World History'. *Scientific American*, 2013. Retrieved from https://www.
scientificamerican.com/article/1816-the-year-without-summer-excerpt/.

4   Helfand, I. 'Nuclear Famine: Two Billion People at Risk?' International
Physicians for the Prevention of Nuclear War, 2, 2013. Retrieved from https://
www.psr.org/wp-content/uploads/2018/04/two-billion-at-risk.pdf.

5   Schultz, G. 'The War That Must Never Be Fought'. Hoover Institution, 12
March 2015. Retrieved from https://www.hoover.org/research/war-must-
never-be-fought-0.

6   Swami Vivekananda. *Sisters & Brothers of America: Speech at World's Parliament
of Religions, Chicago, 1893* (edited by S. Srinivasan). CreateSpace Independent
Publishing Platform, 2015.

7   O'Connor, T. 'Iran Does Not Have Nuclear Weapons, But Here's Why Its
Program Is at the Heart of the Crisis'. *Newsweek*, 3 January 2020. Retrieved
from   https://www.newsweek.com/why-iran-does-not-have-nuclear-
weapons-1480355.

8   Parliament of the World's Religions. 'Responding to the Unique Challenge
of Nuclear Weapons: A Passionate Call From The Parliament of the World's
Religions'. 28 November 2018. Retrieved from https://parliamentofreligions.
org/blog/2019-09-13-1201/responding-unique-challenge-nuclear-
weapons-passionate-call-parliament-world%E2%80%99s?utm_
source=Email%20Updates&utm_campaign=aa83f20c86-EMAIL_
CAMPAIGN_2017_05_04_COPY_01&utm_medium=email&utm_
term=0.

9   Religions for Peace. 'Declaration of the 10th World Assembly of Religions
for Peace'. 23 August 2019. Retrieved from https://rfp.org/declaration-
of-the-10th-world-assembly-of-religions-for-peace%ef%bb%bf/?fbcl

id=IwAR0pMbgFHCfV6GPs4vuTdRcWjSrNLQ7s6V7WjPOWxi-L6vHAEezGoGmRc7E.

10 Christian Campaign for Nuclear Disarmament. 'The Biblical Case against Nuclear Weapons'. September 2019. Retrieved from http://christiancnd.org.uk/wp-content/uploads/2018/05/The-Biblical-Case-Against-Nuclear-Weapons.pdf.

11 *Japan Times*. 'Full Text of Pope Francis' Message in Nagasaki'. 24 November 2019. Retrieved from https://www.japantimes.co.jp/news/2019/11/24/national/full-text-of-pope-francis-nagasaki/#.XtSinTozZPY.

12 Lebow, R. and J. Stein. 'Reagan and the Russians'. *Atlantic*, February 1994. Retrieved from https://www.theatlantic.com/past/docs/politics/foreign/reagrus.htm.

13 Johns, Andrew L. and M.B. Lerner (eds). *The Cold War at Home and Abroad: Domestic Politics and U.S. Foreign Policy since 1945*. US: University Press of Kentucky, 2018, p. 277.

14 Ronald Reagan Presidential Library and Museum. 'Address to the 39th Session of the United Nations General Assembly in New York'. 24 September 1984. Retrieved from. https://www.reaganlibrary.gov/research/speeches/092187b.

15 Weisberg, J. 'Ronald Reagan's Disarmament Dream'. *Atlantic*, 1 January 2016. Retrieved from https://www.theatlantic.com/politics/archive/2016/01/ronald-reagans-disarmament-dream/422244/.

16 'Treaty on Elimination of Intermediate-Range and Shorter-Range Missiles between USA and USSR'. 8 December 1987. Retrieved from https://media.nti.org/documents/inf_treaty.pdf.

17 Negroponte, D.V. 'Would the Soviet Union Have Collapsed without Mikhail Gorbachev?' The Brookings Institution, 17 October 2019. Retrieved from https://www.brookings.edu/blog/order-from-chaos/2019/10/17/would-the-soviet-union-have-collapsed-without-mikhail-gorbachev/.

18 Willy Brandt Online Biografie. (n.d.) 'Willy Brandt'. Retrieved from https://www.willy-brandt-biography.com/.

19 GHDI. (n.d.) 'Agreement on Border Crossing'. 17 December 1963). Retrieved from http://ghdi.ghi-dc.org/sub_document.cfm?document_id=916&language=english.

20 Bernd Rother, K.L. (ed.) *Willy Brandt and International Relations: Europe, the USA and Latin America, 1974–1992*. Bloomsbury, 2019, pp. 5–7.

21 Hofmann, S.J. 'Willy Brandt: German, European and Cosmopolitan'. *DW News*, 18 December 2013. Retrieved from https://www.dw.com/en/willy-brandt-german-european-and-cosmopolitan/a-17300003.

22 Kieninger, S. 'Fifty Years since Ostpolitik. How Willy Brandt's Diplomacy Transformed Europe'. American Institute for Contemporary German Studies, Johns Hopkins University, 21 October 2019. Retrieved from https://

www.aicgs.org/2019/10/fifty-years-since-ostpolitik-how-willy-brandts-diplomacy-transformed-europe/.

23   King, Jr, M.L. '"I Have a Dream", Address Delivered at the March on Washington for Jobs and Freedom'. The Martin Luther King, Jr, Research and Education Institute, Stanford University, 28 August 1963. Retrieved from https://kinginstitute.stanford.edu/king-papers/documents/i-have-dream-address-delivered-march-washington-jobs-and-freedom.

24   Atomic Heritage Foundation. 'The Manhattan Project'. 12 May 2017. Retrieved from https://www.atomicheritage.org/history/manhattan-project.

25   Rust, S. 'How the US Betrayed the Marshall Islands, Kindling the Next Nuclear Disaster'. Los Angeles Times, 10 November 2019. Retrieved from https://www.latimes.com/projects/marshall-islands-nuclear-testing-sea-level-rise/.

26   Geggel, L. 'The Marshall Islands Are 10 Times More "Radioactive" Than Chernobyl'. Live Science, 16 July 2019. Retrieved from https://www.livescience.com/65949-marshall-islands-more-radioactivity-chernobyl.html.

27   Comprehensive Nuclear Test Ban Treaty Organisation. (n.d.) 'The Soviet Union's Nuclear Testing Programme'. Retrieved from https://www.ctbto.org/nuclear-testing/the-effects-of-nuclear-testing/the-soviet-unionsnuclear-testing-programme/.

28   The Nuclear Chain. (n.d.) 'Novaya Zemlya, Russia'. Retrieved from http://www.nuclear-risks.org/en/hibakusha-worldwide/novaya-zemlya.html.

29   Nuclear Threat Initiative. 'Lop Nor Nuclear Weapons Test Base'. 26 July 2012. Retrieved from https://www.nti.org/learn/facilities/710/.

30   Kimbal, D.G. (n.d.) 'In Memoriam: Randall Caroline Forsberg (1943–2007)'. Arms Control Association. Retrieved from https://www.armscontrol.org/act/2007_12/InMemoriam.

31   Robinson, P. 'The American Anti-nuclear Movement'. Oxford Research Encyclopedia, April 2016. Retrieved from https://oxfordre.com/americanhistory/view/10.1093/acrefore/9780199329175.001.0001/acrefore-9780199329175-e-26?mediaType=Article.

32   Klehr, H. Far Left of Center: The American Radical Left Today. US: Transaction Publishers, 1991.

33   Hendrix, K. 'Unlikely Saga of Great Peace March Nears Its Climax'. Los Angeles Times, 9 November 1986. Retrieved from https://www.latimes.com/archives/la-xpm-1986-11-09-vw-24076-story.html.

34   Campaign for Nuclear Disarmament. (n.d.) 'The history of CND'. Retrieved from https://cnduk.org/who/the-history-of-cnd/.

35   'Four Decades of Nuclear Testing: The Legacy of Semipalatinsk'. EClinicalMedicine, 13(1). Elsevier, National Center for Biotechnology Information, 2019. Retrieved from https://www.ncbi.nlm.nih.gov/pmc/articles/PMC6734094/#.

36 Kassenova, T. 'The Lasting Toll of Semipalatinsk's Nuclear Testing'. *Bulletin of the Atomic Scientists*, 28 September 2009. Retrieved from https://thebulletin. org/2009/09/the-lasting-toll-of-semipalatinsks-nuclear-testing/; Yan, W. 'The Nuclear Sins of the Soviet Union Live On in Kazakhstan'. *Nature*, 3 April 2019. Retrieved from https://www.nature.com/articles/d41586-019-01034-8.

37 *BBC.* 'Life after Nuclear Testing'. 19 November 2010. Retrieved from http://www.bbc.co.uk/worldservice/programmes/2010/11/101119_kazakhstan_nuclear_testing.shtml.

38 Gelis, U. 'Against "Sophisticated Barbarianism"'. *Nordic Page*, 22 August 2014. Retrieved from https://www.tnp.no/norway/global/4583-against-sophisticated-barbarianism-25-years-of-the-international-anti-nuclear-movement-nevada-semipalatinsk#_ftn1.

39 Kimball, D. 'Nuclear Testing and Comprehensive Test Ban Treaty (CTBT) Timeline'. Arms Control Association, June 2019. Retrieved from https://www.armscontrol.org/factsheets/Nuclear-Testing-and-Comprehensive-Test-Ban-Treaty-CTBT-Timeline.

40 Reliefweb. 'Landmine Monitor 2019'. 21 November 2019. Retrieved from https://reliefweb.int/report/world/landmine-monitor-2019.

41 International Campaign to Abolish Nuclear Weapons. (n.d.) '*Beatrice Fihn*'. Retrieved from https://www.icanw.org/beatrice_fihn.

42 United Nations. 'Conference to Negotiate Legally Binding Instrument Banning Nuclear Weapons Adopts Treaty by 122 Votes in Favour, 1 against, 1 Abstention'. 7 July 2017. Retrieved from https://www.un.org/press/en/2017/dc3723.doc.htm.

43 International Physicians for the Prevention of Nuclear War. (n.d.) 'Our Mission'. Retrieved from https://www.ippnw.org/mission.html.

44 Campaign to Stop Killer Robots. 'European Parliament Resolution a First'. 27 February 2014. Retrieved from https://www.stopkillerrobots.org/2014/02/europeanparliament/.

45 Conn, A. 'AI Companies, Researchers, Engineers, Scientists, Entrepreneurs, and Others Sign Pledge Promising Not to Develop Lethal Autonomous Weapons'. Future of Life Institute, 18 July 2018. Retrieved from https://futureoflife.org/2018/07/18/ai-companies-researchers-engineers-scientists-entrepreneurs-and-others-sign-pledge-promising-not-to-develop-lethal-autonomous-weapons/.

46 Parliamentarians for Global Action. 'Global Parliamentary Campaign in Support of the Negotiation of a Treaty Prohibiting Fully Autonomous Weapons'. May 2020. Retrieved from https://www.pgaction.org/ips/autonomous-weapons.html.

47 Riley-Smith, B. '3,000 Google Employees Sign Letter Protesting Company's Work with the Pentagon'. *Telegraph*, 5 April 2018. Retrieved from https://

www.telegraph.co.uk/news/2018/04/05/3000-google-employees-sign-letter-protesting-companys-work-pentagon/.

48 Fang, L. 'Google Hedges on Promise to End Controversial Involvement in Military Drone Contract'. *Intercept*, 2 March 2019. Retrieved from https://theintercept.com/2019/03/01/google-project-maven-contract/.

49 World Peace Council. (n.d.) 'Who We Are'. Retrieved from https://www.wpc-in.org/about-wpc.

50 El Baradei, D.M. 'Addressing Verification Challenges'. International Atomic Energy Agency, 16 October 2006. Retrieved from https://www.iaea.org/newscenter/statements/addressing-verification-challenges.

5. Before Daylight: Shaping Peace, Preventing Wars

1   Reuser, I. 'Studying Abroad in the Middle Ages'. Oxford Student, 22 February 2016. Retrieved from https://www.oxfordstudent.com/2016/02/22/studying-abroad-middle-ages/.

2   Waslekar, S. *An Inclusive World in which the West, Islam, and the Rest Have a Stake.* Mumbai, India: Strategic Foresight Group, 2007, pp. 22–23.

3   Surhone, Lambert M., Miriam T. Timpledon and Susan F. Marseken (eds). *Siege of Baghdad (1258)*. Germany: VDM Publishing, 2010.

4   Stanley, M. 'The Man Who Made Einstein World-Famous'. *BBC*, 24 May 2019. Retrieved from https://www.bbc.com/news/science-environment-48369980.

5   Harari, Y.N. *21 Lessons for the 21st Century.* UK: Penguin Random House, 2018.

6   Alighieri, D. *The De Monarchia of Dante Alighieri* (translated by A. Henry). New York: Houghton, Miflin and Company, 1904.

7   Crucé, É. *Nouveau Cyneé de Éméric Crucé* (edited by T.W. Balch). Allen, Lane, and Scott, 1909.

8   Hadjilambrinos, C. 'The Long Path to European Union: A Historical–Institutional Analysis of Proposals for European Integration from 800 to 1938'. *ILIRIA International Review*, 8(2), 2018, p. 132.

9   Hochschild, A. *To End All Wars: A Story of Loyalty and Rebellion, 1914–1918.* New York: Houghton, Mifflin, Harcourt, 2011.

10 Rousseau, J.J. *The Plan for Perpetual Peace, On the Government of Poland, and Other Writings on History and Politics.* US: Dartmouth College Press, 2013, pp. 25–49.

11 Hastie, W. (ed.) *Kant's Principles of Politics, including His Essay on Perpetual Peace. A Contribution to Political Science* (translated by W. Hastie). UK: T. & T. Clark, 1891.

12 Ibid.

13 Friends of Adin Ballou. (n.d.) 'Adin Ballou, Tolstoy, and Gandhi'. Retrieved from http://www.adinballou.org/BallouTolstoyGandhi.shtml.

14 Gandhi, M. 'Speech at Public Meeting, Rangoon'. *Gandhi Sevagram Ashram*, 45(4), 1929, p. 199. Retrieved from https://www.gandhiashramsevagram. org/gandhi-literature/mahatma-gandhi-collected-works-volume-45.pdf.

15 Kripalani, K. (ed.) *All Men Are Brothers: Life and Thoughts of Mahatma Gandhi as Told in His Own Words*. US: UNESCO, 1958.

16 Hudgens, T.A. *Let's Abolish War (Not a New Idea)*. BILR Corporation, 1986, p. 14.

17 Gandhi, M. *Nationalism v. Internationalism*. Bombay Sarvodaya Mandal, 1924. Retrieved from https://www.mkgandhi.org/momgandhi/chap91.htm.

18 Gandhi, M. (n.d.) *The Voice of Truth* (edited by S. Narayan). Ahmedabad, India: Navjivan Publishing House, p. 200.

19 Tendulkar, D. *Mahatma*, Vol. 6 (1940–45). Ministry of Information and Broadcasting, Government of India, 1953, p. 213.

20 Einstein, A. *Out of My Later Years: The Scientist, Philosopher, and Man Portrayed Through His Own Words*, Vol. 2 (1934–50). Open Road Integrated Media, 2011.

21 Einstein, A. *The Albert Einstein Collection*, Vol. 1: *Essays in Humanism, the Theory of Relativity, and the World As I See It*. Open Road Media, 2016.

22 Einstein, A. 'Atomic War or Peace'. *Atlantic*, November 1947. Retrieved from https://www.theatlantic.com/magazine/archive/1947/11/atomic-war-or-peace/305443/.

23 UNOG Library, Registry, Records and Archives Unit. (n.d.) History of the League of Nations. Retrieved from https://www.unog. ch/80256EDD006B8954/(httpAssets)/36BC4F83BD9E4443C1257AF3004 FC0AE/%24file/Historical_overview_of_the_League_of_Nations.pdf.

24 *BBC News*. (n.d.) 'The League of Nations'. Retrieved from https://www. bbc.co.uk/bitesize/guides/z98xj6f/revision/2.

25 Restad, H.E. *American Exceptionalism: An Idea That Made a Nation and Remade the World*. New York: Routledge, 2014.

26 United Nations. 'Charter of the United Nations'. 1945. Retrieved from https://www.un.org/en/charter-united-nations/.

27 Ikeda, D. *Forum for Peace: Daisaku Ikeda's Proposals to the UN*. London: I.B. Tauris & Co., 2014, p. 44.

28 McMahon, R. 'Bosnia: UN Failure to Save Srebrenica Examined'. *Radio Free Europe Radio Liberty*, 7 July 2000. Retrieved from https://www.rferl. org/a/1094332.html.

29 Ahmad, S.Z. 'The UN's Role in the Bosnian Crisis: A Critique'. *Pakistan Institute of International Affairs*, 51(2), April 1998, pp. 83–92. Retrieved from https://www.jstor.org/stable/41394460?seq=1.

30 *UN News*. 'UN Officials Recall "Horror" of Srebrenica as Security Council Fails to Adopt Measure Condemning Massacre'. 8 July 2015. Retrieved from https://news.un.org/en/story/2015/07/503712-un-officials-recall-horror-

srebrenica-security-council-fails-adopt-measure#:~:text=As%20the%20
United%20Nations%20Security,20%20years%20after%20thousands%20of.

31 United Nations. (n.d.) 'Rwanda: A Brief History of the Country'. Retrieved
from https://www.un.org/en/preventgenocide/rwanda/historical-
background.shtml.

32 Maritz, D. 'Rwandan Genocide: Failure of the International Community?'
E-International Relations, 2012. Retrieved from https://www.e-ir.
info/2012/04/07/rwandan-genocide-failure-of-the-international-
community/.

33 Barber, R. 'Syria: The Disgraceful Stain Left by the UN Security Council
Veto'. The Lowy Institute, 24 September 2019. Retrieved from https://www.
lowyinstitute.org/the-interpreter/syria-disgraceful-stain-left-un-security-
council-veto.

34 Gowan, R. 'Three Troubling Trends at the UN Security Council'. International
Crisis Group, 6 November 2019. Retrieved from https://www.crisisgroup.
org/global/three-troubling-trends-un-security-council.

35 Ikeda, D. *Forum for Peace: Daisaku Ikeda's Proposals to the UN*. London: I.B.
Tauris & Co., 2014, p. 165.

36 Rousseau, J.J. *A Treatise on the Social Compact, Or, the Principles of Political Law*.
London: D.I. Eaton, 1795, pp.13–14.

37 Rousseau, J.J. *A Lasting Peace through the Federation of Europe and the State of War*
(translated by C. E. Vaughan). London: Constable and Co., 1917.

6. Morning at Last: A World without War

1 *The Onion*. 'August 5, 1914'. 3 August 2006. Retrieved from https://www.
theonion.com/august-5-1914-1819588242.

2 International Peace Conference. 'Convention (IV) Respecting the Laws and
Customs of War on Land and Its Annex: Regulations Concerning the Laws
and Customs of War on Land'. The Hague Conventions of 1899 (II) and
1907 (IV): Respecting the Laws and Customs of War on Land. The Hague, 18
October 1907.

3 International Court of Justice. 'Legality of the Threat or Use of Nuclear
Weapons, Advisory Opinion'. 1996. Retrieved from https://www.icj-cij.
org/files/case-related/95/095-19960708-ADV-01-00-EN.pdf.

4 United Nations Office for Disarmament Affairs. '67th Session of the General
Assembly'. 2012. Retrieved from https://www.un.org/disarmament/
meetings/firstcommittee-67/.

5 International Committee of the Red Cross. 'Council of Delegates 2011:
Resolution 1. Working towards the Elimination of Nuclear Weapons'. Geneva,
Switzerland, 26 November 2011. Retrieved from https://www.icrc.org/en/
doc/resources/documents/resolution/council-delegates-resolution-1-2011.
htm.

6   Bernhardt, A. et al. 'Pollution Knows No Borders'. *Pure Earth*, January 2019. Retrieved from https://www.pureearth.org/wp-content/uploads/2019/01/PE_PollutionKnowsNoBordersOnline.pdf.

7   Glick, D. 'GeoSigns: The Big Thaw'. *National Geographic*, September 2004. Retrieved from https://www.nationalgeographic.com/science/earth/earths-atmosphere/geo-signs-thaw/.

8   Coyle, M. 'Up in Smoke: Australia Wildfires Are Now So Massive That the Smoke Can Be Seen 7,000 Miles Away in Chile'. *Sun*, 8 January 2020. Retrieved from https://www.thesun.co.uk/news/10694221/australia-bushfires-smoke-reaches-chile-argentina/.

9   Haggeman, H. 'The 1918 Flu Pandemic Was Brutal, Killing More Than 50 Million People Worldwide'. *NPR*, 2 April 2020. Retrieved from https://www.npr.org/2020/04/02/826358104/the-1918-flu-pandemic-was-brutal-killing-as-many-as-100-million-people-worldwide.

10   Centers for Disease Control and Prevention. '1957–1958 Pandemic (H2N2 Virus)'. 2019. Retrieved from https://www.cdc.gov/flu/pandemic-resources/1957-1958-pandemic.html.

11   World Health Organisation. (n.d.) 'SARS (Severe Acute Respiratory Syndrome)'. Retrieved from https://www.who.int/ith/diseases/sars/en/.

12   World Health Organisation. 'Pandemic (H1N1) 2009: Update 112'. 6 August 2010. Retrieved from https://www.who.int/csr/don/2010_08_06/en/.

13   *Sunday Morning Herald*. 'Swine Flu Death Toll Revised to Nearly 300,000 People'. 27 June 2012. Retrieved from https://www.smh.com.au/world/swine-flu-death-toll-revised-to-nearly-300000-people-20120626-210dy.html.

14   Tegmark, Max, et al. 'Research Priorities for Robust and Beneficial Artificial Intelligence'. *Association for the Advancement of Artificial Intelligence*, 111, 2015. Retrieved from https://futureoflife.org/data/documents/research_priorities.pdf.

15   Cellan-Jones, R. 'Stephen Hawking Warns Artificial Intelligence Could End Mankind'. *BBC*, 2 December 2014. Retrieved from https://www.bbc.com/news/technology-30290540.

16   Nowak, R. 'Killer Mousepox Virus Raises Bioterror Fears'. *New Scientist*, 10 January 2001. Retrieved from https://www.newscientist.com/article/dn311-killer-mousepox-virus-raises-bioterror-fears/.

17   See https://www.technologyreview.com/2019/08/01/652/scientists-are-making-human-monkey-hybrids-in-china/.

18   Nussbaum, M.C. 'Beyond the Social Contract: Toward Global Justice'. The Tanner Lectures on Human Values, Canberra, 2002. Retrieved from https://tannerlectures.utah.edu/_documents/a-to-z/n/nussbaum_2003.pdf.

19   International Parliamentary Union. (n.d.) 'The IPU Is the Global Organisation of National Parliaments'. Retrieved from https://www.ipu.org/.

20 EUR-Lex.'The European Parliament'.December 2017.Retrieved from https://
    eur-lex.europa.eu/legal-content/EN/TXT/?uri=LEGISSUM%3Aai0010.

21 Campaign for a United Nations Parliamentary Assembly. (n.d.) 'Who We
    Are'. Retrieved from: https://en.unpacampaign.org/.

22 International Court of Justice. (n.d.) 'How the Court Works'. Retrieved from
    https://www.icj-cij.org/en/how-the-court-works.

23 Permanent Court of Arbitration. (n.d.) 'FAQ: Can the PCA Provide Legal
    Advice or Assistance to Parties Wishing to Bring a Case?' Retrieved from
    https://pca-cpa.org/en/faq/.

24 Peace Palace Library. (n.d.) 'Tsar Nicholas II: Peace and International
    Jurisdiction'. Retrieved from https://www.peacepalacelibrary.nl/library-
    special/tsar-nicholas-ii-peace-and-international-jurisdiction/.

25 Scott, J.B. *The Proceedings of the Hague Peace Conferences* (The Conferences of
    1899 and 1907: Index Volume). New York: Oxford University Press, 1921.
    Retrieved from https://www.loc.gov/rr/frd/Military_Law/pdf/Hague-
    Peace-Conferences_Index.pdf.

26 Baetens, F. *Hague Conferences (1899, 1907)*. *Oxford Bibliographies*, 19 September
    2014. Retrieved from https://www.oxfordbibliographies.com/view/
    document/obo-9780199743292/obo-9780199743292-0115.xml.

27 Alihusain, C. 'International Congress of Women of 1915'. Peace Palace
    Library, 6 February 2015. Retrieved from https://www.peacepalacelibrary.
    nl/2015/02/international-congress-of-women-of-1915/.

28 Science for Peace. 'The Hague Appeal for Peace'. 1 December 1999. Retrieved
    from https://scienceforpeace.ca/the-hague-appeal-for-peace/.

29 'Conference on Security and Co-operation in Europe: Final Act'. Helsinki,
    1975. Retrieved from https://www.osce.org/files/f/documents/5/c/39501.
    pdf.

30 Chiampan, A. 'SALT Treaty'. *Wiley Online Library*, 27 February 2018. Retrieved
    from https://onlinelibrary.wiley.com/doi/full/10.1002/9781118885154.
    dipl0248.

31 'Commission on Security and Cooperation in Europe'. *The Helsinki Final Act*,
    1 August 1975. Retrieved from https://www.csce.gov/international-impact/
    publications/helsinki-final-act?page=18.

32 *New York Times*. 'Atomic Education Urged by Einstein: Scientist in Plea
    for $200,000 to Promote New Type of Essential Thinking'. 25 May 1946.
    Retrieved from https://www.nytimes.com/1946/05/25/archives/atomic-
    education-urged-by-einstein-scientist-in-plea-for-200000-to.html.

33 Einstein, A. *The Albert Einstein Collection*, Volume 1, *Essays in Humanism, The
    Theory of Relativity, and The World As I See It*. New York: Open Road Media,
    2016.

34 Bunzel, D. 'Rational Legal Authority'. *Wiley Online Library*, 2007. Retrieved from https://onlinelibrary.wiley.com/doi/abs/10.1002/9781405165518.wbeosr026.

35 Russell, B. *Power: A New Social Analysis.* London: George Allen & Unwin, 1938.

36 James, J.A. *Hannah Arendt's Theory of Power as Communication: A Feminist Critique.* Fordham University, 1987. Retrieved from https://search.proquest.com/docview/303465319.

37 Arendt, H. 'Reflections on Violence'. *Journal of International Affairs*, 23(1), 1969, pp. 1–35.

38 Toda, J. 'Global Citizenship'. *Josei Toda: Reviving Buddhism in Today's World*, February 1952. Retrieved from https://www.joseitoda.org/vision/global.html.

39 Ikeda, D. *Forum for Peace: Daisaku Ikeda's Proposals to the UN.* London: I.B. Tauris & Co., 2014, p. 39.

40 Eze, M.O. (n.d.) 'I Am Because You Are!' Retrieved from https://www.michaeleze.com/.

41 'Nuclear Darkness, Global Climate Change and Nuclear Famine'. *McCloy–Zorin Accords*, 20 September 1961. Retrieved from http://www.nucleardarkness.org/solutions/mccloyzorinaccordstext/.

42 Jayaprakash, N. 'Conning Humanity in the Name of Disarmament'. *Economic & Political Weekly*, 52(28), July 2017. Retrieved from https://www.epw.in/journal/2017/28/web-exclusives/conning-humanity-name-disarmament.html.

43 'General Assembly Resolution 16/1722, Question of Disarmament, A/RES/16/1722'. 20 December 1961. Retrieved from http://www.un-documents.net/a16r1722.htm.

Index

About the Author

Sundeep Waslekar is a thought leader on the global future. He has worked with sixty-five countries under the auspices of the Strategic Foresight Group, an international think tank he founded in 2002. He is a senior research fellow at the Centre for the Resolution of Intractable Conflicts at Oxford University. He is a practitioner of Track Two diplomacy since the 1990s and has mediated in conflicts in South Asia, those between Western and Islamic countries on deconstructing terror, trans-boundary water conflicts, and is currently facilitating a nuclear risk reduction dialogue between permanent members of the UN Security Council. He was invited to address the United Nations Security Council session 7818 on water, peace and security. He has been quoted in more than 3,000 media articles from eighty countries. Waslekar read Philosophy, Politics and Economics (PPE) at Oxford University from 1981 to 1983. He was conferred D. Litt. (Honoris Causa) of Symbiosis International University by the President of India in 2011.